Chit-Chat Chinese

"Learn the easy way from someone who learned the hard way"

Textbook & Workbook in One:
Beginner Level 1

Rachel Meyer 梅洁如
Kuo-Chung Fu 傅国忠
Hsiao-Chien Huang 黄晓倩
Judy Wu 伍迪佳
Dennis Zhu 朱锋

Using "The Mandarin Building Blocks Approach®"

(Audio CD included)

Free Podcast lessons at **www.chitchatchinese.com**

Published by

The Far East Book Co., Ltd.

www.fareast.com.tw

North America Distributor

U.S. International Publishing, Inc.

www.usipusa.com

ISBN 978-957-612-906-3

Introduction

The Dawn of a New Age in Learning Mandarin

In the olden days, before *Chit-Chat Chinese* existed, hapless students were forced to learn Chinese using a method known as "confusing," it also was a method referred to as "too difficult." With this book we teach you Chinese at a calm pace, building logically on the last linguistic skills learned. It is a skills-based progression known as "The Mandarin Building Blocks Approach®." You will experience a new way of learning a language as we guide you carefully through acquiring the skills necessary to converse in Chinese.

How to Use This Textbook

Chit-Chat Chinese is a guided approach to learning, where you will be taken step-by--step through learning Chinese vocabulary, grammatical structures, practicing dialogues then finally learning cultural and study tips. You should start each lesson from the beginning and progress to each new "locale" in the order it is laid out. Here are the places you will "visit" each lesson:

Pronunciation Plaza—Each lesson starts with pronunciation. Here you learn the sounds of *pinyin* (romanized pronunciation of Chinese) and do pronunciation exercises.

Word Workshop—In this locale you learn vocabulary and expressions. You will stay here to learn enough to practice the dialogues that follow.

Grammar Grove—In this locale you will learn important grammatical points related to that particular lesson.

Chit-Chat Café—This is the place you practice what you have learned through dialogues or other speaking activities. This is followed by a workbook section known as "Chit-Chat Practice." In this section you should first practice the exercises orally, then write them out as homework.

Culture Corner—This section is dedicated to cross-cultural training. It allows you to learn cultural components to speaking and expressing yourself accurately in Chinese.

Advice Alcove—Here you learn how to learn. In other words, here is where you learn study techniques that will make sure you are acquiring skills at a steady pace.

Do you want to hear what you are learning? Take note of the references to your audio CDs (packaged with this book or downloadable online at www.chitchatchinese.com) throughout *Chit-Chat Chinese*. Here is an example of what you will see: 🔘 _____. This means you can find an audio recording of that section on the track number listed. You should also keep an eye out for extra materials and explanations referenced throughout the book in the appendix and online.

How to Learn on Your Own
If you are the go-it-on-your-own, cowboy-style language learner, *Chit-Chat Chinese* is well suited to your needs. It is designed both as a self-study guide as well as a classroom textbook. Without a live teacher, you will need to rely on your audio CDs to learn how to pronounce your vocabulary; you should listen and review frequently the dialogues on the audio CDs as well. Additionally, there are free podcast classes that can guide you through this book, taught by the author and native speakers. Go download your first lesson at www.chitchatchinese.com. Then open your book and get started.

How to Teach from This Book

- Follow the book in the sequence it was written, going to the next section in order.
- Use the dialogues in Chit-Chat Café as a basis for in-class pair practice, and for in--class dialogues between you and your students.
- Save the audio materials for the students to listen to at home. In class time should be used to practice the material taught with live and authentic interaction.
- Speaking and listening is the focus of the *Chit-Chat Chinese*: Textbook & Workbook; however, you may also introduce written Chinese using the *Chit-Chat Chinese*: Character Book, sold separately. All content in the textbook is also provided in characters for students and teachers interested in including a writing curriculum.
- Find lesson plans, in-class games, grammatical support and other teacher resources at www.chitchatchinese.com.

Textbook Overview

You will be learning Mandarin

There are many dialects of Chinese in China, such as Cantonese or Fukienese; however, the official language of China, Taiwan and Singapore is Mandarin. It is the most widely spoken language and most useful to learn.

You will focus on speaking (with the option to include writing)

Chit-Chat Chinese focuses on learning practical, spoken Mandarin. We believe the most important and useful skill when learning any foreign language is the ability to listen and understand, then respond—in other words, the ability to converse. To this end, we concentrate on teaching you Mandarin in its romanized form (that's right, using our alphabet.) This allows you to get up and running in the language without having to spend months or years on learning characters. If you would also like to learn Chinese characters, you may purchase the *Chit-Chat Chinese*: Character Book. For those of you also learning characters in your studies, we have provided the characters for all vocabulary and dialogues in this textbook.

"Simplified" characters will be shown in this book

All romanized words will also have a corresponding character shown for those learners studying the writing system as well. These will be written in "Simplified Chinese." Post-revolution China developed and promulgated a simplification of the Chinese writing system, known as "Simplified Chinese." The older system, now known as "Traditional Chinese," is still used in Taiwan and in some overseas Chinese communities and newspapers, including those in the United States. Here is an example comparison of the two. See if you can tell the difference:

中国	中國
"China" written in	**"China" written in**
Simplified Chinese	**Traditional Chinese**

You will sometimes see a literal translation of each character (free morpheme)

This is to help you see how two or more characters put together can form a word. It also will help you with vocabulary acquisition. Look for this literal translation in parenthesis followed by "*LIT*." If you do not see this, it means we thought adding the literal translation would be too confusing or cumbersome. When you see this (*LIT: for sound*), it means the character was chosen in this word for sound rather than meaning.

This book uses "The Mandarin Building Blocks Approach®"

Finally, a logical way to learn Mandarin! *Chit-Chat Chinese* author and language school owner, Rachel Meyer, noticed that language textbooks tend to organize lessons based on themes or situations, such as "directions," "shopping," or "travel." This works fine for Latin-based languages that share cognates (words that have the same origin and so sound similar) with English. But does that style work for a language that gives you no freebies in the form of cognates? She didn't think so. In theme-based books Mandarin, students are forced into uncomfortable linguistic knots as they are introduced to grammar and vocabulary which they simply are not prepared for and which present no logical progression to the student. *Chit-Chat Chinese*, using the author's own Mandarin Building Blocks Approach®, follows a logical order. You are taught the easy and most useful word parts (morphemes), as we guide you in placing one block of knowledge on top of another until you naturally are able to form sentences and converse. We break the language down into digestible parts, which allow you to piece-by-piece put Mandarin together for yourself. This means less frustration and attaining real skills that allow you to produce language based on a solid and logical foundation.

You will learn using the "*pinyin*" romanization system

In order to write the sounds of Chinese characters for the non-Chinese audience (so we can know that, for example, these characters 北京 are pronounced as "Beijing") romanized systems of writing were invented. The previous most popular one (other than the Yale romanization system) was a system called Wade-Giles. Wade-Giles wrote the Chinese word "Beijing" as "Peking," along with other such words you may be familiar with before the change. In 1958 *pinyin* was adopted by Mainland China as the official romanization system for the Chinese language. Years later, as the system seeped into the west, Westerners began to see names like "Nanking" change to "Nanjing" and "Mao Tse Tong" to "Mao Zedong." Now *Pinyin* is solely used.

Pinyin Overview—Full Chart in Appendix I

The basic sounds of Mandarin are not very complicated. All Chinese words are formed with only 21 initial sounds and 38 finals. In each lesson, we will warm you up by practicing combinations of these initials and finals, along with other pronunciation exercises. You can find a full table of all Mandarin combinations in **Appendix I**.

Table of Contents

"Mandarin Building Blocks Approach®"

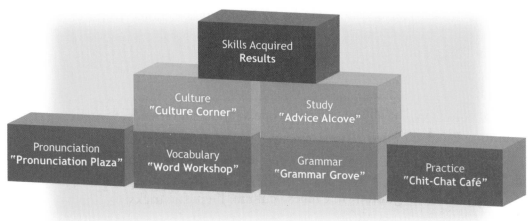

- **Skills Acquired:** The ability to discuss daily habits and activities.
- **Building Blocks:** Tongue twisters; sound differentiation ("j-" vs. "zh-"); tone combination practice (3rd tone + others); daily activities; when ("de shíhou [的时候]"); then ("ránhòu [然后]"); words of frequency; expressing the past (introduction to "le [了]"); expressing the future with "huì & yào (会&要); more time words; hand gestures in Chinese culture; practicing Mandarin by talking to one's self.

- **Skills Acquired:** The ability to discuss food and order in a Chinese restaurant.
- **Building Blocks:** Tongue twister; sound differentiation (q- vs. ch-); challenging sounds (4-letter finals); tone combination practice (4th tone + others); useful expressions; restaurant words; beverages; food; eating & drinking words; food & eating related measure words; dining etiquette in Chinese culture; tips for ordering food in a Chinese restaurant.

- **Skills Acquired:** Ability to make plans and go shopping for clothes.
- **Building Blocks:** A Chinese poem; sound differentiation (x- vs. sh-); natural Chinese intonation; cadence practice; colors; clothes; measure words for clothes; new use of "de (的)"; money and prices; modifiers "yìdiǎnr / yíxià / V. yī V. (一点儿/一下/V. 一 V.)"; shopping; telephone and making plans; expressing "ing" in Chinese; colors in Chinese culture; common Mandarin practice barriers (overcoming learning obstacles [part 1]).

- **Skills Acquired:** The ability to get around and talk about one's daily life.
- **Building Blocks:** Tones in songs; words to "nail"; transportation words; supplementary location words; expressing habits with "huì (会)"; directionals; adverbial "de (得)"; more "le (了)"; work and professions; formal asking and telling of names; culture shock; overcoming learning obstacles (part 2).

Chinese is "Out of This World!"

Imagine a world where just by changing the tone of your voice you form a completely different word. A world where saying the exact same word, only with a different tone, you change the meaning from "mother," to "hemp," to "horse," and then "scold." Welcome, my friend, to the world of Mandarin!

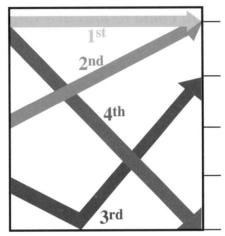

There are four main tones in Mandarin and a fifth neutral tone. The above graph shows the tonal patterns of each of the four main tones. You will see in this book, and anywhere *pinyin* is used, the tone number of each word (morpheme) indicated above the main vowel using the following tone marks as seen for the morpheme "ma":

1st tone = mā   **2nd tone = má**   **3rd tone = mǎ**   **4th tone = mà**

The neutral tone has no tone mark. Here is how each tone basically should sound:

1st tone: This is a high even tone. It sounds like someone holding a steady high note while singing.

2nd tone: This is a rising tone. It sounds almost like the tone of voice we use when asking "huh?".

3rd tone: This is a low dipping tone. Similar to saying "blah" in English when bored, only the sound goes lower in Chinese.

4th tone: This is a sharp falling tone. This sounds similar to when someone yells sharply "Hey!", as in "Hey, stop that!".

The neutral tone: This is said with no marked intonation.

1

Now let's listen to the four main tones on your audio CD (1-1).

mā	má	mǎ	mà
(mother)	(hemp)	(horse)	(scold)

Now that you have learned about tones, let's get rolling with the sounds in Mandarin.

Pronunciation Plaza
– The place you come to practice sounds and tones

(Go to 1-1 to hear:)

Tone Practice
Let's first focus on practicing those four tones!

Note: The English meanings are given below each sound. However, many of the sounds require another character to complete their meaning. When you see "(------)" this means there is no common word for that particular tone.

bā	bá	bǎ	bà
(eight)	(to pull out)	(target)	(father)

pā	pá	pǎ	pà
(to lie)	(to crawl)	(------)	(to fear)

dā	dá	dǎ	dà
(to put up)	(to answer)	(to hit)	(big)

tā	tá	tǎ	tà
(he / she / it)	(------)	(tower)	(to step on)

nā	ná	nǎ	nà
(a surname)	(to take)	(where)	(that)

lā	lá	lǎ	là
(to pull)	(to slash)	(------)	(spicy)

Pinyin Practice

Below is a chart of the sounds we will cover in this lesson, with the initials highlighted in ▢ and the finals highlighted in ▢:

a					
	a	ai	ao	an	ang
b	ba	bai	bao	ban	bang
p	pa	pai	pao	pan	pang
m	ma	mai	mao	man	mang
f	fa			fan	fang
d	da	dai	dao	dan	dang
t	ta	tai	tao	tan	tang
n	na	nai	nao	nan	nang
l	la	lai	lao	lan	lang

Sound Differentiation Practice

bā	bái	bǎo	bàn	bāng
(eight)	(white)	(full)	(half)	(to help)

pā	pái	pǎo	pàn	pāng
(to lie)	(a row)	(to run)	(to judge)	(torrential)

mā	mái	mǎo	màn	māng
(mother)	(to bury)	(mao)	(slow)	(bull)

fā	fàn	fāng		
(to issue)	(meal)	(square)		

dā	dái	dǎo	dàn	dāng
(to put up)	(-----)	(to topple)	(but)	(to act as)

tā	tái	tǎo	tàn	tāng
(he / she / it)	(terrace)	(to demand)	(sigh)	(soup)

nā	nái	nǎo	nàn	nāng
(a surname)	(------)	(brain)	(disaster)	(muttering)

lā	lái	lǎo	làn	lāng
(to pull)	(to come)	(old)	(rotten)	('bang')

Chit-Chat CHINESE

Auditory Exercise

Listen to the following sounds in 🔊 1-2 and write the correct *pinyin* spelling and tones below. See **Appendix IV** for correct answers.

Note: You should expect the first few lessons of auditory transliteration to be challenging and you should use your answer key as an aide. This is meant as an auditory <u>exercise</u> not a test. It is a training ground for your ears and your future receptive ability to distinguish Mandarin sounds and tones.

Part One: Tone Differentiation
Listen to each sound and write down which of the four main tones you hear.

1. tǎi   2. māo   3. pàng   4. dǎ

5. bàn   6. bái   7. pāi   8. pěng

9. láo   10. mā

Part Two: Sounds Differentiation
Listen to each sound and write down the correct *pinyin* spelling.

11. mēng   12. tā   13. nán   14. dāo

15. lāi   16. děng   17. bāo   18. bēng

19. lán   20. māi   ⟩ dān   bǎng

 Word Workshop
– The place you come to learn new words and phrases

(Go to 🔊 1-3 to hear:)

Personal Pronouns

我	你	他/她/它
wǒ	nǐ	tā
(I)	(you)	(he / she / it)

4

我们	你们	他们/她们/它们
wǒmen*	nǐmen*	tāmen*
(we)	(you all)	(they)

Adding the word "men" (们) to pronouns or nouns pluralizes them.

"To be"

This verb, as with all Chinese verbs, does not need to be conjugated. It remains the same no matter to whom or what it is attached as well as whether it is regarding the past, present or future.

是	不	不是
shì	bù	bú* shì
(to be)	(not)	(is not / are not / was not, etc.)
		*We'll explain this change of tone in Lesson Three.

我是	你是	他是/她是/它是
wǒ shì	nǐ shì	tā shì
(I am)	(you are)	(he / she / it is)

我们是	你们是	他们是/她们是/它们是
wǒmen shì	nǐmen shì	tāmen shì
(we are)	(you [all] are)	(they are)

Countries (see **Appendix V** for a wider list of countries)

中国	美国	英国
Zhōngguó	Měiguó	Yīngguó
(China)	(the U.S.A.)	(England, Britain)
(LIT: middle, country)	*(LIT: beautiful, country)*	*(LIT: for sound)*

法国	德国	日本
Fǎguó	Déguó	Rìběn
(France)	(Germany)	(Japan)
(LIT: for sound)	*(LIT: for sound)*	*(LIT: sun, origin)*

1

Nationalities

Nationality names are as easy as pie; just add the following word and you've got it:

人
rén
(person)

Here is how it works:

中国人
Zhōngguórén
(Chinese)
(LIT: China, person)

美国人
Měiguórén
(American)
(LIT: the U.S., person)

英国人
Yīngguórén
(English)
(LIT: England, person)

法国人
Fǎguórén
(French)
(LIT: French, person)

德国人
Déguórén
(German)
(LIT: German, person)

日本人
Rìběnrén
(Japanese)
(LIT: Japanese, person)

Languages

Another set of words simple to form with your building blocks: just add "**wén**" after the first country word (morpheme):

文
wén
(language, culture, writing)

中文
Zhōngwén
(Chinese)

英文
Yīngwén
(English)

法文
Fǎwén
(French)

德文
Déwén
(German)

日文
Rìwén
(Japanese)

Classroom Words

Now, let's give you a few words to communicate with your teacher. (If you are studying on your own, feel free to talk to yourself.) Please note, in the classroom setting you should always call your teacher by the title "teacher ("**lǎoshī**")." You can also add their last name, so if your teacher's last name is "**Wáng**," you should call him or her "**Wáng lǎoshī**," with his or her surname first.

老师
lǎoshī
(teacher)
(LIT: old, master)

学生
xuésheng
(student)
(LIT: study, being)

懂
dǒng
(understand)

不懂
bù dǒng
(not understand)

谢谢
xièxie
(thank you)

不客气
bú kèqi, *yòng xiè*
(you're welcome)
(LIT: [no need], politeness)

 Grammar Grove
— The place you come to learn about structure

Word order

The word order in Chinese for describing nationalities is not different from English: Subject + to be ("shì") + nationality. Just remember, you do not need to conjugate the verb "to be"; leave it as it is and go on your merry way, like so:

我是美国人。
Wǒ shì Měiguórén.　　　　=　　I am American.

你是中国人。
Nǐ shì Zhōngguórén.　　　　=　　You are Chinese.

我们是法国人。
Wǒmen shì Fǎguórén.　　　　=　　We are French.

他是日本人。
Tā shì Rìběnrén.　　　　=　　He is Japanese.

他们是德国人。
Tāmen shì Déguórén.　　　　=　　They are German.

1

Questioning

To ask a question just make a statement and add the word "ma (吗)" at the end. This word means nothing except to function as an out loud question mark. When you hear that at the end of a phrase, you know you are being asked a question.

There is no one word in Chinese for "yes" or "no." Instead the verb, adjective, adverb or other central part to the question is repeated to answer in the affirmative. To answer in the negative you use the word "bù (not)" before this central word. To clarify what that means, I will demonstrate how this works with English words:

<u>Affirmative</u>	<u>Negative</u>
Q: Are you American?	Q: Are you American?
A: Am.	A: Not am.
Q: Do you like China?	Q: Do you like China?
A: Like.	A: Not like.
Q: Do you know Chinese?	Q: Do you know Chinese?
A: Know.	A: Not know.

Now let's look at that in Chinese:

你是美国人吗?

Q: **Nǐ shì Měiguórén ma?**   = Are you American?
(LIT: You are American + ma)

是。

A: **Shì.**   = Yes.
(LIT: to be)

他是中国人吗?

Q: **Tā shì Zhōngguórén ma?**   = Is he Chinese?
(LIT: He is Chinese + ma)

不是。

A: **Bú shì.**   = No.
(LIT: not, to be)

Chit-Chat Café
– The place you come to practice speaking

Module 1.1 - (1-4) / English translation on **Page 18**
Picture this: "Bob" took four weeks of Mandarin lessons and is now in China.
"Lili" bumps into him in Tiananmen Square, Beijing.

Lili:	Nǐ shì Měiguórén ma?	Lili:	你是美国人吗？
Bob:	Shì. Nǐ shì Zhōngguórén ma?	Bob:	是。你是中国人吗？
Lili:	Shì. Nǐ shì lǎoshī ma?	Lili:	是。你是老师吗？
Bob:	Bú shì. Wǒ shì xuésheng. Nǐ shì lǎoshī ma?	Bob:	不是。我是学生。你是老师吗？
Lili:	Shì. Wǒ shì lǎoshī.	Lili:	是。我是老师。
Bob:	Nǐ shì Zhōngwén lǎoshī ma?	Bob:	你是中文老师吗？
Lili:	Bú shì. Wǒ shì Yīngwén lǎoshī.	Lili:	不是。我是英文老师。
Bob:	Nǐ dǒng Yīngwén!	Bob:	你懂英文！
Lili:	Wǒ dǒng Yīngwén. Nǐ dǒng Zhōngwén ma?	Lili:	我懂英文。你懂中文吗？
Bob:	Wǒ dǒng.	Bob:	我懂。

Chit-Chat Practice 1.1
Answer the following questions out loud, then in writing for homework. Be sure to answer in full sentences as in the example (answers in **Appendix IV**.)

Example:

Lili 是中国人吗？

Q: Lili shì Zhōngguórén ma?

是。她是中国人。

A: Shì. Tā shì Zhōngguórén.

1.

Bob 是中国人吗？

Q: Bob shì Zhōngguórén ma?

A: *Bú shì. Tā shì Měiguórén.*

1

2.

Lili 是美国人吗?

Q: Lili shì Měiguórén ma?

A: Bú shì. Ta shì Zhōngguórén

3.

Bob 是学生吗?

Q: Bob shì xuésheng ma?

A: Shì. Tā shì xué sheng.

4.

Lili 是学生吗?

Q: Lili shì xuésheng ma?

A: Bú shì. Tā shì Yīngwen lǎoshī.

5.

Lili 是英文老师吗?

Q: Lili shì Yīngwén lǎoshī ma?

A: Shì. Tā shì Yīngwén lǎoshī

6.

Lili 懂英文吗?

Q: Lili dǒng Yīngwén ma?

Not supposed to be there. Why?

A: Shì. Tā dǒng Yīngwén.

7.

Bob 懂中文吗?

Q: Bob dǒng Zhōngwén ma?

A: Shì. Tā dǒng Zhōngwén.

Word Workshop
– The place you come to learn new words and phrases

(Go to 1-5 to hear:)

Greetings

你好

nǐ hǎo

(hello)

(LIT: you, good)

你好吗?

Nǐ hǎo ma?

(How are you?)

(LIT: you, good, ?)

好　　　　　很好　　　　　不好　　　　　马马虎虎

hǎo　　　　　hěn hǎo*　　　bù hǎo　　　　mǎmahūhū
(good)　　　　(very good)　　(not good)　　(so so)

more modest
& polite
tǐng
(kind of, pretty)

(LIT: horse, horse, tiger, tiger)

我很好。

Wǒ hěn hǎo.
(I am good. / I am fine.)

ba — polite softener

** Even though "hěn hǎo" means very good, it is more common to use this to answer
the question of "How are you?", just as we would use "fine."*

你叫什么名字？　　　　我叫 _____ 。　　　　你呢？

Nǐ jiào shénme míngzi?　　Wǒ jiào _____.　　　Nǐ ne?
(What is your name?)　　　(My name is _____.)　　(And you?)
(LIT: you, called, what, name)　(LIT: I, called, _____)

pronoun third here　　　*What*　　*name*

再见

zàijiàn
(goodbye)
(LIT: again, see)

Possessive Pronouns

我的　　　　　你的　　　　　他的/她的/它的

wǒ de　　　　nǐ de　　　　　tā de
(my)　　　　　(your)　　　　(his / her / its)

我们的　　　　你们的　　　　他们的/她们的/它们的

wǒmen de　　　nǐmen de　　　tāmen de
(our)　　　　　(your [plural])　(their)

Expressions

哇！
Wā!
(Wow!)

1

哪里哪里
nǎli nǎli*
(not so, not so)
(LIT: where?, where?)

i is this coming from

* *It's best not to accept a compliment in Chinese. Otherwise you may "lose face" by appearing too confident or arrogant. Instead, deny the compliment with the above expression "*Nǎli nǎli.*"*

 Chit-Chat Café
– The place you come to practice speaking

Module 1.2 - (1-6) / English translation on **Page 18**

Picture this: "Jen" is taking Chinese classes at the local university. She meets "Xiaomei" in a park in Chinatown.

Jen:	Nǐ shì Zhōngguórén ma?	Jen:	你是中国人吗?
Xiaomei:	Shì. Wā, nǐ de Zhōngwén hěn hǎo!	Xiaomei:	是。哇,你的中文很好!
Jen:	Nǎli nǎli. Wǒ de Zhōngwén bù hǎo.	Jen:	哪里哪里。我的中文不好。
Xiaomei:	Nǐ shì Zhōngwén xuésheng ma?	Xiaomei:	你是中文学生吗?
Jen:	Shì. Nǐ shì lǎoshī ma?	Jen:	是。你是老师吗?
Xiaomei:	Bú shì.	Xiaomei:	不是。
(time lapse)		*(过一会儿)*	
Jen:	Zàijiàn.	Jen:	再见。
Xiaomei:	Zàijiàn.	Xiaomei:	再见。

Chit-Chat Practice 1.2

Fill in the question that should go with these answers (answers in **Appendix IV**). First try the exercise orally, then in writing.

Example:

Q: <u>Xiǎoměi shì Zhōngguórén ma?</u>

A: 是。小美是中国人。
Shì. Xiǎoměi shì Zhōngguórén.

1.

Q: <u>Jen shì Zhōngwén xuésheng ma?</u>

A: 是。Jen是中文学生。
Shì. Jen shì Zhōngwén xuésheng.

2.

Q: <u>Xiǎoměi shì lǎoshī ma?</u>

A: 不是。小美不是老师。
Bú shì. Xiǎoměi bú shì lǎoshī.

3.

Q: <u>Jen de zhōngwen nǎo ma?</u>

A: 好。Jen的中文很好。
Hǎo. Jen de Zhōngwén hěn hǎo.

 Chit-Chat Café
– The place you come to practice speaking

Module 1.3 - (🔘 1-7) / English translation on **Page 19**

Picture this: "Peter" spent a summer in China. Now back in the U.S., he introduces himself to a Chinese coworker, "Wang Bo."

Peter:	Nǐ hǎo ma?	Peter:	你好吗?
Wang Bo:	Wǒ hěn hǎo, xièxie. Nǐ ne?	Wang Bo:	我很好，谢谢。你呢?
Peter:	Wǒ hěn hǎo, xièxie.	Peter:	我很好，谢谢。
Wang Bo:	Nǐ jiào shénme míngzi?	Wang Bo:	你叫什么名字?
Peter:	Wǒ jiào Peter. Nǐ ne?	Peter:	我叫Peter。你呢?

1

Wang Bo: Wǒ jiào Wáng Bō. Nǐ de Zhōngwén hěn hǎo!	Wang Bo: 我叫王波。你的中文很好！
Peter: Nǎli nǎli. Nǐ de Yīngwén hěn hǎo!	Peter: 哪里哪里。你的英文很好！
Wang Bo: Wǒ de Yīngwén bù hǎo.	Wang Bo: 我的英文不好。
(time lapse)	(过一会儿)
Peter: Zàijiàn.	Peter: 再见。
Wang Bo: Zàijiàn.	Wang Bo: 再见。

Chit-Chat Practice 1.3

Answer the following questions about yourself. You can find example answers to these questions in **Appendix IV**.

1.
你好吗？
Q: Nǐ hǎo ma?   A: _Wǒ hěn hǎo, xièxiè._

2.
你叫什么名字？
Q: Nǐ jiào shénme míngzi?   A: _Wǒ jiào Will._

3.
你是美国人吗？
Q: Nǐ shì Měiguórén ma?   A: _Wǒ shì Měiguórén._

4.
你是中国人吗？
Q: Nǐ shì Zhōngguórén ma?   A: _Bú shì Zhōngguórén._

5.
你是学生吗？
Q: Nǐ shì xuésheng ma?   A: _Wǒ shì Zhōngwén xuésheng._

6.
你的英文好吗？
Q: Nǐ de Yīngwén hǎo ma?   A: _Mǎmahūhū._

7.
你的中文好吗?

Q: Nǐ de Zhōngwén hǎo ma?

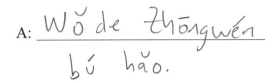
A: Wǒ de Zhōngwén bú hǎo.

1

 Grammar Grove
– The place you come to learn about structure

KISS = "Keep It Simple, Stupid."

Think of us poor westerners conjugating verbs for each different pronoun and tense, and sprinkling our language with articles, such as "the" and "a," and using different prepositions after different verbs. While Chinese speakers glide through their linguistic life with little or no need for any of the above. Here is some of what you will not have to worry about with Chinese:

No verb conjugation — Chinese verbs only have one form, no matter what noun or pronoun you use or time the event takes place. So, verbs remain the same whether you are discussing today, yesterday or tomorrow. Time is indicated using a time word such as "tomorrow," "soon," or "2 years ago." Here is how the structure works (written out in English words, so you get the picture):

- I tomorrow go store.
- I yesterday ride bike.
- I now work.

There are no articles — As you can see from the above sentences, there is also no need for "the" or "a."

Prepositions are used less — Prepositions do exist, but are not nearly as prevalent as in western languages. Have a look at this sentence written in English, then with English words with Chinese grammar:

- **English:** She looks **at the** dog.
- **Mock Chinese:** She look dog.

Pronouns remain the same — Pronouns remain the same whether they are direct or indirect. For example, "wǒ" means "I" and "me," "tā" means "he" and "him," etc.

15

Culture Corner
– The place you come to learn more than just language

入境随俗
rù jìng suí sú
"When in a new environment, do as the locals do."
Chinese saying

Meeting and greeting

Now that you can do the meet and greet in Chinese, it's important to know some cultural aspects to your first interactions. In particular, how should you greet someone? Is it with a bow, a handshake or nothing at all?

- **Bowing?** — This is not nearly as common or formal in China as it is in Japan. The Chinese reserve bowing for very formal situations such as being in the presence of a high authority (e.g. a high government official), when worshiping a deity, or for certain funeral rites. You may notice an abbreviated kind of bow from time to time, or just a gentle lowering of the head to show respect, without actually bending from the waist.

- **Shaking hands?** — Although the Chinese do not traditionally shake hands when meeting, this has changed in the last couple of decades. With greater contact with the west, more and more Chinese will shake hands when meeting a foreigner (but not as common amongst themselves). Generally in the urban centers, if you are non-Asian and are meeting someone Chinese they may, out of courtesy for western culture, extend a hand. Minimally most will know what to do if you are the one who extends a hand. Shaking hands will tend to take place only when meeting, and a wave will suffice when saying goodbye. If you are doing business in Asia, it is best to assume all business people are familiar with the common international practice of shaking hands when meeting and when saying goodbye.

- **Just stand there?** — If you are not in an urban center, and / or are meeting someone elderly, likely the person will not be accustomed to shaking hands. Smiling and slightly nodding your head is enough.

- **How about a kiss on the cheek?** — There is a simple answer to this question: "NO!". This is not common practice and most people will not be familiar or comfortable with this western tradition, whether it be the European two-kisses when meeting and when saying goodbye or the American single kiss on the cheek when saying goodbye. Hold off on your smooches.

Just as with any new person you meet, no matter the nationality, you should tap into your EQ (emotional quotient) and try to read what the person is accustomed to. Chinese people travel and live all over the world, you may, by chance, meet someone who lived in France for years, or the U.S. Generally, anytime you are abroad and in doubt of the customs, let the other person take the lead: If a hand extends, shake it; if a head is lowered, lower yours too; if a kiss is offered, offer one back. Just mirror back the locals' behavior and you can't go wrong.

 **Advice Alcove**
– The place you come to learn how to learn

师傅领进门，修行在个人

shīfu lǐnqìn mén, xiūxíng zài gèrén
"The teacher opens the door, but you must enter on your own."
Chinese proverb

Although memorizing is out of fashion when it comes to learning languages, do not underestimate the importance of doing just that when learning a non-Latin based language. Memorizing means knowing the material "like the back of your hand," not just being able to recall with some thought. When learning a Latin-based language, it is easier for us to learn through context and educated guessing. Non-Latin based languages, you have got to start from scratch. This means initially putting some of these new and strange sounds to memory. Here are some ideas on how to do it:

1st: Make Flashcards — Buy index cards, or even fold and tear regular printer paper (8 pieces per sheet). Write the English word or sentence on one side and the Chinese on the other.

2nd: Memorize until "the cows come home" — This means when you hold up a flashcard and cannot produce the word or sentence, either in Chinese or English, within one second, it should go into the "NOT KNOW" pile. You should be able to do this both ways: English to Chinese, and Chinese to English. If it takes you longer than one second, you don't have the speed for regular conversation.

1

3rd: **Consistently memorize** — Put aside 15 minutes or more every day to simply memorize your vocabulary and sentences.

Chinese will sound strange to you at first. Memorization helps you get past this "alien" feeling. Later on, you will not need to memorize as much; you will have the basic sounds and tools to incorporate new words and phrases without rote memorization.

English Translation

Module 1.1

Lili:	Are you American?
Bob:	Yes. Are you Chinese?
Lili:	Yes. Are you a teacher?
Bob:	No. I am a student. Are you a teacher?
Lili:	Yes. I am a teacher.
Bob:	Are you a Chinese teacher?
Lili:	No. I am an English teacher.
Bob:	You understand English!
Lili:	Yes, I understand English. Do you understand Chinese?
Bob:	Yes, I understand.

Module 1.2

Jen:	Are you Chinese?
Xiaomei:	Yes. Wow, your Chinese is very good!
Jen:	Not so. My Chinese is not good.
Xiaomei:	Are you a student of Chinese?
Jen:	Yes. Are you a teacher?
Xiaomei:	No.
(time lapse)	
Jen:	Goodbye.
Xiaomei:	Goodbye.

Module 1.3

Peter:	How are you?
Wang Bo:	I am very good. Thank you. And you?
Peter:	I am very good. Thank you.
Wang Bo:	What is your name?
Peter:	My name is Peter. And you?
Wang Bo:	My name is Wang Bo. Your Chinese is very good!
Peter:	Not so, not so. Your English is very good.
Wang Bo:	My English is not good.
(time lapse)	
Peter:	Goodbye.
Wang Bo:	Goodbye.

NOTE

Pronunciation Plaza
— The place you come to practice sounds and tones

(Go to 🔘 2-1 to hear:)

Pinyin Practice

Below is a chart of the pronunciation focus for this lesson, with the initials highlighted in ▨ and the finals highlighted in ▨ :

	a	a	a	a	a	o	o	e	e	e	e	i
	a	ai	ao	an	ang	ong	ou	e	ei	en	eng	i
z	za	zai	zao	zan	zang	zong	zou	ze	zei	zen	zeng	zi
c	ca	cai	cao	can	cang	cong	cou	ce	cei	cen	ceng	ci
s	sa	sai	sao	san	sang	song	sou	se		sen	seng	si

Mixed Tone Practice

zá	zài	zǎo	zàn	zāng	zǒng
(mixed)	(at)	(early)	(to praise)	(dirty)	(chief)

zǒu	zé	zéi	zěn	zēng	zì
(to walk)	(to pick)	(thief)	(how)	(to increase)	(word)

cā	cài	cǎo	cán	cáng	cóng
(to wipe)	(vegetable)	(grass)	(incomplete)	(to hide)	(from)

còu	cè	cèi	cēn	céng	cí
(assemble)	(booklet)	(to smash)	(-------)	(storey)	(porcelain)

sǎ	sài	sào	sān	sāng	sòng
(to scatter)	(competition)	(broom)	(three)	(funeral)	(to send)

sōu	sè	sēn	sēng	sì	
(to search)	(color)	(forest)	(monk)	(four)	

21

Sound Differentiation

Initials "*c*" vs. "*s*"

The "s" initial sound in Chinese is like that of the English "s." The "c" sound, on the other hand, does not exist in English. The sound for the initial "c" in Chinese is somewhere between a "t" and an "s" sound in English.

Pronounce the sound for "t," and now for "s," and then try to say them at the same time: "ts." Listen to your audio and see if you can distinguish these two sounds and hear that "ts" sound for the "c" initials and the "s" sound for the "s" initials:

sā – cā	sāi – cāi	sāo – cāo	sān – cān
sāng – cāng	sōng – cōng	cōu – sōu	cē – sē
sēn – cēn	sēi – cēi	sēng – cēng	cī – sī

The final "*i*"

The final "i" has 2 different sounds: One sounds like the long "ee" in English, as in the Chinese surname "Lǐ" (pronounced Lee); the other is like a shortened vowel of someone beginning to pronounce "uh" and getting cut off. For the initials you have just focused on, z, c, s, as well as for these initials, zh, ch, sh, r, you will need to pronounce that shortened vowel sound. Let's practice with just the initials we have learned:

zi   ci   si

Combination Practice:

zìsī (selfish)	sì cì (four times)	sīzì (private)
zǐsì (male offspring)	zìsì (unrestrained)	cìzǐ (the second son)
cìsī (stinging thread)	cìzì (brand a criminal by tattooing)	zìcí (characters and words)

Sound Differentiation Exercise

Listen to the following sounds in 2-2 and write the correct *pinyin* spelling and tones below. See **Appendix IV** for correct answers:

Remember: This section is for training your little ears. If you find it challenging, use your answer key as your aide. Remember to listen either for sound first or tone, then listen more times to get all the answers.

1. sòng   2. cǎo   3. sái   4. zái

5. cèn (zì)   6. sèn (sì)   7. zàng   8. zào

9. cā   10. zǒng (sàng)   11. sàn   12. cé (zè)

13. zēng   14. zén   15. cén (à)   16. cái (zài)

17. sào   18. cóng   19. cè (ì)   20. zén

2. zǒu   3. à

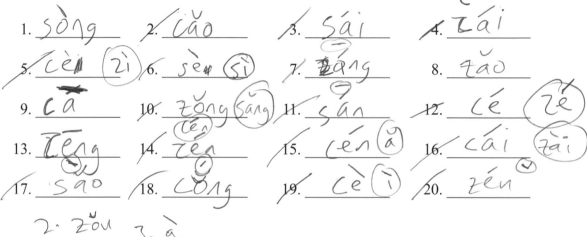

Word Workshop

– The place you come to learn new words and phrases

(Go to 2-3 to hear:)

Verbs

学		我学中文。
xué	**Example:**	Wǒ xué Zhōngwén.
(to study, to learn)		(I study Chinese.)
说		他说英文。
shuō	**Example:**	Tā shuō Yīngwén.
(to say, to speak)		(He speaks English.)
看		我看她。
kàn	**Example:**	Wǒ kàn tā.
(to see, to read, to look at)		(I look at her.)

watch, visit

2

写
xiě
(to write)

Example: 他们写中文。
Tāmen xiě Zhōngwén.
(They write Chinese.)

会
huì
(to know [a skill])

Example: 你会中文吗?
Nǐ huì Zhōngwén ma?
(Do you know Chinese?)

知道
zhīdao
(to know [about something])

Example: 我不知道。
Wǒ bù zhīdao.
(I don't know.)

会说
huì shuō
(to know how to speak)

Example: 我会说中文。
Wǒ huì shuō Zhōngwén.
(I know how to speak Chinese.)

会看
huì kàn
(to know how to read)

Example: 我不会看中文。
Wǒ bú huì kàn Zhōngwén.
(I can't read Chinese.)

会写
huì xiě
(to know how to write)

Example: 他会写中文。
Tā huì xiě Zhōngwén.
(He knows how to write Chinese.)

喜欢
xǐhuān
(to like)

Example: 我喜欢中国。
Wǒ xǐhuan Zhōngguó.
(I like China.)

要
yào
(to want) determined
(I'm going to have to)

Example: 我们要学中文。
Wǒmen yào xué Zhōngwén.
(We want to study Chinese.)

教
jiāo
(to teach)

Example: 我教你们中文。
Wǒ jiāo nǐmen Zhōngwén.
(I teach you [all] Chinese.)

听
tīng
(to listen)

Example: 我喜欢听。
Wǒ xǐhuan tīng.
(I like to listen [to it].)

Supplementary Vocabulary

一点儿
yìdiǎnr*
(a little [bit])
(said in northern accent)

一点
yìdiǎn
(a little [bit])
(said in southern or Taiwanese accent)

* This "r" on the end of this word is a common sound added to the end of words in Mainland China, primarily in the north, and particularly in Beijing. It doesn't have a linguistic purpose and is only there to express an accent. The actual character added is "er (儿)." In *pinyin* when this morpheme is added, one should remove the last consonant sound of the previous character and add the letter "r." Linguists refer to this as the "retroflex" ending.

只
zhǐ*
(only)

Example: Tā zhǐ huì shuō Zhōngwén, bú huì shuō Yīngwén.
(He only knows how to speak Chinese, and doesn't know English.)

他只会说中文，不会说英文。

也
yě*
(also)

Example: Tā huì shuō Zhōngwén yě huì shuō Yīngwén.
(He knows Chinese and also knows how to speak English.)

他会说中文也会说英文。

*"Zhǐ" and "yě" come before the verb.

Grammar Grove
– The place you come to learn about structure

When using verbs in a basic Chinese sentence, you place them in the same spot you would with English. You may have noticed this already, that a basic Chinese declarative sentence has the same word order as English.

Subject + Verb + Object

Here are some examples with the English translation written below:

Wǒ   xué   Zhōngwén.
S.   V.   O.
(I   study   Chinese.)

Tā	xiě	Yīngwén.
S.	V.	O.
(He	writes	English.)

2

Wǒ	xǐhuan	nǐ.
S.	V.	O.
(I	like	you.)

This pattern should come naturally to you.

 ***Chit-Chat Café***
– The place you come to practice speaking

Module 2.1 - (🔊 2-4) / English translation on **Page 35**
Picture this: "Lucy" is a beginner student of Mandarin. She starts talking to a Chinese woman, named "Qiqi" sitting next to her on the bus.

Lucy:	Nǐ shì Zhōngguórén ma?	Lucy:	你是中国人吗？
Qiqi:	Shì. Wā, nǐ huì shuō Zhōngwén!	Qiqi:	是。哇，你会说中文！
Lucy:	Wǒ huì yìdiǎnr.	Lucy:	我会一点儿。
Qiqi:	Nǐ de Zhōngwén hěn hǎo!	Qiqi:	你的中文很好！
Lucy:	Nǎli nǎli. Wǒ de Zhōngwén bù hǎo.	Lucy:	哪里哪里。我的中文不好。
Qiqi:	Nǐ shì Měiguórén ma?	Qiqi:	你是美国人吗？
Lucy:	Shì.	Lucy:	是。
Qiqi:	Nǐ xǐhuan xué Zhōngwén ma?	Qiqi:	你喜欢学中文吗？
Lucy:	Wǒ hěn xǐhuan xué.	Lucy:	我很喜欢学。
Qiqi:	Nǐ huì kàn, huì xiě Zhōngwén ma?	Qiqi:	你会看、会写中文吗？
Lucy:	Wǒ bú huì kàn, bú huì xiě. Wǒ zhǐ huì shuō.	Lucy:	我不会看、不会写。我只会说。

Qiqi:	Wǒ de Yīngwén hěn bù hǎo.	Qiqi:	我的英文很不好。
Lucy:	Nǐ yào xué ma?	Lucy:	你要学吗？
Qiqi:	Wǒ yào xué. Nǐ yào jiāo wǒ ma?	Qiqi:	我要学。你要教我吗？
Lucy:	Hǎo, wǒ jiāo nǐ Yīngwén, nǐ jiāo wǒ Zhōngwén.	Lucy:	好，我教你英文，你教我中文。
Qiqi:	Xièxie.	Qiqi:	谢谢。
Lucy:	Bú kèqi.	Lucy:	不客气。

Chit-Chat Practice 2.1

Here are some questions to answer about yourself in Chinese. Try to answer in full sentences and first try it out loud before writing your answer out. You can find example answers to these questions in **Appendix IV**.

Example:

你喜欢美国吗？　　　　喜欢。我很喜欢美国。

Q: Nǐ xǐhuan Měiguó ma?　A: Xǐhuan. Wǒ hěn xǐhuan Měiguó.

1.

你喜欢中国吗？

Q: Nǐ xǐhuan Zhōngguó ma?　A: *Xǐhuan. Wǒ hěn xǐhuan Zhōngguó.*

2.

你学中文吗？

Q: Nǐ xué Zhōngwén ma?　A: *Xué. Wǒ xué Zhōngwén.*

3.

你会英文吗？

Q: Nǐ huì Yīngwén ma?　A: *Huì. Wǒ huì shuō Yīngwén.*

4.

你会说中文吗？

Q: Nǐ huì shuō Zhōngwén ma?　A: *Bù huì. Wǒ zhǐ xué.*

2

5.

你要学法文吗?

Q: Nǐ yào xué Fǎwén ma? A: _Xué. Wǒ xué Fǎwén._

6.

你会写中文吗?

Q: Nǐ huì xiě Zhōngwén ma? A: _Bú Xué. Wǒ bú huì xiě_
Zhōngwén.

Chit-Chat Practice 2.1 - Brain Stretcher

All right, now let's get you to stretch the ole "noggin." Here are sentences all written with words and grammatical structures you know in Chinese. Let's see if you can figure out their meanings (don't forget to check your answers against the correct ones in **Appendix IV**). Translate the following into English:

Note: Tenses are often determined by context, so there may be more than one right answer in English. You only need to write one answer that would work.

Example:

Chinese: English:

他不好吗?

Tā bù hǎo ma?   Is he not good?

1.

Chinese: English:

我们看他们。

Wǒmen kàn tāmen.   _We see/visit them._

2.

Chinese: English:

他说"你好"。

Tā shuō "Nǐ hǎo."   _He/she says "Hello."_

3.

Chinese: English:

我写我的名字。

Wǒ xiě wǒ de míngzi.   _I write my name._

4.

Chinese:
我要说德文。
Wǒ yào shuō Déwén.

English: I want
I'm going to speak German.

5.

Chinese:
我听老师说中文。
Wǒ tīng lǎoshī shuō
Zhōngwén.

English:
I am listening to my teacher speaking Chinese.

6.

Chinese:
他不会写。
Tā bú huì xiě.

English: doesn't know how to write.
He doesn't know

7.

Chinese:
他只会说。
Tā zhǐ huì shuō.

English:
He only knows how to speak.

 # *Grammar Grove*
– The place you come to learn about structure

Questioning

Part 1
There is another way to ask a question, other than using "ma (嗎)." You may do this with the following formula:

Subject + Verb + "bù" + Verb?

2

Here is how that works:

	Subject	Verb	**bù**	Verb	Object
1)	Nǐ	shì	bú	shì	Měiguórén?
2)	Nǐ	xué	bù	xué	Zhōngwén?
3)	Tā	shuō	bù	shuō	Yīngwén?

1)   Are you American?
2)   Do you study Chinese?
3)   Does he speak English?

Part 2

If the verb has more than one character, you can use the same pattern using both characters (morphemes), like so:

Subject + M_1M_2 * + "bù" + M_1M_2 + Object?

Subject	M_1M_2*	**bù**	M_1M_2	Object
Nǐ	xǐhuan	bù	xǐhuan	Měiguó?

Do you like the U.S.?

*M_1M_2 = morpheme 1 of the combination and morpheme 2

It is more common; however, to use the above pattern and omit the second morpheme in the first combination. This is how that works:

Subject + M_1 + "bù" + M_1M_2 + Object?

Subject	M_1	**bù**	M_1M_2	Object
Nǐ	xǐ	bù	xǐhuan	Měiguó?

Do you like the U.S.?

Note: You should initially use whichever combination comes more naturally to you. But, you should expect to hear and understand the second version more frequently.

More Examples:

	Subject	M₁	bù	M₁M₂	Object
1)	Tā	zhī	bù	zhīdao?	
2)	Tāmen	huì	bú	huì xiě	Zhōngwén?
3)	Lǎoshī	huì	bú	huì shuō	Yīngwén?

1) Does he know?
2) Do they know how to write Chinese?
3) Does teacher know how to speak English?

 Chit-Chat Café
– *The place you come to practice speaking*

Module 2.2 - (2-5) / English translation on **Page 36**
Picture this: "Tim" is Chinese American and a beginner student of Mandarin. He meets "Junli" at a party and thinks she might be Chinese.

Tim: Nǐ hǎo. Nǐ shì Zhōngguórén ma?	Tim: 你好。你是中国人吗？
Junli: Shì. Nǐ ne?	Junli: 是。你呢？
Tim: Wǒ bú shì. Wǒ shì Měiguórén, kěshì (but) wǒ huì shuō Zhōngwén.	Tim: 我不是。我是美国人，可是我会说中文。
Junli: Nǐ huì shuō Zhōngwén. Hěn hǎo!	Junli: 你会说中文。很好！
Tim: Wǒ zhǐ huì yìdiǎnr.	Tim: 我只会一点儿。
Junli: Nǐ huì bú huì xiě Zhōngwén?	Junli: 你会不会写中文？
Tim: Bú huì.	Tim: 不会。
Junli: Nǐ xǐ bù xǐhuan xué Zhōngwén?	Junli: 你喜不喜欢学中文？
Tim: Wǒ hěn xǐhuan xué Zhōngwén.	Tim: 我很喜欢学中文。

Junli: Nǐ jiào shénme míngzi?	Junli: 你叫什么名字？
Tim: Wǒ jiào Tim.	Tim: 我叫Tim。
Junli: Ò, nǐ de Yīngwén míngzi jiào Tim. Wǒ de Yīngwén míngzi jiào Susan. Wǒ de Zhōngwén míngzi shì Jūnlì.	Junli: 哦，你的英文名字叫 Tim。我的英文名字叫 Susan。我的中文名字 是君莉。
Tim: Nǐ huì bú huì shuō Yīngwén?	Tim: 你会不会说英文？
Junli: Wǒ bú huì. Wǒ yào xué.	Junli: 我不会。我要学。
Tim: Hǎo, wǒ jiào nǐ Yīngwén, nǐ jiāo wǒ Zhōngwén. Hǎo bù hǎo?	Tim: 好，我教你英文，你 教我中文。好不好？
Junli: Hǎo, xièxie.	Junli: 好，谢谢。

Chit-Chat Practice 2.2

Ask the question that goes to these answers, and put down BOTH ways to ask.

Example:

Answer:

君莉是中国人。

Jūnlì shì Zhōngguórén.

Two ways to ask the question:

1. Jūnlì shì Zhōngguórén ma?
2. Jūnlì shì bú shì Zhōngguórén?

1.
Answer:

Tim是美国人。

Tim shì Měiguórén.

Two ways to ask the question:

1. Tim shì Měiguórén ma?
2. Tim shì bú shì Měiguórén?

2.
Answer:

Tim学中文。

Tim xué Zhōngwén.

Two ways to ask the question:

1. Tim xué Zhōngwén ma?
2. Tim xué bú xué Zhōngwén?

Tim huì bú huì xiě Zhōngwén huì

3.

Answer:

Tim不会写中文。

Tim bú huì xiě Zhōngwén.

Two ways to ask the question:

1. *Tim huì bú huì xiě Zhōngwén ma?*
2. *Tim bú huì xiě bú xiě Zhōngwén?*

4.

Answer:

Tim喜欢学中文。

Tim xǐhuan xué Zhōngwén.

Two ways to ask the question:

1. *Tim xǐhuan xué Zhōngwén na?*
2. *Tim xǐ bú xǐhuan xué Zhōngwén?*

5.

Answer:

君莉不会说英文。

Jūnlì bú huì shuō Yīngwén.

Two ways to ask the question:

1. *Jūnlì bú huì shuō Yīngwén ma?*
2. *Jūnlì huì bú huì shuō Yīngwén?*

Check your answers in **Appendix IV**.

 ## Culture Corner
– The place you come to learn more than just language

打破沙锅问到底。

dǎpò shāguō wèn dào dǐ

"You get to the bottom of things by asking a lot of questions."

Chinese saying

Asking questions in Chinese

"How much money do you make?"
"How much is your rent?"
"How old are you?"
"Are you married?"
"Why aren't you married?"
"How much do you weigh?"
"How much did that cost you?"

2

These are all questions that are acceptable in Chinese culture, and may require some getting used to for a westerner. The questioner by no means is being rude or nosey in the context of Chinese culture. So try to answer politely and not take offense.

"But," you may protest, "I don't want to tell someone I don't know well how much money I make or my marital status." And, that is understandable, but to not be rude to your new Chinese friends you may have to do some fancy footwork to get around the questions. You could just "When in Rome do as the Romans do," and answer the question. Or, if you really can't bear to answer the question, sidestep it or turn it into a joke. Here is one approach:

Q: "How much is your rent?" A: "Too much."
Q: "How old are you?" A: "I've stopped counting."
Q: "Why aren't you married?" A: "Why haven't you found me a husband?"

Many Chinese who have contact with westerners will know certain questions are not polite in western culture, so, if you are in an urban center, likely you will not be bombarded with too many of these kinds of questions. If you do, remember they are not taking the question so seriously and it won't be that big a deal to just answer honestly.

 ## *Advice Alcove*
– The place you come to learn how to learn

学无止境
xué wú zhǐjìng
"There is no end to learning."
Chinese saying

Study habits are important to learning any language, but particularly important for the western learner who is learning a non-western language. You are not happily handed a plateful of cognates, as you would be with say Spanish or French. Instead, each word and phrase must be memorized from scratch. Add to that sounds and concepts, such as tones, which don't exist in your native language, which also must be learned and incorporated into your speech. Consistency in your studies is crucial to moving forward. Here are some ways to make sure you are on track with your studying:

- Dedicate a short period of time every day for memorization and review of your material, even if it is as short as 15 minutes.
- Dedicate one or more longer periods each week to sit down for 2 or more hours to study.
- Schedule your study time and put it in your calendar. Make sure you have a specific day and time, for example, Sunday from 4 p.m.-6 p.m., that you always study.
- Use down time, such as while riding public transportation, driving, or any other time you are waiting or in transit, to pull out your flashcards, listen to your audio CD, or listen to a podcast class.
- Remember to review constantly. Learning new material is good, but you will forget the old material if it is not also a part of your study schedule.
- Make study a priority as you would with an exercise regime or other such commitment.

Owning a language school for over a decade, I have been able to observe what amounts in the end to a successful language student, and the one prominent thing they all have in common is consistency. Consistently study, practice and review.

English Translation

Module 2.1

Lucy:	Are you Chinese?
Qiqi:	Yes. Wow, you know how to speak Chinese!
Lucy:	I know a little bit.
Qiqi:	Your Chinese is very good.
Lucy:	Not so. My Chinese isn't good.
Qiqi:	Are you American?
Lucy:	Yes.
Qiqi:	Do you like studying Chinese?
Lucy:	I like to study it very much.
Qiqi:	Do you know how to read and write Chinese?
Lucy:	I don't know how to read or write. I only know how to speak.
Qiqi:	My English is not good.

2

Lucy:	Do you want to study it?
Qiqi:	Yes, I want to study it. Do you want to teach me?
Lucy:	OK. I'll teach you English. You teach me Chinese.
Qiqi:	Thank you.
Lucy:	You're welcome.

Module 2.2

Tim:	Hello. Are you Chinese?
Junli:	Yes, and you?
Tim:	I am not. I am American, but I know how to speak Chinese.
Junli:	You know how to speak Chinese. That's great.
Tim:	I only know a little.
Junli:	Do you know how to write Chinese?
Tim:	No, I don't.
Junli:	Do you like studying Chinese?
Tim:	I like studying Chinese a lot.
Junli:	What is your name?
Tim:	My name is Tim.
Junli:	Oh, Your English name is Tim. My English name is Susan. My Chinese name is Junli.
Tim:	Do you know how to speak English?
Junli:	I don't know how to. I want to study it.
Tim:	Good, I'll teach you English and you teach me Chinese. All right?
Junli:	Great, thanks.

Pronunciation Plaza
— The place you come to practice sounds and tones

(Go to 🔘 3-1 to hear:)

Tone Exceptions

In Chinese there are some tone exceptions, where the tone of the character will change based on the tone of the character that follows it. Not to worry, there are very few of these. Here is one basic exception you should be aware of:

The "bù" Exception

"Not" in Chinese, or "bù," is typically said in the 4th tone. However, this changes from a 4th to a 2nd tone when the following character (morpheme) is a 4th tone. Allow me to show you how this works with words you already know:

Behold! All these "bu" stick to their original 4th tone. Why? Because none of the second characters are a 4th tone:

不好	不写	不说	不听
bù hǎo	bù xiě	bù shuō	bù tīng
(not good)	(not write)	(not speak)	(not hear)

Now, look. "Bu" suddenly can't stand being a 4th tone. It must morph itself into a 2nd tone. Why? Because the following character is a 4th tone and that's just what "bu" likes to do when the next character is a 4th tone:

不是	不会	不看	不要
bú shì	bú huì	bú kàn	bú yào
(is not)	(not know)	(not read)	(not want)

Note: In some textbooks the tone change is not printed and the student is expected to remember to change it when speaking. In this book we will make the change for you.

Pinyin Practice

Below is a chart of the pronunciation focus for this lesson, with the initials highlighted in ▢ and the finals highlighted in ▢ :

	a					o		e				u							
	a	ai	ao	an	ang	ong	ou	e	ei	en	eng	u	ua	uo	ui	uai	uan	un	uang
g	ga	gai	gao	gan	gang	gong	gou	ge	gei	gen	geng	gu	gua	guo	gui	guai	guan	gun	guang
k	ka	kai	kao	kan	kang	kong	kou	ke	kei	ken	keng	ku	kua	kuo	kui	kuai	kuan	kun	kuang
h	ha	hai	hao	han	hang	hong	hou	he	hei	hen	heng	hu	hua	huo	hui	huai	huan	hun	huang

Mixed Tone Practice

gā (*onomat.*)	gāi (should)	gāo (tall)	gǎn (to catch up)	gāng (steel)	gòng (altogether)
gǒu (dog)	gē (song)	gěi (to give)	gēn (root)	gèng (more)	gǔ (drum)
guā (melon)	guó (country)	guì (expensive)	guài (strange)	guān (to close)	gǔn (to roll)
guāng (light)					
kǎ (card)	kāi (to open)	kǎo (to test)	kàn (to see)	kàng (to resist)	kōng (empty)
kǒu (mouth)	kě (thirsty)	kēi (to beat)	kěn (to be willing to)	kēng (hole)	kǔ (bitter)
kuā (to praise)	kuò (to include)	kuì (ashamed)	kuài (fast)	kuān (wide)	kǔn (to bundle up)
kuáng (crazy)					
hā (to breath out)	hǎi (sea)	hǎo (good)	hán (cold)	háng (a row)	hóng (red)

hòu	hé	hēi	hěn	héng	hù
(back)	(river)	(black)	(very)	(horizontal)	(to protect)

huā	huó	huí	huài	huān	hūn
(flower)	(to live)	(to return)	(bad)	(cheerful)	(marriage)

huáng
(yellow)

Sound Differentiation

What's this "woo" sound I am hearing?

If you find your ears ringing with the sound of "*woo*" every time you hear a word with "u" in it followed by another final, you don't need to go see a doctor. Notice the difference:

gu = sounds like "goo"
ku = sounds like "koo"
hu = sounds like "who" ("*hoo*")

While these are pronounced as so:

gui = sounds like "g-woo-ay"
kuan = sounds like "k-woo-an"
huang = sounds like "h-woo-ang"

Any time you have a letter following that "u," you will have to get that "*woo*" sound in for it to sound correct, let's practice that sound in isolation:

guā	guó	guì	guài	guān	gǔn
(melon)	(country)	(expensive)	(strange)	(to close)	(to roll)

guāng	kuā	kuò	kuī	kuài	kuǎn
(light)	(to praise)	(to include)	(to lose)	(fast)	(sincere)

kùn	kuàng	huā	huó	huí	huài
(in distress)	(condition)	(flower)	(to live)	(to return)	(bad)

huān	hūn	huáng
(cheerful)	(marriage)	(yellow)

Note: Later you will learn the "ü" sound, sometimes written simply as "u." In those cases, it will not have a "w" sound to it. We will go over that when we get to it.

Sound Differentiation Exercise

Listen to the following sounds in 🔘 3-2 and write the correct *pinyin* spelling and tones below. See **Appendix IV** for correct answers:

1. _____   2. _____   3. _____   4. _____

5. _____   6. _____   7. _____   8. _____

9. _____   10. _____   11. _____   12. _____

13. _____   14. _____   15. _____   16. _____

17. _____   18. _____   19. _____   20. _____

 *Grammar Grove*
– *The place you come to learn about structure*

Adjectives

You do not need the verb "shì (to be)" in Chinese with adjectives. You can just say the subject and then the adjective as in "She pretty," "We happy," "He tall." You should also say "hěn (very)" before the adjective when speaking in the affirmative, whether you mean "very" or not. In the negative or in questions this is not necessary.

Q: So why do I have to say "hěn" even when I don't mean "very"? And, how can I express something, for example, that is "pretty," but not "very pretty"?

A: Why? Unfortunately, no one knows why. That is just the way it is done and it just won't sound right if you don't add in "hěn." If you really want to make sure the person knows you don't mean "very," simply say the negative version: So, instead of saying "Chinese is very difficult," say "Chinese isn't easy."

When asking questions with adjectives, you may do so by adding "ma (吗)" or by using the same sentence pattern you used to ask questions with verbs. So with adjectives containing one character you may ask a question like so:

Subject + Adj. + ma?   OR   Subject + Adj. + bù + Adj.?

Also, just like asking a verb question, adjectives with two morphemes you may ask a question using "ma" or like so:

Subject + M_1M_2 + bù + M_1M_2?   OR   Subject + M_1 + bù + M_1M_2?

Word Workshop
– *The place you come to learn new words and phrases*

3

(Go to 3-3 to hear:)

Adjectives

大
dà
(big)

⇔

小
xiǎo
(small)

Example: 中国很大。
Zhōngguó hěn dà.
(China is big.)

高
gāo
(tall / high)

⇔

矮
ǎi
(short)

Example: 他很高。
Tā hěn gāo.
(He is tall.)

美/漂亮
měi / piàoliang
(beautiful)

⇔

丑
chǒu
(ugly)

Example: 她很漂亮。
Tā hěn piàoliang.
(She is beautiful.)

好看
hǎokàn
(good-looking)
(LIT: good, look)

⇔

难看
nánkàn
(unattractive)
(LIT: difficult, look)

Example: 他很好看。
Tā hěn hǎokàn.
(He is good-looking.)

gāoxìng

快乐 vs
kuàilè
(happy)
(LIT: quick, happy)

⇔ 难过
nánguò
(sad)
(LIT: difficult, pass)

我不难过。
Example: Wǒ bù nánguò.
(I am not sad.)

3

胖
pàng
(fat)

⇔ 瘦
shòu
(thin)

你不胖。
Example: Nǐ bú pàng.
(You are not fat.)

难
nán
(difficult)

⇔ 容易
róngyì
(easy)

中文不难。
Example: Zhōngwén bù nán.
(Chinese is not difficult.)

聪明
cōngmíng
(intelligent)

⇔ 笨
bèn
(stupid)

你很聪明。
Example: Nǐ hěn cōngmíng.
(You are very intelligent.)

Chit-Chat Café
– The place you come to practice speaking

Module 3.1 - (3-4) / English translation on **Page 54**
Picture this: "Jack" is talking to his Chinese friend "Yuanyuan" about Kate Winslet.
For the sake of simplicity we will keep Kate Winslet's name in English.

Yuanyuan: Kate Winslet shì Měiguórén ma?	Yuanyuan: Kate Winslet是美国人吗?
Jack: Bú shì. Tā shì Yīngguórén.	Jack: 不是。她是英国人。
Yuanyuan: Nǐ xǐhuan tā ma?	Yuanyuan: 你喜欢她吗?

Jack:	Wǒ hěn xǐhuan.	Jack:	我很喜欢。
Yuanyuan:	Tā piào bú piàoliang?	Yuanyuan:	她漂不漂亮？
Jack:	Tā hěn piàoliang.	Jack:	她很漂亮。
Yuanyuan:	Tā pàng bú pàng?	Yuanyuan:	她胖不胖？
Jack:	Tā bú pàng yě bú shòu.	Jack:	她不胖也不瘦。
Yuanyuan:	Tā cōng bù cōngmíng?	Yuanyuan:	她聪不聪明？
Jack:	Tā hěn cōngmíng.	Jack:	她很聪明。
Yuanyuan:	Tā huì bú huì shuō Zhōngwén?	Yuanyuan:	她会不会说中文？
Jack:	Tā bú huì. Tā shuō Yīngwén.	Jack:	她不会。她说英文。
Yuanyuan:	Tā yào xué Zhōngwén ma?	Yuanyuan:	她要学中文吗？
Jack:	Wǒ bù zhīdao.	Jack:	我不知道。

Module 3.2 - (3-5) / English translation on **Page 54**

Picture this: "Amy" is talking to her friend "Dijia" about "Gong Li," China's most famous actress.

Amy:	Gǒng Lì shì Zhōngguórén ma?	Amy:	巩俐是中国人吗？
Dijia:	Shì. Tā shì Zhōngguórén.	Dijia:	是。她是中国人。
Amy:	Tā hěn piàoliang. Nǐ xǐhuan tā ma?	Amy:	她很漂亮。你喜欢她吗？
Dijia:	Wǒ hěn xǐhuan. Tā hěn cōngmíng yě hěn piàoliang.	Dijia:	我很喜欢。她很聪明也很漂亮。
Amy:	Tā gāo bù gāo?	Amy:	她高不高？
Dijia:	Tā bù gāo yě bù ǎi.	Dijia:	她不高也不矮。
Amy:	Tā huì shuō Yīngwén ma?	Amy:	她会说英文吗？

Dijia: Tā huì shuō. Tā de Yīngwén hěn hǎo.	Dijia: 她会说。她的英文很好。
Amy: Tā huì bú huì xiě Yīngwén.	Amy: 她会不会写英文？
Dijia: Wǒ bù zhīdao.	Dijia: 我不知道。
Amy: Tā pàng bú pàng?	Dijia: 她胖不胖？
Dijia: Tā bú pàng yě bú shòu.	Dijia: 她不胖也不瘦。

Chit-Chat Practice 3.1 & 3.2

Questions about famous people, places & things
Now that you have heard a couple of conversations about famous people, let's see what you think about the following famous people, places and things. Note that names which you haven't learned will be kept in English, or in parenthesis in English, for simplicity. You can find example answers to these questions in **Appendix IV**.

Example:

中国大不大？
Q: Zhōngguó dà bú dà?
中国很大。
A: Zhōngguó hěn dà.

1.

Scarlett Johansson 漂不漂亮？
Q: Scarlett Johansson piào bú piàoliang?
A: Shì, SJ piàoliang.

2.

姚明高不高？
Q: Yáo Míng gāo bù gāo?
A: Shì, YM hěn gāo.

3.

George Clooney 好不好看？

Q: George Clooney hǎo bù hǎokàn?

A: Shì, GC hǎokàn.
hěn

4.

孔子聪不聪明？

Q: Kǒngzǐ (Confucius) cōng bù cōngmíng?

A: Shì, Kǒngzǐ hěn cōngmíng.

5.

Paris Hilton 胖不胖？

Q: Paris Hilton pàng bú pàng?

A: Bú shì, PH bú pàng.

6.

功夫容不容易？

Q: Gōngfu (kungfu) róng bù róngyì?

A: Bú shì, gōngfu bù róngyì.

7.

Britney Spears 难不难过？

Q: Britney Spears nán bù nánguò?

A: Tā bù nánguò yě bú kuàilè.

8.

"Mini Me" 矮不矮？

Q: "Mini Me" ǎi bù ǎi?

A: Shì, Tā hěn ǎi.

3

45

9.

美国美不美?

Q: Měiguó měi bù měi?

A: <u>Shì, Měiguó *hěn* měi.</u>

3

10.

成龙快不快乐?

Q: Chéng Lóng (Jackie Chan) kuài bú kuàilè?

A: <u>Chéng Lóng *hěn* kuàilè</u>

Further discussion: Now on your own or in your class look at the above pictures and ask and answer as many questions as you can, such as "Is Britney Spears American?", "Is she tall?", "Is she smart?", etc.

 Grammar Grove
– The place you come to learn about structure

Comparatives

In Chinese you use the word "bǐ (比)" to compare two things, to say something is more something than the other (e.g. "taller," "smarter," "shorter," etc.). Here is the construction you will use:

A	bǐ	B	Adj.	Whichever comes first is the "more" of the two.

Let me show how that works by illustrating the sentence pattern with English words:

You bǐ me tall. = You are taller than me.

He bǐ you smart. = He is smarter than you.

Now in Chinese:

他比我矮。
Tā bǐ wǒ ǎi. = He is shorter than me.

Can put hěn, other ma líbǎo after

中文比英文难。

Zhōngwén bǐ Yīngwén nán. = Chinese is more difficult than English.

他比我快乐。

Tā bǐ wǒ kuàilè. = He is happier than me.

你的中文比我的英文好。

Nǐ de Zhōngwén bǐ wǒ de Yīngwén hǎo.

= Your Chinese is better than my English.

Let's now practice this in a drill. Read the following out loud pausing to make sure you have understood each sentence. You may check an English translation in **Appendix IV**, to make sure. Remember in this case A is always more the adjective than B:

"Bǐ (比)" Pattern Drill

A	bǐ	B	adj.
Měiguó		Yīngguó	dà.

1. : The U.S. is bigger than England.

Yīngguó	bǐ	Měiguó	xiǎo.

2. : England is smaller than America.

Lǎoshī	bǐ	xuésheng	cōngmíng.

3. : The teacher is more intelligent then the student.

Nǐ de Yīngwén	bǐ	wǒ de Zhōngwén	hǎo.

4. : Your English is much better than my China

Tāmen	bǐ	wǒmen	pàng.

5. : They are fatter than us.

Nǐmen **bǐ** tāmen ǎi.

6.: You all are taller than them.

Běijīng **bǐ** Shànghǎi měi.

7.: Běijīng is more beautiful than Shanghai.

Xué Zhōngwén **bǐ** xué Yīngwén nán.

8.: Studying Chinese is more difficult than studying English.

Shuō Zhōngwén **bǐ** shuō Yīngwén róngyì.

9.: Speaking Chinese is easier than speaking English.

Déguórén **bǐ** Měiguórén gāo.

10.: Germans are taller than Chinese. Americas

Fǎwén **bǐ** Yīngwén nán xué.

11.: French is harder than English to study.

Kàn Yīngwén **bǐ** kàn Zhōngwén róngyì.

12.: Reading English is more difficult than reading chinese

Superlatives

To say something is the "most" or the "_____ est," as in "tallest," "most difficult," "smartest," etc., you use the word "zuì" before the adjective or verb:

他最高。
Tā zuì gāo. = He is the tallest.

我们最快乐。
Wǒmen zuì kuàilè. = We are the happiest.

我最喜欢中文。
Wǒ zuì xǐhuan Zhōngwén. = I like Chinese the best.

Chit-Chat Café
– *The place you come to practice speaking*

Module 3.3 - (3-6) / English translation on **Page 55**
Picture this: "Tim" completed a beginner's course in Mandarin. He is in China traveling for a month, when he meets a teacher named "Wang laoshi."

Wang:	Nǐ shì Měiguórén ma?	Wang:	你是美国人吗？
Tim:	Shì. Nǐ ne?	Tim:	是。你呢？
Wang:	Wǒ bú shì. Wǒ shì Zhōngguórén. Nǐ huì shuō Zhōngwén ma?	Wang:	我不是。我是中国人。你会说中文吗？
Tim:	Huì. Nǐ huì shuō Yīngwén ma?	Tim:	会。你会说英文吗？
Wang:	Wǒ zhǐ huì yìdiǎnr. Nǐ de Zhōngwén bǐ wǒ de Yīngwén hǎo. Nǐ bǐ wǒ cōngmíng.	Wang:	我只会一点儿。你的中文比我的英文好。你比我聪明。
Tim:	Nǎli nǎli. Wǒ zhǐ huì yìdiǎnr. Wǒ de Zhōngwén hěn bù hǎo.	Tim:	哪里哪里。我只会一点儿。我的中文很不好。
Wang:	Zhōngwén nán bù nán xué?	Wang:	中文难不难学？
Tim:	Zhōngwén hěn bù róngyì. Zhōngwén bǐ Yīngwén nán xué.	Tim:	中文很不容易。中文比英文难学。
Wang:	Yīngwén yě hěn nán xué.	Wang:	英文也很难学。
Tim:	Xiě Yīngwén bǐ xiě Zhōngwén róngyì.	Tim:	写英文比写中文容易。

3

| Wang: | Xiě Zhōngwén hěn nán. Kàn Zhōngwén bǐ kàn Yīngwén nán. | Wang: | 写中文很难。看中文比看英文难。 |
| Tim: | Kěshì (but), Zhōngwén bǐ Yīngwén piàoliang! Wǒ zuì xǐhuan Zhōngwén. | Tim: | 可是，中文比英文漂亮！我最喜欢中文。 |

3

Chit-Chat Practice 3.3

The last dialogue may have required some tricky mental gymnastics. Let's make sure you understood it all correctly. Below write a translation of the entire dialogue into English. You should compare your answers to the English translation on **Page 55**. Here we have started the first line for you:

Wang: Are you American?

Tim: I am. And you?

Wang: I'm not. I'm Chinese. Do you know how to

Tim: I know. Can you speak English? *Speak Chinese?*

Wang: I only know a little. Your Chinese is better than my English

Tim: No, no, I only know a little. My Chinese is not very good

Wang: Chinese is difficult to study?

Tim: Chinese is not very easy. Chinese is harder

Wang: English is also not easy to study

Tim: Writing English is harder than Chinese

Wang: Writing Chinese is very difficult too

Tim: But Chinese is more beautiful than English! I like Chinese the best.

Culture Corner
– The place you come to learn more than just language

Now that you have learned some adjectives and can describe others and yourself, and even give and receive compliments, it is time to learn about something central to Chinese culture and politesse: humility. The act of remaining, or at least appearing to remain, humble in all circumstances is a very important social skill. If you have had any contact with people from China, you probably already recognize this trait: reluctance to brag, a deflection of any and all compliments, a willingness to put anyone else above oneself. However, there may have been or will come other times when this humility manifests itself in a way that leaves the westerner scratching his head and wondering what exactly is going on. For example, how would you feel if a friendly mother at your child's school said, "Your son is so smart and diligent, but my son is so lazy and slow"? You would probably feel shocked and sorry for that poor boy with such a mean mother.

In fact, in Chinese culture this woman has shown great humility in not bragging about her son. By complimenting your son and putting her own son down she has gained "face" for both herself and her son. (The concept of "face" is something I will discuss in Lesson Four.) You may see a similar thing between spouses and wonder if the husband or wife would get an earful later back at home. In fact, the opposite is true; the spouse is more at ease because socially as a couple they are demonstrating humility. So, for example, when I (the author here) was visiting a Chinese couple with my then boyfriend (also fluent in Mandarin), the husband and wife both frequently outlined each other's faults while delineating our own talents or good looks. This time the husband said: "If my wife were half as beautiful as your girlfriend, then I would be happy." Luckily, we were familiar with how to respond and my boyfriend said: "But, if my girl friend could cook half as well as your wife, then I would be happy." We all laughed and no one took offense. The humility-complimentary-face-gaining game can be light-hearted and does not hold the weight an outsider might mistake it to have. In fact, in this situation the wife feels good her husband is making the guests feel complimented. The family unit has shown humility and respect.

Here are some guidelines for showing humility and for responding to the humility of others:

Displaying humility:

- Never talk about what you think you are good at (e.g. "I learn languages fast."); this is seen as bragging, even if what you say is true.
- Avoid saying how great, smart or good-looking any family member is.
- Don't discuss how great your country is for any reason.
- Deny any compliments as untrue or an exaggeration (you will learn more expressions for this; but "nǎli nǎli" is a good blanket deflector).
- Don't try to win a discussion or debate in public.
- Don't show off a talent, unless you have been asked many times by your hosts (e.g. playing the piano, etc.)
- Be quick to think of a reply compliment for any compliment you receive.

Responding to humility:

- Don't be put off if someone seems to be criticizing themselves, their child or spouse; remember this is just a societal way of showing humility for the whole family unit.
- Don't agree with anyone's self-criticism; deny it and offer a compliment.
- Remember no one is taking it too seriously; it's just a social grace.
- Be astute in noticing positive things about your friends, so you are ready to offer up compliments.

Advice Alcove
– The place you come to learn how to learn

学以致用
xué yǐ zhì yòng
"Study something to put it into use."
Chinese proverb

Now that you have a system for memorizing your vocabulary and sentences, it is time to start to get in the habit of using your language skills. You will only be able to say a few greetings and some simple sentences, but it is important to start using your skills. "Doing," or actively using, your language skills is the cornerstone to retaining what you have learned and progressing forward. Language learning is more akin to learning a physical skill, rather than an intellectual pursuit. If you wanted to learn windsurfing, you could sit on the shore and learn all the techniques in the world. However, it doesn't amount to anything until you actually get on the board on the water and try it. Also, like learning a sport, there can be some embarrassment in trying out your fledgling skills. You will fall off, trip over yourself and generally feel like an uncoordinated toddler. Getting past this fear is very important to gaining speaking skills. You simply have to put it out of your mind and get started even when your skills are at their lowest.

Here are ways to begin using Chinese in your day-to-day life:

- Write out and practice imaginary conversations you could have with Chinese speakers in your life (e.g. in your school or office, with friends you know, in a Chinese restaurant, etc.).
- Start a conversation with a Chinese speaker and get as far as you can before switching back to English.
- Even if the person speaks English very well, ask for a "favor" to try speaking Chinese for just a little while.
- Remember people appreciate your effort in learning their language. Even if you can't have a full conversation, they will understand you are trying.
- After the conversation, go over what was said in your head. Take notes when you get home on how you could have taken the conversation further. Look up words that you needed but couldn't produce in the conversation.
- Carry a dictionary with you. If you start a conversation with someone who doesn't know English, you may need to look up a word in order to continue forward. The Chinese value education and studiousness. You will be surprised at the positive and patient response you get when you need to stop and look something up. They will probably say you are "hěn rènzhēn (very diligent)."

Typically a language learner will need to hear and use a word or phrase 20 times before it is "learned." This means you will need to start to practice the same conversation many times before it becomes second-hand. Once it is truly learned you will not need to think about it and new words and phrases will become the challenge. This is how language learning progresses.

English Translation

Module 3.1

Yuanyuan:	Is Kate Winslet American?
Jack:	No. She is English.
Yuanyuan:	Do you like her?
Jack:	I like her a lot.
Yuanyuan:	Is she pretty?
Jack:	She is very pretty.
Yuanyuan:	Is she fat?
Jack:	She is not fat, but also not thin.
Yuanyuan:	Is she smart?
Jack:	She is very smart.
Yuanyuan:	Does she know how to speak Chinese?
Jack:	She doesn't know. She speaks English.
Yuanyuan:	Does she want to study Chinese?
Jack:	I don't know.

Module 3.2

Amy:	Is Gong Li Chinese?
Dijia:	Yes. She is Chinese.
Amy:	She is very pretty. Do you like her?
Dijia:	I like her a lot. She is smart and also pretty.
Amy:	Is she tall?
Dijia:	She is not tall, but also not short.
Amy:	Does she know how to speak English?
Dijia:	Yes, she does. Her English is very good.
Amy:	Does she know how to write English?
Dijia:	I don't know.
Amy:	Is she fat?
Dijia:	She is not fat, but also not thin.

Module 3.3 & Chit Chat Practice 3.3

Wang:	Are you American?
Tim:	Yes. And you?
Wang:	I am not. I am Chinese. Do you know how to speak Chinese?
Tim:	Yes. Do you know how to speak English?
Wang:	I only know a little bit. Your Chinese is better than my English. You are smarter than me.
Tim:	Not so, not so. I only know a little. My Chinese is not good.
Wang:	Is Chinese difficult to learn?
Tim:	Chinese is really not easy. Chinese is harder to learn than English.
Wang:	English is also very difficult to learn.
Tim:	Writing English is easier than writing Chinese.
Wang:	Writing Chinese is very difficult. Reading Chinese is more difficult than reading English.
Tim:	But, Chinese is more beautiful than English! I like Chinese the most.

3

NOTE

LESSON 4

 Pronunciation Plaza
– The place you come to practice sounds and tones

4

(Go to 4-1 to hear:)

Tone Exceptions

Here is another tone change that you will need to be aware of: when a third tone is immediately followed by another third tone, it should be pronounced as a second tone. The tone mark as shown in textbooks; however, will remain unchanged. So, you will see the third tone mark "ⱴ", but will be expected to remember to pronounce the character as a second tone.

Examples:

你好
nǐ hǎo   should be pronounced as = ní hǎo
(hello)

很好
hěn hǎo   should be pronounced as = hén hǎo
(very good)

很矮
hěn ǎi   should be pronounced as = hén ǎi
(very short)

也好
yě hǎo   should be pronounced as = yé hǎo
(also good)

Just remember to keep this change in mind since you won't see the tone change indicated.

Pinyin Practice

Below is a chart of the sounds we will cover in this lesson, with the initials highlighted in [ ] and the finals highlighted in [ ]:

	a					o		e			
	a	ai	ao	an	ang	ong	ou	e	ei	en	eng
zh	zha	zhai	zhao	zhan	zhang	zhong	zhou	zhe	zhei	zhen	zheng
ch	cha	chai	chao	chan	chang	chong	chou	che		chen	cheng
sh	sha	shai	shao	shan	shang		shou	she	shei	shen	sheng
r			rao	ran	rang	rong	rou	re		ren	reng
j											
q											
x											

	i									
	i	ia	iao	ie	iu	ian	iang	in	ing	iong
zh	zhi									
ch	chi									
sh	shi									
r	ri									
j	ji	jia	jiao	jie	jiu	jian	jiang	jin	jing	jiong
q	qi	qia	qiao	qie	qiu	qian	qiang	qin	qing	qiong
x	xi	xia	xiao	xie	xiu	xian	xiang	xin	xing	xiong

Mixed Tone Practice

zhá (deep-fry)	zhài (debt)	zhǎo (to look for)	zhǎn (exhibition)	zhāng (to spread)	zhōng (clock)
zhōu (continent)	zhè (this)	zhèi (this)	zhēn (really)	zhèng (politics)	zhǐ (only)
chá (to check)	chái (firewood)	chāo (to exceed)	chǎn (to produce)	cháng (long)	chōng (to fill)
chòu (smelly)	chē (vehicle)	chén (to sink)	chéng (to become)	chī (to eat)	
shā (sand)	shài (to shine on)	shǎo (less)	shān (mountain)	shàng (up)	shǒu (hand)
shé (snake)	shéi (who)	shēn (body)	shēng (to give birth to)		shí (ten)

58

rào	rǎn	ràng	róng	ròu
(to coil)	(to dye)	(to yield)	(to contain)	(meat)

rè	rén	réng	rì
(hot)	(human being)	(still)	(day)

jǐ	jiā	jiào	jié	jiù	jiàn
(oneself)	(home)	(to call)	(knot)	(just)	(to see)

jiǎng	jìn	jīng	jiǒng
(award)	(to enter)	(to go past)	(embarrassed)

qǐ	qià	qiáo	qiē	qiú	qián
(to rise)	(appropriate)	(bridge)	(to cut)	(ball)	(money)

qiáng	qīn	qíng	qióng
(strong)	(relative)	(sunny)	(poor)

xī	xià	xiǎo	xiě	xiū	xiàn
(west)	(down)	(small)	(to write)	(to repair)	(to appear)

xiǎng	xīn	xíng	xióng
(to think)	(heart)	(to walk)	(bear)

Sound Differentiation

The short final "i"

As mentioned in the last lesson, any "i" final preceded by these initials, z, c, s, zh, ch, sh, and r, should be pronounced as a short vowel. Notice how these words in this lesson focus are pronounced:

zhǐ	chī	shí	rì
(only)	(to eat)	(ten)	(day)

The longer final "i"

Any final "i" preceded by these initials, b, p, m, d, t, n, l, j, q, x, on the other hand, should be pronounced as a longer "ee" sound, as in "bee" or "fee." Here are the three words in this lesson focus with that sound:

jǐ	qǐ	xī
(oneself)	(to rise)	(west)

Combination Practice:

qíshí (in fact)	sījī (driver)	zǐxì (attentively)	rìqī (date)
cíqì (porcelain)	jīqì (machine)	zìsī (selfish)	xīqí (rare)
zhíjí (job rank)	jīchì (chicken wings)	rìshí (solar eclipse)	zīshì (posture)

4 Sound Differentiation Exercise

Listen to the following sounds in 🔘 4-2 and write the correct *pinyin* spelling and tones below. See **Appendix IV** for correct answers:

1. _____ 2. _____ 3. _____ 4. _____

5. _____ 6. _____ 7. _____ 8. _____

9. _____ 10. _____ 11. _____ 12. _____

13. _____ 14. _____ 15. _____ 16. _____

17. _____ 18. _____ 19. _____ 20. _____

 Word Workshop
– The place you come to learn new words and phrases

(Go to 🔘 4-3 to hear:)

Verbal Preposition - (to be) in / at / on

在
zài
([to be] in, at, on)

Example:

我在美国。
Wǒ zài Měiguó.
(I am in the U.S.)

Note: The verb "to be" is implicit in the meaning of this preposition, therefore it is known as a "verbal preposition." There is no need to say "shì" in sentences with "zài."

"Zài" should be placed after the subject and before the location:

Subject + zài + Location

Caution Learners! The location of "zài" is not where you would expect it as an English speaker. It should go directly after the subject and before the verb:

Subject + zài + Location + verb

Example:
我在美国学中文。
Wǒ zài Měiguó xué Zhōngwén.
(I study Chinese in the U.S.)

Verb - To live

住
zhù
(to live [reside])

住在
zhù zài
(to live [reside] in / at)

Example: 我住在美国。
Wǒ zhù zài Měiguó.
(I live in the U.S.)

Question Words (interrogative pronouns)

谁
shéi / shuí*
(who)
* both forms acceptable

Example: 你是谁?
Nǐ shì shéi?
(Who are you?)

什么
shénme
(what)

Example: 你要什么?
Nǐ yào shénme?
(What do you want?)

哪
nǎ / něi
(which)

Example: 你是哪国人?
Nǐ shì něi guó rén?
(What country are you from?)
(LIT: You are which country person?)

哪儿/哪里
nǎr / nǎli*
(where)
* both forms acceptable

Example: 你住在哪儿?
Nǐ zhù zài nǎr?
(Where do you live?)

4

_____ 哪儿/哪里?
_____ nǎr / nǎli*

(Where in _____ ...?)

Example:

你住美国哪里?
Nǐ zhù Měiguó nǎli?
(Where in the U.S. do you live?)

* Both forms of "where" in Chinese are acceptable; "nǎr" is more popular on mainland China, particularly in the north, while "nǎli" is more popular in Taiwan and in parts of southern China.

Grammar Grove
– The place you come to learn about structure

4

When asking a question with WHAT, WHERE, WHEN, WHY, HOW, and WHICH in Chinese, there is no need for "ma (吗)" at the end of the sentence or to use the V. bù V. construction.

The word order in a question is the same as a regular sentence (declarative sentence), only you replace where the missing information would be with your WHAT, WHERE, WHEN, WHY, HOW, WHICH word. In other words, you place your question pronoun in the part of the sentence to which the interrogative pronoun corresponds. Here is how it works:

Statement		Question
她是我的老师。 Tā shì wǒ de lǎoshī. (She is my teacher.)	*To ask WHO* place here →	她是谁? Tā shì shéi? (Who is she?)
我要学中文。 Wǒ yào xué Zhōngwén. (I want to learn Chinese.)	*To ask WHAT* place here →	你要学什么? Nǐ yào xué shénme? (What do you want to learn?)
我是美国人。 Wǒ shì Měiguórén. (I am American.)	*To ask WHICH* place here →	你是哪国人? Nǐ shì něi guó rén? (What country are you from?)
我住在中国。 Wǒ zhù zài Zhōngguó. (I live in China.)	*To ask WHERE* place here →	你住在哪儿? Nǐ zhù zài nǎr? (Where do you live?)

Word Workshop
– The place you come to learn new words and phrases

(Go to 🔘 4-4 to hear:)

Locational Prepositions

那里/那儿 这里/这儿
nàli / nàr* zhèli / zhèr*
(there) (here)

As mentioned earlier, both forms are acceptable. You'll find more people in mainland China, particularly in the north using "nàr" and "zhèr."

World Cities (See **Appendix V** for a longer list of cities)

Canada
Jiā ná dà

纽约 芝加哥 *ancient rather than old person* 洛杉矶
Niǔyuē Zhījiāgē 旧金山 Luòshānjī
(New York) (Chicago) ↳ Jiùjīnshān (Los Angeles)
(LIT: for sound) *(LIT: for sound)* (San Francisco) *(LIT: for sound)*
  (LIT: old, gold, mountain)

伦敦 巴黎 北京 上海
Lúndūn Bālí Běijīng Shànghǎi
(London) (Paris) (Beijing) (Shanghai)
(LIT: for sound) *(LIT: for sound)* *(LIT: northern, capital)* *(LIT: on, the sea)*

California
Jiā lǐ fú níjà

台北 香港 东京 *Jiā zhōu*
Táiběi Xiānggǎng Dōngjīng *(slang for CA)*
(Taipei) (Hong Kong) (Tokyo)
(LIT: terrace, northern) *(LIT: fragrant, harbor)* *(LIT: eastern, capital)*

Would you like to find out how to say your city or country in Chinese? You may look it up in the online Chinese-English dictionary on this website:
www.yellowbridge.com

Huá shèng dùn – Washington

Supplementary Vocabulary & Expressions

对	不对	对不对?
duì	bú duì	Duì bú duì?
(correct / right)	(not correct)	(Correct? / Right?)

4

对不起
duìbuqǐ
(sorry)

bù hǎo yì sī
(I feel bad)

没关系
méi guānxi
(that's OK, it doesn't matter)
(LIT: no, relationship)   *(connection)*

请问
qǐngwèn
(Excuse me. / May I ask?)
(LIT: please, ask)

可是
kěshì
(but)

Chit-Chat Café
– The place you come to practice speaking

Module 4.1 - (4-5) / English translation on **Page 73**
Picture this: "Ann" is talking to "Xiaomei" between classes at a university in
Chicago when they see Ann's teacher walk by.

Xiaomei:	Tā shì shéi?	Xiaomei:	她是谁?
Ann:	Tā shì wǒ de lǎoshī.	Ann:	她是我的老师。
Xiaomei:	Tā shì něi guó rén?	Xiaomei:	她是哪国人?

Ann:	Tā shì Táiwānrén.	Ann:	她是台湾人。
Xiaomei:	Tā jiāo nǐ Zhōngwén, duì bú duì?	Xiaomei:	她教你中文，对不对？
Ann:	Duì. Tā shì wǒ de Zhōngwén lǎoshī.	Ann:	对。她是我的中文老师。
Xiaomei:	Tā jiào shénme míngzi?	Xiaomei:	她叫什么名字？
Ann:	Tā de Yīngwén míngzi jiào Nancy. Wǒ bù zhīdao tā de Zhōngwén míngzi. Wǒmen jiào tā "lǎoshī."	Ann:	她的英文名字叫Nancy。我不知道她的中文名字。我们叫她"老师"。
Xiaomei:	Tā hěn piàoliang.	Xiaomei:	她很漂亮。
Ann:	Duì. Tā yě hěn cōngmíng.	Ann:	对。她也很聪明。
Xiaomei:	Nǐ xǐhuan tā ma?	Xiaomei:	你喜欢她吗？
Ann:	Wǒ hěn xǐhuan.	Ann:	我很喜欢。
Xiaomei:	Tā zhù zài nǎr?	Xiaomei:	她住在哪儿？
Ann:	Tā zhù zài zhèr.	Ann:	她住在这儿。
Xiaomei:	Ò, tā zhù zài Zhījiāgē.	Xiaomei:	哦，她住在芝加哥。
Ann:	Duì. Tā zhù zài Zhījiāgē. Wǒ yě zhù zài Zhījiāgē.	Ann:	对。她住在芝加哥。我也住在芝加哥。
Xiaomei:	Nǐ xǐhuan zhù zhèr ma?	Xiaomei:	你喜欢住这儿吗？
Ann:	Wǒ hěn xǐhuan. Zhījiāgē hěn hǎo.	Ann:	我很喜欢。芝加哥很好。

4

Chit-Chat Practice 4.1

Answer the following questions regarding the above dialogue. You can find correct answers to these questions in **Appendix IV**.

Example:

Ann的老师是美国人吗？

Q: Ann de lǎoshī shì Měiguórén ma?

不。Ann的老师不是美国人。

A: Bù. Ann de lǎoshī bú shì Měiguórén.

4

1. Ann的老师是哪国人？

Q: Ann de lǎoshī shì něi guó rén?

A: Ann de lǎoshī ~~Zhōngwén~~ Táiwānrén, kěshì tā zhù zài Měiguó

2. Ann的老师教英文吗？

Q: Ann de lǎoshī jiāo Yīngwén ma?

A: ~~Ann de lǎoshī jiāo Nancy.~~ Bu duì, ta jiāo zhōngwén.

3. Ann的老师教中文，对不对？

Q: Ann de lǎoshī jiāo Zhōngwén, duì bú duì?

A: Duì, Ann de lǎoshī jiāo zhōngwén.

4. 她老师的英文名字叫什么？

Q: Tā lǎoshī de Yīngwén míngzi jiào shénme?

A: Tā lǎoshī de Yīngwén míngzi jiào Nancy.

5. Ann知不知道她老师的中文名字？

Q: Ann zhī bù zhīdao tā lǎoshī de Zhōngwén míngzi?

A: Ann bù zhīdao tā lǎoshi de zhōngwén míngzi.

6. Ann的老师漂不漂亮？

Q: Ann de lǎoshī piào bú piàoliang?

A: Ann de lǎoshi hěn piàoliang.

7.   Ann 的老师住在哪儿?

Q: Ann de lǎoshī zhù zài nǎr?

A: _Ann de lǎoshī zhù zài Zhījiāgē_

8.   Ann 不喜欢芝加哥，对不对?

Q: Ann bù xǐhuan Zhījiāgē, duì bú duì?

A: ~~Wǒ shì~~ Bú duì, Ann xǐhuan Zhījiāgē.

Module 4.2 - (💿 4-6) / English translation on **Page 74**
Picture this: "Sam" is living and studying in Shanghai, when a woman named "Chen Liang" approaches him.

Chen: **Qǐngwèn, nǐ shì něi guó rén?**	Chen: 请问，你是哪国人?
Sam: **Wǒ shì Měiguórén. Nǐ shì Zhōngguórén, duì bú duì?**	Sam: 我是美国人。你是中国人，对不对?
Chen: **Duì. Nǐ zhù zài Zhōngguó ma?**	Chen: 对。你住在中国吗?
Sam: **Shì. Wǒ zhù zài Shànghǎi. Nǐ ne? Nǐ zhù zài Zhōngguó nǎli?**	Sam: 是。我住在上海。你呢? 你住在中国哪里?
Chen: **Wǒ zhù zài Běijīng. Wǒ shì Běijīngrén.**	Chen: 我住在北京。我是北京人。
Sam: **Běijīng hǎo bù hǎo?**	Sam: 北京好不好?
Chen: **Hǎo. Běijīng hěn dà, yě hěn piàoliang. Nǐ yào qù Běijīng ma?**	Chen: 好。北京很大，也很漂亮。你要去北京吗?
Sam: **Shénme? Duìbuqǐ, wǒ bù dǒng.**	Sam: 什么? 对不起，我不懂。

4

4

Chen: Wǒ shuō (I was saying.... / I mean....), nǐ yào bú yào qù Běijīng?	Chen: 我说，你要不要去北京？
Sam: Wǒ yào qù, wǒ yě yào qù Xiānggǎng.	Sam: 我要去，我也要去香港。
Chen: Nǐ zài Shànghǎi xué Zhōngwén ma?	Chen: 你在上海学中文吗？
Sam: Shì. Wǒ zài zhèr xué Zhōngwén.	Sam: 是。我在这儿学中文。
Chen: Zhōngwén nán bù nán xué?	Chen: 中文难不难学？
Sam: Zhōngwén bù nán, yě bù róngyì.	Sam: 中文不难，也不容易。
Chen: Nǐ xǐhuan Shànghǎi ma?	Chen: 你喜欢上海吗？
Sam: Wǒ hěn xǐhuan. Shànghǎirén hěn hǎo.	Sam: 我很喜欢。上海人很好。

Chit-Chat Practice 4.2

Ask the following questions in Chinese:

Example:

Question: What country are you from?

Translation: **Nǐ shì něi guó rén?**

1.
Question: Do you know how to speak Chinese?

Translation: Nǐ hùi shuō zhōngwén ma?

2.
Question: Where do you study Chinese?

Translation: Nǐ xué zhōngwen nǎr?

in back is
Nǐ zài nǎr xué zhǎngwú (more proper)

3.

Question: Where in the U.S. do you live?

Translation: Nǐ zhù zài Měiguó ~~zhù~~ nǎr?

4.

Question: Is Chinese difficult to learn?

Translation: Zhōngwén Xué Hàn ma?

in back,
zhōngwén
nán bú nán Xué?

5.

Question: Do you want to go to China?

Translation: Nǐ gǔ Yào qù Zhōngguó ma?

4

6.

Question: Where in China do you live?

Translation: Nǐ zhù zài Zhōngguó nǎr?

7.

Question: Do you like to study English?

Translation: Nǐ xǐhuan xué Yīngwén ma?

8.

Question: Is Beijing large?

Translation: Běijīng hěn dà ma?

9.

Question: Is Chinese more difficult than English?

Translation: Zhōngwén ~~bǐ~~ Yīngwén ma?

Check your answers in **Appendix IV**.

Zhōngwén bǐ Yīngwén nán ma?

Culture Corner
– The place you come to learn more than just language

"Face it, 'face' is important."

The Face Game

"Face" is an overarching and important component in Chinese culture to which a Westerner must pay attention if he or she intends to make friends and not make enemies. The concept of "face," or "miànzi" roughly translates as "honor," "good reputation," or "respect." Likewise, in Chinese culture one can "lose face," "gain face," "give face," and even "retain face."

Here are the four types of "face":

1) diū miànzi = losing face

   You have "lost face" when you have not followed protocol, insulted another person, were not humble, or made other such social errors revealing yourself as unrespectable.

2) gěi miànzi = giving face

   You have "given face" when you have followed the proper protocol, flattered your hosts, shown respect to another person, or other successful social graces which flatter others. In other words, you have shown your respect for your counterpart(s) and now they have more "face."

3) liú miànzi = retaining face

   You have avoided social errors and sidestepped situations in which you could have potentially lost face. As such, you have retained, or held on to your "face."

4) jiǎng miànzi = gaining face

   Others have shown you respect, or given you "face" and now you have "gained face." You can also gain face by giving face, since the honorable person is skilled in the art of giving face.

Unfortunately, the rules of the face game are so complicated that if you have not grown up in or around Chinese culture, you are bound to frequently lose your face and even make others lose theirs. So, what are we to do to hold on to our poor faces?

First thing to do is to be passive and observant in social situations; closely watch how Chinese people socially interact to learn what is polite and acceptable. Be sensitive to gestures and copy them: If someone hands you a business card with two hands, accept it with two; if someone offers to have you start to eat or drink first, return the gesture. You can't go wrong with mimicry.

On the other hand, it will be very hard to tell what is an impolite gesture since part of being polite in Chinese culture is not to embarrass the person losing face by pointing it out. Do not take laughter to mean you are a big hit either! Laughter is often invoked to lighten up a bad situation in which a person is losing face and losing it big time. I have seen this situation many times: the unseasoned Westerner says or does something that horrifies his or her Chinese counterparts. When the Westerner sees the uproarious laughter it is met with, the visitor then grows proud of what a great sense of humor the Chinese seem to think he or she has, and may even repeat the same action for the extra laughs.

Lastly, do not worry about making sure everything you do perfectly follows Chinese customs. The Chinese have a lot of contact with and exposure to western culture. They are usually forgiving and will often understand you are not familiar with Chinese customs.

Advice Alcove
– The place you come to learn how to learn

When learning a second language you should be a linguistic sponge. Learn everything and anything you can. Do not discard or skip words or grammar you think it is too difficult or obscure. It will come up eventually and may be the key to you understanding and not understanding. The more exposure you get to different words, grammar, different ways that every unique human being speaks, the better equipped you are to speak and understand fluently. In the language school I own we sometimes get complaints if the teacher has changed: "But I won't learn because I won't have a consistent program." In fact, switching teachers is the best thing that can happen to a student. Now they will get exposure to a different voice, a different lexicon (we all have our own) and a different way of speaking. I'm not suggesting students skip around with materials, classes or programs, but that you remain flexible to changes and realize you can learn from any book, any class and any teacher. In other words, "ask not what your class can do for you, but what you can do for your class." Take charge of your learning by organizing it and amplifying it beyond your textbook, class or teacher. Keep a schedule of how much time you will spend with each resource. Go through this book from beginning to end, but also mix up your learning with other resources. It will keep it interesting and keep you motivated. Here are some suggestions:

- **Podcasts:** Listen to your podcast lessons while jogging, commuting to work or while taking a walk. Any down time can be filled with learning Chinese through audio. Download your free lessons here www.chitchatchinese.com.

- **Language Exchange Partner:** Find a language exchange partner and meet to speak one hour in English and one hour in Chinese. You can find one by going on Craig's List (www.craigslist.org) and searching or posting in the community section. If you live in a non-urban center and cannot find a local exchange partner, try an online one through www.mylanguageexchange.com.

- **Free Language Groups:** Join a Chinese language group and practice what you have learned. There are many such groups you can find through www.meetup.com. Just type in your zip code and "Chinese language."

- **Access web tools:** There is a plethora of materials on the web to be accessed. A good place to start as one of the larger clearing housing for Mandarin tools and information is www.mandarintools.com.

- **Connect with other learners:** Connecting with other learners helps you share ideas and keeps you motivated to stay the course. Here are a couple of sites that can help you do just that:

  Live Mocha: Social Language Learning - Online!
  http://www.livemocha.com/

  Voxswap: The social network for learning languages
  http://www.voxswap.com/

Surf the web and see what you can find. Anything that continues your exposure to Mandarin is worthy. Even materials too easy or too difficult always hold something to either review or learn.

English Translation

Module 4.1

Xiaomei:	Who is she?
Ann:	She is my teacher.
Xiaomei:	Where is she from?
Ann:	She is Taiwanese.
Xiaomei:	She teaches you Chinese, right?
Ann:	Right. She is my Chinese teacher.
Xiaomei:	What is her name?
Ann:	Her English name is Nancy. I don't know her Chinese name. We call her "teacher."
Xiaomei:	She is very pretty.
Ann:	Yes. She is also very smart.
Xiaomei:	Do you like her?
Ann:	I like her a lot.
Xiaomei:	Where does she live?
Ann:	She lives here.
Xiaomei:	Oh, she lives in Chicago.
Ann:	Right. She lives in Chicago. I also live in Chicago.
Xiaomei:	Do you like living here?
Ann:	I like it a lot. Chicago is great.

4

Module 4.2

Chen:	Excuse me, what country are you from?
Sam:	I am American. You are Chinese, right?
Chen:	Right. Do you live in China?
Sam:	Yes. I live in Shanghai. How about you? Where in China do you live?
Chen:	I live in Beijing. I am a "Beijinger."
Sam:	How is Beijing?
Chen:	Good. Beijing is large, and very beautiful. Do you want to go to Beijing?
Sam:	What? Sorry, I don't understand.
Chen:	I said, do you want to go to Beijing?
Sam:	I want to go. I also want to go to Hong Kong.
Chen:	Do you study Chinese in Shanghai?
Sam:	Yes. I study Chinese here.
Chen:	Is Chinese difficult to learn?
Sam:	Chinese is not difficult, but also not easy.
Chen:	Do you like Shanghai?
Sam:	I like it a lot. The Shanghainese are great.

4

LESSON 5

Pronunciation Plaza
– The place you come to practice sounds and tones

(Go to ⊙ 5-1 to hear:)

Pinyin Practice

Below is a chart of the pronunciation focus for this lesson, with the initials highlighted in ▢ and the finals highlighted in ▢:

	i										u								
	i	ia	iao	ie	iu	ian	iang	in	ing	iong	u	ua	uo	ui	uai	uan	un	uang	ueng
(no initial)	yi	ya	yao	ye	you	yan	yang	yin	ying	yong	wu	wa	wo	wei	wai	wan	wen	wang	weng
b	bi		biao	bie		bian		bin	bing		bu								
p	pi		piao	pie		pian		pin	ping		pu								
m	mi		miao	mie	miu	mian		min	ming		mu								
f											fu								
d	di	dia	diao	die	diu	dian			ding		du		duo	dui		duan	dun		
t	ti		tiao	tie		tian			ting		tu		tuo	tui		tuan	tun		
n	ni		niao	nie	niu	nian	niang	nin	ning		nu		nuo			nuan	nun		
l	li	lia	liao	lie	liu	lian	liang	lin	ling		lu		luo			luan	lun		

Mixed Tone Practice

yī (one)	yà (Asia)	yào (to want)	yě (also)	yǒu (to have)	yǎn (eyes)
yàng (shape)	yīn (because)	yǐng (shadow)	yòng (to use)		
wù (thing)	wǎ (roof tile)	wǒ (I)	wéi (to do)	wài (outside)	wān (to bend)
wèn (to ask)	wàng (to forget)	wēng (onomat.)			

bǐ (to compare)	biǎo (surface)	bié (other)	biàn (to change)	bīn (guest)	bìng (illness)

bù
(no)

pí (skin)	piào (ticket)	piē (to cast away)	piàn (a slice)	pǐn (quality)	píng (level)

pǔ
(general)

mì (dense)	miào (wonderful)	miè (to extinguish)	miù (wrong)	miàn (face)	mín (people)

míng (bright)	mǔ (mother)

5

fù
(father)

dì (land)	diǎ (coquettish)	diào (to drop)	dié (butterfly)	diū (to lose)	diàn (electricity)

dìng (to settle)	dù (degree)	duō (many)	duì (correct)	duàn (to cut off)	dūn (ton)

tǐ (body)	tiào (to jump)	tiě (iron)	tiān (sky)	tīng (to hear)	tǔ (soil)

tuō (to undress)	tuī (to push)	tuán (group)	tūn (to swallow)

nǐ (you)	niǎo (bird)	niē (to pinch)	niú (cattle)	nián (year)	niáng (mother)

nín (you[respect])	níng (peaceful)	nù (anger)	nuò (promise)	nuǎn (warm)	nún (fragrance)

lì (power)	liǎ (two)	liào (to expect)	liè (a row)	liú (to flow)	lián (to link)

liáng	lín	lǐng	lù	luò	luàn
(to measure)	(forest)	(to lead)	(road)	(to fall)	(in disorder)

Lún
(Analects)

Sound Differentiation

"OK, now I am hearing a "*yee*" sound!"

There is another little sound you may hear interjected into certain words. Just like that "*woo*" sound you need to make with certain words, this "*yee*" sound you will need to make with certain words. Any word written with "i" in it and followed by other final <u>vowels</u>, you will need to preserve that long "ee" sound even as you pronounce the other vowel(s).

Beginning learners of Chinese often introduce themselves, instead of saying "Nǐ hǎo. Wǒ jiào Robert.", and will say "Nǐ hǎo. Wǒ zhào Robert.". This, unfortunately, makes no sense, unless he meant to say "Hello. I shine on Robert."

Here is how you will need to say these words:

biao = should be "b-yee-ow"
pian = should be "p-yee-en"
mian = should be "m-yee-en"
diu   = should be "d-yee-oh"
lie   = should be "l-yee-eh"

Let's practice that "*yee*" sound in isolation:

biǎo	bié	biàn	piào	piē	piàn
(surface)	(other)	(to change)	(ticket)	(to cast away)	(a slice)

miào	miè	miàn
(wonderful)	(to extinguish)	(face)

diǎ	diào	dié	diū	diàn
(coquettish)	(to drop)	(butterfly)	(to lose)	(electricity)

tiào	tiě	tiān
(to jump)	(iron)	(sky)

liǎ	liào	liè	liú	lián	liáng
(two)	(to expect)	(a row)	(to flow)	(to link)	(to measure)

Revisiting your "*woo*" sound

Let's practice that "*woo*" sound again as it relates to the pronunciation focus of this lesson:

duō	duì	duàn	dùn
(many)	(correct)	(to cut off)	(pause)

tuō	tuán	tūn
(to undress)	(group)	(to swallow)

luò	luàn	Lún
(to fall)	(in disorder)	(Analects)

5

Sound Differentiation Exercise

Listen to the following sounds in 🔊 <u>5-2</u> and write the correct *pinyin* spelling and tones below. See **Appendix IV** for correct answers:

1. _____   2. _____   3. _____   4. _____

5. _____   6. _____   7. _____   8. _____

9. _____   10. _____   11. _____   12. _____

13. _____   14. _____   15. _____   16. _____

17. _____   18. _____   19. _____   20. _____

Word Workshop
– The place you come to learn new words and phrases

(Go to 🔊 <u>5-3</u> to hear:)

Verb - to have

nǎr yǒu – there is

有	没有	你有没有＿＿＿＿＿＿＿＿?
yǒu	méiyǒu*	Nǐ yǒu méiyǒu ＿＿＿＿＿＿＿＿?
(to have)	(to not have)	(Do you have ＿＿＿＿＿＿＿＿?)

* Although most verbs are negated with "bù (不)," "yǒu (有)" is negated with the word "méi (没)."

还有
hái yǒu
(also have, there also is)

Family & Friends Terms

家
jiā
(family, home)

家人
jiārén
(family member)

妈妈
māma
(mother)

爸爸
bàba
(father)

爸爸妈妈
bàba māma
(parents)

男
nán
(male)

女
nǚ
(female)

孩子
háizi
(child)

男孩子
nánháizi
(boy)

女孩子
nǚháizi
(girl)

女儿
nǚ'ér
(daughter)

儿子
érzi
(son)

哥哥
gēge
(older brother)

弟弟
dìdi
(younger brother)

姐姐
jiějie
(older sister)

妹妹
mèimei
(younger sister)

5

兄弟姐妹
xiōng-dì-jiě-mèi
(siblings)

太太
tàitai
(wife, Mrs.,
ma'am)

先生
xiānsheng
(husband,
Mr., sir)

goes after family names

小姐
xiǎojie
(Miss)
*(LIT: little,
older sister)*

(not popular in mainland, slang word for prostitute)

朋友
péngyou
(friend)

男朋友
nánpéngyou
(boyfriend)

女朋友
nǚpéngyou
(girlfriend)

5

Grammar Grove
– The place you come to learn about structure

xiǎo péngyou
– little kids

More about the possessive "de" in Chinese

Point 1

The possessive "de" can be omitted when the possessor is a personal pronoun (I, you, he, she, etc.) and the possessed is a "personal" noun such as relatives or your teacher. Both using "de" and not using "de" are correct:

我的妈妈		我妈妈
wǒ de māma	or say	wǒ māma
他的哥哥		他哥哥
tā de gēge	or say	tā gēge
我们的老师		我们老师
wǒmen de lǎoshī	or say	wǒmen lǎoshī

Point 2

If there is more than one item being possessed then the "de" is placed after the last possessor. Let's have a look at that starting with a simple possessive phrase and increasingly adding possessors:

Increasingly adding possessors:

他的爸爸……

Tā de bàba......

(His father...)

他爸爸的朋友……

Tā bàba de péngyou......

(His father's friend...)

他爸爸朋友的老师……

Tā bàba péngyou de lǎoshī......

(His father's friend's teacher...)

他爸爸朋友老师的太太……

Tā bàba péngyou lǎoshī de tàitai......

(His father's friend's teacher's wife...)

Final full sentence:

他爸爸朋友老师的太太是中国人。

Tā bàba péngyou lǎoshī de tàitai shì Zhōngguórén.

(His father's friend's teacher's wife is Chinese.)

Chit-Chat Café
– The place you come to practice speaking

Module 5.1 - (5-4) / English translation on **Page 97**

Picture this: "Andy" is in China and showing his friend "Siyong" photos of his family back in the U.S.

Siyong: **Tā shì shéi?**	Siyong: 他是谁？
Andy: **Tā shì wǒ gēge.**	Andy: 他是我哥哥。
Siyong: **Nà shì nǐ jiějie ma?**	Siyong: 那是你姐姐吗？

Andy:	Bú shì, nà shì wǒ gēge de tàitai.	Andy:	不是，那是我哥哥的太太。
Siyong:	Tā hěn piàoliang. Tā shì něi guó rén?	Siyong:	她很漂亮。她是哪国人？
Andy:	Tā shì Zhōngguórén.	Andy:	她是中国人。
Siyong:	Ò, nǐ gēge de tàitai shì Zhōngguórén! Nǐ gēge huì bú huì shuō Zhōngwén?	Siyong:	哦，你哥哥的太太是中国人！你哥哥会不会说中文？
Andy:	Tā bú huì, kěshì tā yào xué.	Andy:	他不会，可是他要学。
Siyong:	Nǐ gēge de tàitai huì bú huì Yīngwén?	Siyong:	你哥哥的太太会不会英文？
Andy:	Huì. Tā de Yīngwén hěn hǎo.	Andy:	会。她的英文很好。
Siyong:	Nǐ gēge zhù zài nǎr?	Siyong:	你哥哥住在哪儿？
Andy:	Tā zhù zài Jiùjīnshān.	Andy:	他住在旧金山。
Siyong:	Tā xǐ bù xǐhuan Jiùjīnshān?	Siyong:	他喜不喜欢旧金山？
Andy:	Tā hěn xǐhuan. Tā shuō Jiùjīnshān hěn piàoliang.	Andy:	他很喜欢。他说旧金山很漂亮。
Siyong:	Nǐ bàba māma yě zhù zài Jiùjīnshān ma?	Siyong:	你爸爸妈妈也住在旧金山吗？
Andy:	Bù. Tāmen zhù zài Niǔyuē. Wǒ jiějie mèimei yě zhù zài Niǔyuē.	Andy:	不。他们住在纽约。我姐姐妹妹也住在纽约。
Siyong:	Ò, nǐ yě yǒu jiějie mèimei. Nǐ yǒu méiyǒu dìdi?	Siyong:	哦，你也有姐姐妹妹。你有没有弟弟？
Andy:	Wǒ yě yǒu dìdi.	Andy:	我也有弟弟。

5

Chit-Chat Practice 5.1

Answer these questions about the dialogue. You can find the answers in **Appendix IV**.

1. Andy有没有哥哥?

   Q: Andy yǒu méiyǒu gēge?

   A: Andy yǒu gēge.

2. 他哥哥有没有太太?

   Q: Tā gēge yǒu méiyǒu tàitai?

   A: Tā gēge yǒu tàitai.

3. 他的太太漂亮吗?

   Q: Tā de tàitai piàoliang ma?

   A: Duì, ~~Shì,~~ tā de tàitai piàoliang.

4. 他太太是美国人吗?

   Q: Tā tàitai shì Měiguórén ma?

   A: Tā tàitai zhù zài Měiguo, kèshì tā shì Zhōngguórén.

5. 他哥哥会不会说中文?

   Q: Tā gēge huì bú huì shuō Zhōngwén?

   A: Tā gēge bú huì shuō zhōngwén, keshi tā hái yào xué.

6. 他哥哥的太太英文好不好?

   Q: Tā gēge de tàitai Yīngwén hǎo bù hǎo?

   A: Tā gēge de tàitai Yīngwén hěn hǎo.

7. Andy 的爸爸妈妈住在哪儿?

Q: Andy de bàba māma zhù zài nǎr?

A: *Andy bàba māma zhù zài Niǔyuē.*

8. Andy 有没有姐姐妹妹?

Q: Andy yǒu méiyǒu jiějie mèimei?

A: *Andy yǒu jiějie ye mèimei.*

9. 他姐姐妹妹住在哪儿?

Q: Tā jiějie mèimei zhù zài nǎr?

A: *Tā jiějie mèimei zhù zài Niǔyuē.*

5

Word Workshop
– The place you come to learn new words and phrases

(Go to 5-5 to hear:)

Numbers
Numbers are easy in Chinese. If you can count to ten, then you can count to 99.
Here is how it works:

0

零
líng
(0)

1-10

一	二	三	四	五	六	七	八	九	十
yī	èr	sān	sì	wǔ	liù	qī	bā	jiǔ	shí
(1)	(2)	(3)	(4)	(5)	(6)	(7)	(8)	(9)	(10)

11-19

Now, for the numbers above 10 just say "10" then say "1" to say the number 11, and "10, 2" to say 12; likewise to say 20 you say "2" then "10" and 22 is "2, 10, 2." Have a look:

十一	十二	十三	十四	十五
shíyī	shí'èr	shísān	shísì	shíwǔ
(11)	(12)	(13)	(14)	(15)

十六	十七	十八	十九
shíliù	shíqī	shíbā	shíjiǔ
(16)	(17)	(18)	(19)

20s

二十	二十一	二十二	二十三	二十四
èrshí	èrshíyī	èrshí'èr	èrshísān	èrshísì
(20)	(21)	(22)	(23)	(24)

二十五	二十六	二十七	二十八	二十九
èrshíwǔ	èrshíliù	èrshíqī	èrshíbā	èrshíjiǔ
(25)	(26)	(27)	(28)	(29)

30s

三十	三十一	三十二	三十三	三十四
sānshí	sānshíyī	sānshí'èr	sānshísān	sānshísì
(30)	(31)	(32)	(33)	(34)

三十五	三十六	三十七	三十八	三十九
sānshíwǔ	sānshíliù	sānshíqī	sānshíbā	sānshíjiǔ
(35)	(36)	(37)	(38)	(39)

And so on.... Continue with the same pattern all the way to 99. Here is how to say 100:

yìbǎi líng yī – 101

一百
yìbǎi
(100)

yì bǎi yī shí
110

85

Chit-Chat Café
– The place you come to practice speaking

Module 5.2 - (🔘 5-6)

This Chit-Chat Café is simple. Here we want you to simply count from one to hundred several times. Listen to your Audio CD to hear this done. Then do it yourself several times and you will never forget your numbers.

After counting out loud to 100 several times practice saying all these numbers out loud:

16	42	90	11	6	40
32	9	33	21	14	86
91	20	5	57	75	69
38	41	13	2	0	77
29	88	30	52	94	100
3	23	87	45	35	72
55	70	22	34	44	73
50	82	78	30	53	22
19	99	48	17	40	26

Grammar Grove
– The place you come to learn about structure

Measure Words & Counting

In Chinese when something is counted, or the number of things is said, you need a "measure word." The first measure word you will learn in Chinese is also the most popular and most general:

个

ge

(measure word for saying the number of things)

All numbers combined with "ge (个)" remain the same except for the number 2 (èr); this becomes "liǎng (两)."

Examples:

一个人	两个人	三个人
yí ge rén	liǎng ge rén	sān ge rén
(1 person)	(2 people)	(3 people)
四个人	五个人	六个人
sì ge rén	wǔ ge rén	liù ge rén
(4 people)	(5 people)	(6 people)

and so on...

Measure words function somewhat as we would use counter words in English such as "a piece of paper," "a loaf of bread," or "a cup of water." Only, in Chinese it is necessary to use them. Later in this textbook we will explain more about measure words and teach you others. If you are curious you can skip ahead to **Lesson Ten's Grammar Grove** and you can learn more.

5

Word Workshop
– The place you come to learn new words and phrases

(Go to 5-7 to hear:)

Asking Number Questions

几
jǐ
(How many?)

几个
jǐ ge
(How many [of something]?)

Example:
你家有几个人?
Nǐ jiā yǒu jǐ ge rén?
(How many people are there in your family?)

几岁
jǐ suì
(How many years old?)

Example:
你几岁?
Nǐ jǐ suì?
(How old are you?)

岁
_____suì
(age, years old)

Example:
我二十五岁。
Wǒ èrshíwǔ suì.
(I am 25 years old.)

Supplementary Vocabulary

都
dōu
(all, both, entirely)

关系
guānxi
(relations, connections, to matter)

没有关系
méiyǒu guānxi
(it doesn't matter, it's OK)

意思
yìsi
(meaning)

bú hǎo yìsi
(I'm embarrassed)

有意思
yǒu yìsi
(interesting)
(LIT: have, meaning)

没有意思
méiyǒu yìsi
(not interesting, boring)
(LIT: not have, meaning)

Chit-Chat Café
– The place you come to practice speaking

5

Module 5.2 - (5-8) / English translation on **Page 98**
Picture this: "Wang Jian" is in New York and speaking with his friend "Nancy" in Chinese.

Nancy:	Nǐ jiā yǒu jǐ ge rén?	Nancy:	你家有几个人？
Wang Jian:	Wǒ jiā yǒu liù ge rén: wǒ bàba māma, liǎng ge mèimei, yí ge dìdi, hái yǒu wǒ.	Wang Jian:	我家有六个人：我爸爸妈妈、两个妹妹、一个弟弟，还有我。
Nancy:	Nǐ zuì dà, duì bú duì?	Nancy:	你最大，对不对？
Wang Jian:	Duì. Wǒ zuì dà.	Wang Jian:	对。我最大。
Nancy:	Shéi zuì xiǎo?	Nancy:	谁最小？
Wang Jian:	Wǒ dìdi zuì xiǎo.	Wang Jian:	我弟弟最小。
Nancy:	Tā jǐ suì?	Nancy:	他几岁？
Wang Jian:	Tā shí'èr suì.	Wang Jian:	他十二岁。
Nancy:	Nǐ ne? Nǐ jǐ suì?	Nancy:	你呢？你几岁？
Wang Jian:	Wǒ èrshíwǔ suì. Wǒ bǐ wǒ dìdi dà shísān suì.	Wang Jian:	我二十五岁。我比我弟弟大十三岁。

Nancy:	Tā yě huì shuō Yīngwén ma?	Nancy:	他也会说英文吗？
Wang Jian:	Tā zhǐ huì yìdiǎnr.	Wang Jian:	他只会一点儿。
Nancy:	Nǐ de mèimeimen* ne?	Nancy:	你的妹妹们呢？
Wang Jian:	Wǒ liǎng ge mèimei yě huì yìdiǎnr. Kěshì wǒ bàba māma dōu bú huì shuō Yīngwén.	Wang Jian:	我两个妹妹也会一点儿。可是我爸爸妈妈都不会说英文。
Nancy:	Méiyǒu guānxi, wǒ bàba māma de Yīngwén yě bù hǎo.	Nancy:	没有关系，我爸爸妈妈的英文也不好。
Wang Jian:	Kěshì, nǐ bàba māma shì Měiguórén, bú shì ma?	Wang Jian:	可是，你爸爸妈妈是美国人，不是吗？
Nancy:	Wǒ bàba māma zhù zài Měiguó, kěshì tāmen bú shì Měiguórén. Tāmen shì Fǎguórén. Zài wǒmen jiā, wǒmen shuō Fǎwén.	Nancy:	我爸爸妈妈住在美国，可是他们不是美国人。他们是法国人。在我们家，我们说法文。
Wang Jian:	Hěn yǒu yìsi!	Wang Jian:	很有意思！

* *"men"* here is used to pluralize *"mèimei,"* so that changes it to "sisters" instead of just the singular "sister."

Chit-Chat Practice 5.2

Answer these questions about the dialogue. You can find the answers in **Appendix IV**.

1. 王坚的家有几个人？
   Q: Wáng Jiān de jiā yǒu jǐ ge rén?
   A: Tā de jiā yǒu liù ge rén.

2. 谁最大?
   Q: Shéi zuì dà?

   A: Wang Jian zuì dà.

3. 谁最小?
   Q: Shéi zuì xiǎo?

   A: Tā de dìdi zuì xiǎo.

4. 王坚几岁?
   Q: Wáng Jiān jǐ suì?

   A: Tā èrshíwǔ suì.

5. 王坚的弟弟几岁?
   Q: Wáng Jiān de dìdi jǐ suì?

   A: Tā yòu zhǐ yì (ge?)

6. 王坚的妹妹们会不会说英文?
   Q: Wáng Jiān de mèimeimen huì bú huì shuō Yīngwén?

   A: Huì, tāmen huì yìdiǎn Yīngwén.

7. 王坚的爸爸妈妈会说英文吗?
   Q: Wáng Jiān de bàba māma huì shuō Yīngwén ma?

   A: Bú huì, tāmen bú huì shuō Yīngwén.

8. Nancy的爸爸妈妈是美国人吗?
   Q: Nancy de bàba māma shì Měiguórén ma?

   A: tāmen zhù zài hali (shuō) kěshì tāmen Fǎwén.

9. 在Nancy的家他们说英文吗?
   Q: Zài Nancy de jiā tāmen shuō Yīngwén ma?

   A: Bú shuō, tāmen shuō Fǎwén.

5

91

Module 5.3 - (5-9) / English translation on **Page 99**

Picture this: "John" is studying Chinese in Shanghai; he is speaking with a new friend of his "Lian."

Lian:	Zhōngwén nán xué ma?	Lian:	中文难学吗?
John:	Zhōngwén nán xué, kěshì wǒ xǐhuan xué. Zhōngwén hěn yǒu yìsi.	John:	中文难学,可是我喜欢学。中文很有意思。
Lian:	Nǐ bàba māma huì bú huì shuō Zhōngwén?	Lian:	你爸爸妈妈会不会说中文?
John:	Tāmen bú huì.	John:	他们不会。
Lian:	Nǐ yǒu xiōng-dì-jiě-mèi ma?	Lian:	你有兄弟姐妹吗?
John:	Yǒu. Wǒ yǒu yí ge gēge, hái yǒu yí ge mèimei.	John:	有。我有一个哥哥,还有一个妹妹。
Lian:	Nǐ jiārén zhù zài nǎr?	Lian:	你家人住在哪儿?
John:	Wǒ bàba, māma zhù zài Niǔyuē, wǒ gēge, mèimei zhù zài Zhījiāgē.	John:	我爸爸、妈妈住在纽约,我哥哥、妹妹住在芝加哥。
Lian:	Zhījiāgē hǎo bù hǎo?	Lian:	芝加哥好不好?
John:	Zhījiāgē hěn hǎo, hěn yǒu yìsi. Nǐ jiārén zài nǎr?	John:	芝加哥很好,很有意思。你家人在哪儿?
Lian:	Wǒ jiārén dōu zài Shànghǎi.	Lian:	我家人都在上海。
John:	Nǐ xǐhuan zhù zài Shànghǎi ma?	John:	你喜欢住在上海吗?
Lian:	Wǒ xǐhuan, kěshì wǒ yào qù Měiguó xué Yīngwén.	Lian:	我喜欢,可是我要去美国学英文。
John:	Nǐ yào qù Měiguó nǎr xué?	John:	你要去美国哪儿学?
Lian:	Wǒ yào qù Luòshānjī. Kěshì wǒ nǚpéngyou bú yào	Lian:	我要去洛杉矶。可是我女朋友不要去那儿。

qù nàr. Tā shuō Luòshānjī bù hǎo. Tā shuō Jiùjīnshān bǐ Luòshānjī hǎo.	她说洛杉矶不好。她说旧金山比洛杉矶好。
John: Jiùjīnshān hěn piàoliang, kěshì Jiùjīnshān bǐ Luòshānjī xiǎo. Luòshānjī bǐ Jiùjīnshān yǒu yìsi.	John: 旧金山很漂亮，可是旧金山比洛杉矶小。洛杉矶比旧金山有意思。

Chit-Chat Practice 5.3

In-class: Separate students into pairs and have them ask and answer the below questions in Chinese. The questions are written in English as prompts and the students may refer to the prompts while they practice. However, they should ask and answer all questions in Chinese.

Self-study and outside class homework: Take the below questions and write out the question and answer in Chinese to each question as it pertains to you.

Note: This is to practice language. You do not have to give real answers in class about your age and whether you have a boyfriend / girlfriend or not. Although these questions may be asked of you in Chinese in real life, in the classroom you may answer with real or made-up answers.

1. What is your name?

2. Where do you live?

3. Where are you from?

4. Where are your parents from?

5. How old are you?

6. How old are your parents?

7. How many people are in your family?

8. How many brothers and sisters do you have?

9. What are their names?

10. How old are they?

11. Where do they live?

12. Do you have a boyfriend / girlfriend?

13. Do you have a wife / husband?

14. What is his / her name?

15. Do you have children?

16. How old are your children?

Now ask and answer any other questions you can think of in class or as homework.

 ## Culture Corner
– The place you come to learn more than just language

5

"Guānxi yǒu guānxi."

Connections matter!

In this lesson you learned the term "guānxi" meaning connections or to matter. There is also an important cultural connotation to the word "guānxi." Having "guānxi" also means having important social, political or business connections. Traditionally the Chinese have used "guānxi" to get many different things done. It is a kind of network of social connections, which people rely on to either work around the system or to get something done faster or more efficiently. If you do business in China knowing people who have "guānxi" can make the difference between closing a deal or not. Connections are important in the west, but in China they are central to getting things done. Just as you may expect connections to work to your advantage, you may also expect to be called upon to use your position or power to help others. Westerners successful in business or socially adept in China are aware of "guānxi" and keep a careful eye on using "guānxi" or avoiding its drawbacks.

Here is how the BBC Beijing correspondent, Rupert Wingfield Hayes, describes "guānxi" in modern day China:

"If you want to understand who runs China today you have to understand the meaning of the word 'guānxi.' Literally translated, 'guānxi' means connections. But it is much more than having the same old school tie. In Europe or America who you know might help you get a job, or get your child into a decent school. In China who you have 'guānxi' with can mean the difference between freedom and jail, justice or discrimination, wealth or poverty."

Oh no, it's that "face" thing again!

Developing "guānxi" and maintaining it brings us back to the overarching concept of **face**. In order to even begin to foster "guānxi" you will have to give and save face when associating with business contacts or even casually in social situations. Saving face by avoiding blunders, giving face by saying and doing the right thing are paramount in developing your relations.

 Advice Alcove
— The place you come to learn how to learn

Learning linguistic tricks can help you get up and running in a language even before you have all the proper pieces. Often you can indicate that you aren't certain and the listener (if a native speaker) will naturally correct you. The important thing is to keep your ears tuned for the correct version and to try to self-correct yourself next time. Here is an example of this:

Student: 我家有四人。
                Wǒ jiā yǒu sì rén. *— incorrect way*
                (There are four people in my family.)

Native Speaker: 哦，你家有四个人。
                Ò, nǐ jiā yǒu sì ge rén. *— correct way*
                (Oh, you have four people in your family.)

Student perks up his / her ears, hears the correct way and repeats the correct version.

Student: 对，我家有四个人。
                Duì, wǒ jiā yǒu sì ge rén. *— corrected version*
                (Right. There are four people in my family.)

Don't let not knowing everything stop you from simply starting to speak and starting to use your language skills. This is the only way to learn how to speak any language. It just is not going to all be perfect in the beginning. You will have to rely on native speakers to help you along by speaking more slowly and repeating sentences or words for you. One way to get a native speaker to slow down is to repeat the question or sentence at the speed you will need it. This has the dual purpose of buying you time to think about what was just said and also to indicate what speed works for you. Here is how this can work:

Native Speaker:

你父母是哪国人？

Nǐ fù-mǔ shì něi guó rén?

(What is the nationality of your parents?)

— *said very fast*

Here the student is lost. He / she has never learned the word "fù-mǔ" for parents. The rest of the words sound familiar but just a bit too fast to grasp and respond yet. Here the student will repeat the sentence slowly and then indicate which part was confusing.

Student:

我父母是哪国人？ 父母？

Wǒ fù-mǔ shì něi guó rén? Fù-mǔ?

(My parents are which nationality? Parents?)

— *said slowly, the student not understanding*

The native speaker realizes which part is confusing and also realizes he / she spoke too quickly and alters his / her approach:

Native Speaker:

你爸爸妈妈是哪国人？

Nǐ bàba māma shì něi guó rén?

(What is the nationality of your parents?)

— *said more slowly, using different words to see if that will work*

This is a way you can indicate to the native speaker what speed and level of complexity and the speed you can handle.

English Translation

Module 5.1

Siyong:	Who is he?
Andy:	He is my older brother.
Siyong:	Is that your older sister?
Andy:	No, that is my older brother's wife.
Siyong:	She is very pretty. What country is she from?
Andy:	She is Chinese.
Siyong:	Oh, your brother's wife is Chinese! Does your brother know how to speak Chinese?
Andy:	He does not. But, he wants to learn.
Siyong:	Does your brother's wife know English?
Andy:	Yes. Her English is very good.
Siyong:	Where does your brother live?
Andy:	He lives in San Francisco.
Siyong:	Does he like San Francisco?
Andy:	He likes it a lot. He says San Francisco is very pretty.
Siyong:	Do your father and mother also live in San Francisco?
Andy:	No. They live in New York. My older and younger sisters also live in New York.
Siyong:	Oh, you also have sisters. Do you have a younger brother?
Andy:	I also have a younger brother.

5

Module 5.2

Nancy:	How many people are in your family?
Wang Jian:	There are six people in my family: My father and mother, two younger sisters, one younger brother and me.
Nancy:	You are the oldest, right?
Wang Jian:	Right. I am the oldest.
Nancy:	Who is the youngest?
Wang Jian:	My younger brother is the youngest.
Nancy:	How old is he?
Wang Jian:	He is 12 years old.
Nancy:	How about you? How old are you?
Wang Jian:	I am 25 years old. I am 13 years older than my younger brother.
Nancy:	Does he also know how to speak English?
Wang Jian:	He only knows a little bit.
Nancy:	How about your younger sisters?
Wang Jian:	My two younger sisters also know a little. But my father and mother don't know how to speak any English.
Nancy:	That's all right. My father and mother's English is not good either.
Wang Jian:	But, your father and mother are American. Isn't that so?
Nancy:	My father and mother live in the U.S., they are not American. They are French. In my home we speak French.
Wang Jian:	How interesting!

Module 5.3

Lian:	Is Chinese difficult to learn?
John:	Chinese is difficult, but I like studying it. Chinese is very interesting.
Lian:	Do your father and mother know how to speak Chinese?
John:	They don't know (how to speak it).
Lian:	Do you have any brothers or sisters?
John:	Yes. I have an older brother and a younger sister.
Lian:	Where does your family live?
John:	My father and mother live in New York. My brother and sister live in Chicago.
Lian:	How is Chicago?
John:	Chicago is great; it's very interesting. Where is your family?
Lian:	My family is all in Shanghai.
John:	Do you like living in Shanghai?
Lian:	I like it, but I want to go to the U.S. to study English.
John:	Where in the U.S. do you want to go to study?
Lian:	I want to go to Los Angeles. But my girlfriend doesn't want to go there. She says Los Angeles is not good. She says San Francisco is better than Los Angeles.
John:	San Francisco is very beautiful, but it is smaller than Los Angeles. Los Angeles is more interesting than San Francisco.

5

NOTE

 Pronunciation Plaza
— The place you come to practice sounds and tones

(Go to 6-1 to hear:)

Chinese Tongue Twister

Now that you know your numbers, let's try a Chinese tongue twister involving numbers to help you practice sounds and tones. You know all the words in this tongue twister. So, let's see if you can understand the meaning before looking at the translation below:

Sì shì sì, shí shì shí	四是四，十是十
Shísì shì shísì, sìshí shì sìshí	十四是十四，四十是四十
Shísì bú shì sìshí, sìshí bú shì shísì	十四不是四十，四十不是十四
Sìshísì shì sìshísì	四十四是四十四
Shì bú shì, lǎoshī?	是不是，老师？

Translation:

Four is four, ten is ten

Fourteen is fourteen, forty is forty

Fourteen is not forty, forty is not fourteen

Forty four is forty four

Right, teacher?

6

Tone Exception - (6-2)

This is the last important tone exception you should be aware of. The number one (yī) changes tone depending on the words following it. Here are the tone exception rules:

1: "Yī" becomes a 4th tone when followed by a character (morpheme) that is a 1st, 2nd or 3rd tone.

Examples:

yì bēi (one glass)	yì tiān (one day)	yì biān (one side)
yì píng (one bottle)	yìshí (temporary)	yì nián (one year)
yì wǎn (one bowl)	yìbǎi (one hundred)	yìdiǎnr (a little bit)

2: "Yī" becomes a second tone when followed by a character that is a 4th tone.

Examples:

yídìng   yí jiàn   yí duì
(definitely)   (a piece [of clothing]) (a pair of)

Note: "Yī" (for the word meaning "one" only) always changes tone, unless it is said alone or is followed by a neutral tone.

Pinyin Practice

Below is a chart covering the pronunciation focus for this lesson, with the initials highlighted in   and the finals highlighted in   :

	o			e			
	o	ong	ou	e	ei	en	eng
b	bo				bei	ben	beng
p	po		pou		pei	pen	peng
m	mo		mou		mei	men	meng
f	fo		fou		fei	fen	feng
d		dong	dou	de	dei	den	deng
t		tong	tou	te	tei		teng
n		nong	nou	ne	nei	nen	neng
l		long	lou	le	lei		leng

Mixed Tone Practice

bō
(wave)

běi
(north)

běn
(origin)

bēng
(to collapse)

pò
(broken)

pōu
(to dissect)

pèi
(to match)

pēn
(to spurt)

péng
(friend)

mó
(model)

móu
(scheme)

měi
(beautiful)

mén
(door)

mèng
(dream)

fó
(Buddha)

fǒu
(to negate)

fēi
(to fly)

fēn
(to divide)

fēng
(wind)

dòng
(to move)

dōu
(all)

de
(*modifier particle*)

děi
(need)

dèn
(to tug)

dēng
(lamp)

tóng
(same)

tóu
(head)

tè
(special)

tēi
(*onomat.*)

téng
(to ache)

nóng
(agriculture)

nòu
(to weed)

ne
(*question particle*)

nèi
(inside)

nèn
(tender)

néng
(ability)

lóng
(dragon)

lóu
(floor)

lè
(joyous)

lèi
(tired)

lěng
(cold)

Sound Differentiation

Ben bú Bèn = Ben is not stupid

There is the temptation for the English speaker to look at *pinyin* with "en" in it and pronounce it as we would the words for the name "Ben," the animal "hen," or the writing utensil "pen." In fact, this "en" should sound like the "en" in "taken," almost like a "un" sound. So, you will be closer to the correct pronunciation if you say "bun," "hun" or "pun" instead. Listen closely to the following sounds, since that analogy is not perfect (there is a bit of an "e" sound in it just as in the "en" in "taken"):

běn
(origin)

pēn
(to spurt)

mén
(door)

fēn
(to divide)

dèn
(to tug)

nèn
(tender)

zěn	cēn	sēn	zhēn	chén	shēn
(how)	(-------)	(forest)	(really)	(to sink)	(body)

rén	gēn	kěn	hěn
(human being)	(to follow)	(to be willing to)	(very)

Now, retain that same vowel sound and add an "ng" at the end to get the sound for *pinyin* morphemes ending in "eng":

bēng	péng	mèng	fēng	dēng	téng
(to collapse)	(friend)	(dream)	(wind)	(lamp)	(to gallop)

néng	lěng	zēng	céng	sēng	zhèng
(ability)	(cold)	(to increase)	(storey)	(monk)	(politics)

chéng	shēng	réng	gèng	kēng	héng
(to become)	(to give birth to)	(still)	(more)	(hole)	(horizontal)

6

Sound Differentiation Exercise

Listen to the following sounds in 🔘 6-3 and write the correct *pinyin* spelling and tones below. See **Appendix IV** for correct answers:

1. _____   2. _____   3. _____   4. _____

5. _____   6. _____   7. _____   8. _____

9. _____   10. _____   11. _____   12. _____

13. _____   14. _____   15. _____   16. _____

17. _____   18. _____   19. _____   20. _____

Word Workshop
– The place you come to learn new words and phrases

(Go to 6-4 to hear:)

Time

In Chinese, time always goes from the larger to the smaller unit. So a date and time in English, for example, would be:

June 5, 2010

In Chinese, however, that same date would go in this order:

2010, June, 5

The largest unit, the year, is first; the month is next and the day last. Any other units to follow, such as hour, minute, second, follow the same pattern: larger to smaller.

6

Year

As always, anything involving numbers is straightforward and easy in Chinese. To say the year you simple say the individual numbers in order plus the word "year" after. So, for example, to say the year 2008, you would not say "two thousand and eight" you would say "two, zero, zero, eight year" in Chinese. Here is how it works:

Year = nián (年) *does not need measure word*

1998 = yī jiǔ jiǔ bā nián
1955 = yī jiǔ wǔ wǔ nián
2003 = èr líng líng sān nián
2006 = èr líng líng liù nián

Months

Likewise, you will see how easy months are. Simply say a number and then the word "moon" to name the month. So "8 moon" is August, and "5 moon" is May, like so:

月
yuè
(moon, month)

一月	二月	三月	四月	五月	六月
Yīyuè	Èryuè	Sānyuè	Sìyuè	Wǔyuè	Liùyuè
(Jan.)	(Feb.)	(Mar.)	(Apr.)	(May)	(Jun.)

七月	八月	九月	十月	十一月	十二月
Qīyuè	Bāyuè	Jiǔyuè	Shíyuè	Shíyīyuè	Shí'èryuè
(Jul.)	(Aug.)	(Sept.)	(Oct.)	(Nov.)	(Dec.)

Note: To count months you should say the following:

一个月	两个月	三个月	四个月	五个月……
yí ge yuè	liǎng ge yuè	sān ge yuè	sì ge yuè	wǔ ge yuè
(1 month)	(2 months)	(3 months)	(4 months)	(5 months)

This is how you can distinguish whether you are saying how many months, rather than the month's name. Note as well, you should use "èr" not "liǎng," when saying February—since this is the month name, not something you are counting.

Days of the month

To say the day of the month, such as the 5th of December, you just say the number then add the word "hào (号)."

号
hào
(number, date)

Examples:

January 5th = Yīyuè wǔ hào

December 25th = Shí'èryuè èrshíwǔ hào

March 15th = Sānyuè shíwǔ hào

Weeks / Days of the week

To say the day of the week you say the word "week" in Chinese then the number of the day for all days except Sunday. Sunday is referred to as "heavenly day" or "sun day."

星期
xīngqī
(week)
(LIT: star, period of time)

星期一	星期二	星期三	星期四
Xīngqīyī	Xīngqī'èr	Xīngqīsān	Xīngqīsì
(Monday)	(Tuesday)	(Wednesday)	(Thursday)

星期五	星期六	星期天/星期日
Xīngqīwǔ	Xīngqīliù	Xīngqītiān / Xīngqīrì
(Friday)	(Saturday)	(Sunday)
		(LIT: week, heaven / week, sun)

Counting the weeks is done with "**ge**" as well.

一个星期	两个星期	三个星期	四个星期
yí ge xīngqī	liǎng ge xīngqī	sān ge xīngqī	sì ge xīngqī
(one week)	(two weeks)	(three weeks)	(four weeks)

Time of Day

早上	中午	下午	晚上
zǎoshang	zhōngwǔ	xiàwǔ	wǎnshang
(morning)	(midday, noon)	(afternoon)	(evening)

[handwritten: means 12-2?M instead of just 12?M]

Hours

The hours are expressed by saying the number followed by "**diǎn**."

点
diǎn
(o'clock) *[handwritten: (does not mean hour)]*
(LIT: point, clock)

一点	两点	三点	四点
yì diǎn	liǎng diǎn	sān diǎn	sì diǎn
(1 o'clock)	(2 o'clock)	(3 o'clock)	(4 o'clock)

Minutes

Expressing minutes is equally logical.

分
fēn
(minute[s])

 一点十分
yì diǎn shí fēn

 两点二十五分
liǎng diǎn èrshíwǔ fēn

"Bàn" can be used in place of "30" to express "half past" the hour:

半
bàn
(half)

 五点半
wǔ diǎn bàn
(5:30, or half past five)

6 Chit-Chat Café
– The place you come to practice speaking

Below you will see two calendars with dates highlighted. You should practice saying out loud each date, day of the week, time of day and time. Remember to start with the largest unit and finish with the smallest.

Here are the first two; you do the rest:

1. 二零零九年，九月一号，星期二，下午三点二十分
   èr líng líng jiǔ nián, Jiǔyuè yī hào, Xīngqī'èr, xiàwǔ sān diǎn èrshí fēn
   (September 1, 2009; Tuesday at 3:20 in the afternoon)

2. 二零零九年，九月四号，星期五，晚上六点半
   èr líng líng jiǔ nián, Jiǔyuè sì hào, Xīngqīwǔ, wǎnshang liù diǎn bàn
   (September 4, 2009; Friday at 6:30 in the evening)

Now, say the below dates and times out loud, then check your answers with the audio and the *pinyin* transcript in the appendix to see if you did it correctly.

SEPTEMBER 2009

Sunday	Monday	Tuesday	Wednesday	Thursday	Friday	Saturday
		① 1 3:20 p.m.	2	3	② 4 6:30 p.m.	5
6	③ 7 9:10 a.m.	8	9	④ 10 1:40 p.m.	11	⑤ 12 2:20 p.m.
13	14	15	⑥ 16 11:45 a.m.	17	⑦ 18 12:20 p.m.	19
⑧ 20 12:00 p.m.	21	22	23	⑨ 24 9:30 p.m.	25	26
27	28	⑩ 29 10:25 a.m.	30			

JUNE 2010

Sunday	Monday	Tuesday	Wednesday	Thursday	Friday	Saturday
		⑪ 1 8:10 p.m.	2	3	4	⑫ 5 2:20 p.m.
⑬ 6 7:35 a.m.	7	8	⑭ 9 8:50 p.m.	10	11	12
13	⑮ 14 8:30 a.m.	15	16	17	⑯ 18 11:28 p.m.	19
20	21	⑰ 22 12:00 p.m.	23	⑱ 24 6:40 p.m.	25	26
⑲ 27 2:35 a.m.	28	29	⑳ 30 10:35 p.m.			

3) èr líng líng jiǔ nián, Jiǔyuè liù hào, Xīngqīyī, zǎoshang liù diǎn sān shí wǔ fēn

6

109

Word Workshop
– The place you come to learn new words and phrases

(Go to 🔘 6-6 to hear:)

More time words

现在
xiànzài
(now)

今天
jīntiān
(today)

明天
míngtiān
(tomorrow)

昨天
zuótiān
(yesterday)

生日
shēngrì
(birthday)

Time questions

什么时候?
Shénme shíhou?
(When?)

哪一年?
Nǎ yì nián?
(What year?)

几月?
Jǐ yuè?/ *Nǎ yì ge yuè?*
(What month?)

几个月?
Jǐ ge yuè?
(How many months?)

几号?
Jǐ hào?
(What day [of the month]?)

星期几?
Xīngqī jǐ?
(What day [of the week]?)

几个星期?
Jǐ ge xīngqī?
(How many weeks?)

几点?
Jǐ diǎn?
(What time?)

110

New Expressions

听不懂

tīng bù dǒng

(not understand)

(LIT: hear, not, understand)

就是

jiù shì

(happens to be [emphasizes that something is precisely or exactly what is stated])

真的	真的吗？
zhēn de	Zhēn de ma?
(really)	(Really?)

interchangeable w/ hen

 Chit-Chat Café
— *The place you come to practice speaking*

6

Module 6.2 - (💿 6-7) / English translation on **Page 120**

Picture this: "Lisa" is in Shanghai and talking to her friend "Wang Qin" in a tea house. "Lisa" is still struggling with Chinese and doesn't understand everything "Wang Qin" is saying.

Wang Qin:	Lisa, nǐ de shēngrì shì jǐ yuè jǐ hào?	Wang Qin:	Lisa，你的生日是几月几号？
Lisa:	Wǒ de shēngrì shì Sānyuè yī hào.	Lisa:	我的生日是三月一号。
Wang Qin:	Zhēn de ma? Jīntiān jiù shì nǐ de shēngrì!	Wang Qin:	真的吗？今天就是你的生日！
Lisa:	Duì, jīntiān shì wǒ de shēngrì.	Lisa:	对，今天是我的生日。
Wang Qin:	Nǐ jǐ suì?	Wang Qin:	你几岁？
Lisa:	Wǒ jīnnián èrshíwǔ suì.	Lisa:	我今年二十五岁。

111

Wang Qin:	Zhù nǐ shēngrì kuàilè!	Wang Qin:	祝你生日快乐！
Lisa:	Shénme? Duìbuqǐ. Wǒ tīng bù dǒng.	Lisa:	什么？对不起，我听不懂。
Wang Qin:	Méiyǒu guānxi. Wǒ jiāo nǐ: "Zhù nǐ shēngrì kuàilè" shì Zhōngwén de "happy birthday."	Wang Qin:	没有关系。我教你："祝你生日快乐"是中文的"happy birthday"。
Lisa:	Xièxie. Nǐ ne? Nǐ de shēngrì shì jǐ yuè jǐ hào?	Lisa:	谢谢。你呢？你的生日是几月几号？
Wang Qin:	Wǒ de shēngrì shì Bāyuè èrshíbā hào.	Wang Qin:	我的生日是八月二十八号。
Lisa:	Nà shì wǒ māma de shēngrì!	Lisa:	那是我妈妈的生日！
Wang Qin:	Zhēn de ma? Nǐ bàba ne? Tā de shēngrì shì jǐ yuè jǐ hào?	Wang Qin:	真的吗？你爸爸呢？他的生日是几月几号？
Lisa:	Tā de shēngrì shì Liùyuè shíjiǔ hào.	Lisa:	他的生日是六月十九号。

Chit-Chat Practice 6.2

Answer the following questions about the above dialogue then about yourself. You can find the correct answers in **Appendix IV**.

1. Lisa 的生日是几月几号？

Q: Lisa de shēngrì shì jǐ yuè jǐ hào?

A: ~~Lisa birth~~ Lisa de shēnrì shì Sānyuè yī hào.

你呢？你的生日是几月几号？

Q: Nǐ ne? Nǐ de shēngrì shì jǐ yuè jǐ hào?

A: Wǒ de shēngrì shì Shíyīyuè shíbā hào.

2.　　Lisa几岁？

Q:　Lisa jǐ suì?

A: <u>Lisa èrshíwǔ suì</u>

你呢？你几岁？

Q:　Nǐ ne? Nǐ jǐ suì?

A: <u>Wǒ er shí yíng suì.</u>

3.　　Lisa妈妈的生日是几月几号？

Q:　Lisa māma de shēngrì shì jǐ yuè jǐ hào?

A: <u>Lisa māma de shēngrì shì Bā yuè èrshíba hào.</u>

你妈妈呢？她的生日是几月几号？

Q:　Nǐ māma ne? Tā de shēngrì shì jǐ yuè jǐ hào?

A: <u>Wǒ māma de shēngrì shì Bayuè shísi hào.</u>

6

4.　　Lisa 爸爸的生日是几月几号？

Q:　Lisa bàba de shēngrì shì jǐ yuè jǐ hào?

A: <u>Lisa bàba de shēngrì shì Liùyuè shíjiǔ hào.</u>

你爸爸呢？他的生日是几月几号？

Q:　Nǐ bàba ne? Tā de shēngrì shì jǐ yuè jǐ hào?

A: <u>Wǒ bàba de shēngrì shì Sìyuè shí hào.</u>

 *Grammar Grove*
— The place you come to learn about structure

Time in Chinese is laid out in a logical fashion. Let's have a look at how that works. Here is a layout of some time words you have learned and some new ones. You will see a pattern to many of them:

	Previously	Before	Now	After	Later
Time	qián (first, prior)	yǐqián (before)	xiànzài (now)	yǐhòu (after)	hòulái (later)
Day	qiántiān (day before yesterday)	zuótiān (yesterday)	jīntiān (today)	míngtiān (tomorrow)	hòutiān (day after tomorrow)
Week	shàngshàng ge xīngqī (week before last)	shàng ge xīngqī (last week)	zhèige xīngqī (this week)	xià ge xīngqī (next week)	xiàxià ge xīngqī (week after next)
Month	shàngshàng ge yuè (month before last)	shàng ge yuè (last month)	zhèige yuè (this month)	xià ge yuè (next month)	xiàxià ge yuè (month after next)
Year	qiánnián (year before last)	qùnián (last year)	jīnnián (this year)	míngnián (next year)	hòunián (year after next)

The Chinese Concept of Up as "Before" and Down as "After"

Perhaps because Chinese used to be only written from up to down, the Chinese connote up with "before" and down with "after." Much in the way the words "up" were ones already written while the words to come would be down. Note the words for each in Chinese:

上 shàng = up
下 xià = down

So, "shàng ge xīngqī" is literally "up week," and means last week. The "ge" here is the measure word you learned for counting things. Then "shàngshàng ge xīngqī" means "up, up week" and means the week before last. Likewise, "xià ge xīngqī" is "down week," or next week, and "xiàxià ge xīngqī" is literally "down, down week" and means the week after next. You can see this same pattern for months as well.

Grammar Reminder Regarding Time

Subject + Time + Place + Event

Remember your time words come after the subject. You may also place the time word before your subject. Those are the only two places time may go in a declarative sentence:

Example:

我今天学中文。   or   今天我学中文。

Wǒ jīntiān xué Zhōngwén.   Jīntiān wǒ xué Zhōngwén.

(I am studying Chinese today.)   (Today I am studying Chinese.)

6

You may be tempted to place the time word at the end, as in "I am studying Chinese today." But, unfortunately, that is not where to put the time word in Chinese.

Chit-Chat Café
– The place you come to practice speaking

Chit-Chat Practice 6.3
Answer the following time questions with a short answer following the English prompt.

Example:

星期几?   Xīngqī yī.

Xīngqī jǐ?   (Monday)

1. 什么时候?   *Míngtiān.*

    Shénme shíhou?   (Tomorrow)

2. 哪一年?
   Nǎ yì nián?

   Yīng jiǔ jiǔ bā nián.
   (1998)

3. 几月几号?
   Jǐ yuè jǐ hào?

   Jiǔ yuè èrshí sān hào.
   (September 23rd)

4. 几点?
   Jǐ diǎn?

   Xiàwǔ sān diǎn bàn.
   (3:30 in the afternoon)

5. 星期几?
   Xīngqī jǐ?

   Xīngqī tiān.
   (Sunday)

6. 什么时候?
   Shénme shíhou?

   Xiànzài.
   (Now)

7. 几月?
   Jǐ yuè?

   Shí yue.
   (October)

8. 几个星期?
   Jǐ ge xīngqī?

   Sān ge xīngqī.
   (3 weeks)

9. 几点?
   Jǐ diǎn?

   Zǎoshang qī dian èrshí fēn.
   (7:20 in the morning)

10. 几个月?
    Jǐ ge yuè?

    Liǔ ge yuè.
    (6 months)

11. 哪一年?
    Nǎ yì nián?

    Èr líng líng yī nián.
    (2001)

12. 什么时候?
    Shénme shíhou?

    Xià ge xīngqī.
    (Next week)

Chit-Chat Practice 6.4

Draw a line to connect the Chinese time words with their English meaning. The first one is done for you.

去年三月
qùnián Sānyuè

上上个星期三
shàngshàng ge Xīngqīsān

下个月五号
xià ge yuè wǔ hào

晚上八点三十五分
wǎnshang bā diǎn
sānshíwǔ fēn

六个月
liù ge yuè

下个星期日
xià ge Xīngqīrì

今年五月
jīnnián Wǔyuè

下下个星期一
xiàxià ge Xīngqīyī

明年六月
míngnián Liùyuè

这个月七号
zhèi ge yuè qī hào

两个月
liǎng ge yuè

后年二月
hòunián Èryuè

8:35 at night

next Sunday

June of next year

March of last year

Wednesday of the week
before last

two months

the 7th of this month

the 5th of next month

six months

February of the year after next

Monday of the week after next

May of this year

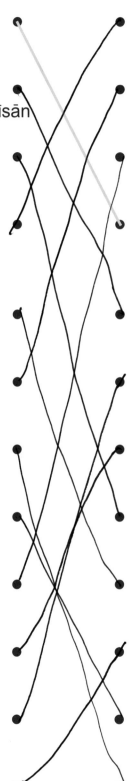

6

Culture Corner
– *The place you come to learn more than just language*

Luck and Numbers in Chinese Culture

In Chinese culture some numbers are considered lucky, or auspicious, while others are considered unlucky, or inauspicious. The degree to which this is believed varies from person to person, yet it is good to be aware of in order to understand behavior and avoid the perception of giving bad luck to others. Typically, the good luck numbers sound similar to something good in Chinese and are therefore considered lucky, while the unlucky numbers sound similar to something bad. Here are some numbers to be aware of:

Lucky Numbers

6:

The number 6 in Chinese, pronounced "liù," sounds similar to the word "liú," which means "smooth" or "flowing." The Chinese believe this number can help things go well or run smoothly, so it is considered an auspicious number. Unlike the devilish connotations that "666" can have in the west, in China you may see in some shop windows a "666" prominently displayed as a luck charm that the business will go well.

8:

The number 8 in Chinese culture is known as among the luckiest. In some dialects "bā," number 8, sounds like "wealth" or "make a fortune." Having this number in your address, telephone number or as the date of an important event, such as a wedding or grand opening for a business is considered very lucky. The Beijing Olympics opened on the auspicious date and time of 8/8/08 at 8:08:08 p.m. Real estate and telephone numbers containing 8 sell at higher prices. The telephone number 8888-8888 sold for USD 280,000 in Chengdu, Sichuan, China.

Unlucky Numbers

4:

Four is probably the most well-known unlucky number in Chinese culture. It is considered unlucky because the number four in Chinese (sì) sounds much like the word death (sǐ). It has a similar level of infamy in Chinese culture to that of the number 13 in western culture. Telephone numbers, addresses, and the like are avoided that contain this number.

5:

Five (wǔ) can be considered an unlucky number since it sounds like a word meaning "not" or "none (无)," giving the impression that you will not make money or things will not go well. Generally it is avoided, but if combined with the right number it can then become a lucky number as in 54 (wǔ, sì), sounding like "not, die."

Advice Alcove
– The place you come to learn how to learn

Discovering Your Learning Style

As you likely know, everyone learns very differently; this is particularly apparent when it comes to learning foreign languages. Here you see a wide spectrum of the students who just "get it" and start speaking, while others easily grasp the grammar but can't speak, and still others who must write down and see every word written out before they can learn it. So, what kind of learner are you? And how can your learning style and type of intelligence be leveraged to speed up your learning and help you approach your studies in a way that will yield results?

First allow me to discuss learning styles, to figure out which kind of learner you are. There are three common types of learners:

- **The Visual Learners:** This type of learners learns through seeing. They tend to take notes while learning and prefer to see things in writing before trying to say or understand it out loud. They learn faster with pictures, diagrams or video where they can make a connection between something visual and a word or concept. You may see this type of student taking many notes in class and referring to the book when lost.

- **The Auditory Learners:** The auditory learners learn best through listening. They can pick up new words and phrases by hearing them and through spontaneous dialogue. It is easy for them to encounter new words in a sentence and learn them through context alone. They tend to be good at picking up the pronunciation in a new language. You may see this style of student taking a tape recorder to class or picking up language skills "in the street."

- **The Kinesthetic Learners:** The kinesthetic learners learn through doing and actively using information. They tend to get the most out of role-plays and active in-class activities that put language in context through actually using it in realistic situations. This type of students may find it hard to sit through grammar and vocabulary lessons, but shines when the language comes to life through interaction.

All learners employ a bit of each style to learn, but you will likely find one of the above styles easiest to utilize. Once you realize which method is most effective for you, you can tailor your studies to emphasize this. Employing a learning style that comes most naturally to you means streamlining your learning so you get the most out of the time you put into studying.

English Translation

Module 6.2

Wang Qin:	Lisa, when is your birthday?
Lisa:	My birthday is March 1st.
Wang Qin:	Really? Today then happens to be your birthday!
Lisa:	Right, today is my birthday.
Wang Qin:	How old are you?
Lisa:	This year (I turn) 25 years old.
Wang Qin:	Happy birthday!
Lisa:	What? Sorry, I don't understand.
Wang Qin:	That's all right. I'll teach you: "Zhù nǐ shēngrì kuàilè" is Chinese for "happy birthday."
Lisa:	Thanks. How about you? When is your birthday?
Wang Qin:	My birthday is August 28th.
Lisa:	That is my mother's birthday!
Wang Qin:	Really? How about your father? When is his birthday?
Lisa:	His birthday is June 19th.

LESSON 7

Pronunciation Plaza
– The place you come to practice sounds and tones

(Go to 🔘 <u>7-1</u> to hear:)

Pinyin Practice

Below is a chart of the sounds we will cover in this lesson, with the initials highlighted in   and the finals highlighted in   :

	ü			
	ü	üe	üan	ün
no intial	yu	yue	yuan	yun
n	nü	nüe		
l	lü	lüe		
j	ju	jue	juan	jun
q	qu	que	quan	qun
x	xu	xue	xuan	xun

The Umlaut Sound

The umlaut is a sound found in German (as in "**ü**ben") and French (as in "t**u**" or "r**ue**"), and which can also be found in Mandarin. If you are not familiar with this sound in either of those languages, think of Kermit the Frog speaking in English and saying "you." It's a guttural "you" sound. So, where and when do you speak like Kermit?

1: Any "u" following these initials should be pronounced as an umlauted "u" (even though the "u" does not have two dots above it):

j-, q-, x-, y-

2: Any other "u" that has two dots above it like this "ü," should be pronounced as an umlauted "u."

The reason these two dots appear above some umlauted "u"s and not over others is that the assumption is any "u" preceded by a j, q, x or y is going to be pronounced as an umlaut. However, some "u"s after an l or an n are pronounced as a regular "u" and some as an umlauted "u." Therefore, there is a need to differentiate and to place the two dots above the "u" to clarify.

Mixed Tone Practice

yú (fish)	yuè (moon)	yuàn (yard)	yùn (to transport)
nǚ (female)	nüè (cruel)		
lǚ (travel)	lüè (strategy)		
jǔ (to raise)	jué (to decide)	juān (to donate)	jūn (military)
qù (to go)	què (but)	quán (whole)	qún (crowd)
xǔ (to permit)	xué (to learn)	xuǎn (to choose)	xún (to seek)

Sound Differentiation
Let's practice differentiating between the regular "u" and the umlauted form:

Non-Umlaut "u"	Umlauted "u"
lù (road)	lǜ (green)
nú (slave)	nǚ (female)

zhū (pig)	jú (orange)
zhuǎn (to turn)	juān (to donate)
zhǔn (to permit)	jūn (military)
chū (to exit)	qù (to go)
chuān (to wear)	quān (circle)
chūn (springtime)	qún (skirt)
shū (book)	xū (to need)
shuān (bolt)	xuǎn (to choose)
shùn (smooth-flowing)	xùn (information)

Tone Combination Practice

Now it's time to work on your pronunciation when combining two tones. The intonation will change slightly when a tone is said in combination rather than in isolation. So listen closely for what each combination should sound like. First we will start with tone combinations beginning with the first tone:

1st tone + 1st tone

sījī	pīnyīn	fēijī	xīngqī	qīngwā
(driver)	(pinyin)	(plane)	(week)	(frog)

1st tone + 2nd tone

jiārén	pīpíng	bāngmáng	gōngpíng	fācái
(family)	(criticize)	(help out)	(fair)	(get rich)

1st tone + 3rd tone

jiānbǎng	gōngxǐ	hē jiǔ	chūqiǔ	xīnlǐ
(shoulders)	(congratulations)	(drink alcohol)	(mistake)	(psychology)

1st tone + 4th tone

bīngkuài	fāngbiàn	tiānqì	shēngqì	yīnyuè
(ice cube)	(convenient)	(weather)	(angry)	(music)

1st tone + neutral tone

zhīdao	qīngchu	chuānghu	gēge	yīfu
(to know)	(clear)	(window)	(older brother)	(clothes)

Sound Differentiation Exercise

Listen to the following sounds in 7-2 and write the correct *pinyin* spelling and tones below. See **Appendix IV** for correct answers:

1. _____ 2. _____ 3. _____ 4. _____

5. _____ 6. _____ 7. _____ 8. _____

9. _____ 10. _____ 11. _____ 12. _____

13. _____ 14. _____ 15. _____ 16. _____

17. _____ 18. _____ 19. _____ 20. _____

Word Workshop
– The place you come to learn new words and phrases

(Go to 7-3 to hear:)

Activity Verbs & Objects

Most activity verbs in Chinese are transitive (in other words, they must take an object). This follows the logical pattern of "verb + object." Here are some common activities using some verbs you have already learned as well as some new verbs and nouns.

Verb [1]	Verb [2]	Noun / Object	Activity
看 kàn (to read)		书 shū (book)	看书 kànshū (to read a book)
Example sentence: 我喜欢看书。 Wǒ xǐhuan kànshū. (I like to read books.)			
去 qù (to go)	看 kàn (to watch)	电影 diànyǐng (movie)	去看电影 qù kàn diànyǐng (to go to the movies)
Example sentence: 她去看电影。 Tā qù kàn diànyǐng. (She is going to the movies.)		*electricity*	
要 yào (to want)	看 kàn (to watch)	电视 diànshì (television)	要看电视 yào kàn diànshì (to want to watch television)
Example sentence: 你要看电视吗？ Nǐ yào kàn diànshì ma? (Do you want to watch TV?)			

7

Verb [1]	Verb [2]	Noun / Object	Activity
去 qù (to go)	看 kàn (to see)	朋友 péngyou (friend[s]).	去看朋友 qù kàn péngyou (to go see friends)
Example sentence: 你几点去看朋友? Nǐ jǐ diǎn qù kàn péngyou? (What time are you going to see friends?)			
去 qù (to go)	吃 chī (to eat)	饭 fàn (rice / meal)	去吃饭 qù chīfàn (to go out to eat)
Example sentence: 你们去哪儿吃饭? Nǐmen qù nǎr chīfàn? (Where are you all going out to eat?)			
去 qù (to go)		玩儿 wánr (to play, to have fun) *hǎo wánr?* *Is it fn?*	去玩儿 qù wánr (to go out, to go have fun)
Example sentence: 你晚上要去哪里玩儿? Nǐ wǎnshang yào qù nǎli wánr? (Where do you want to go out tonight?)			
做 zuò (to make / do)		饭 fàn (rice / meal)	做饭 zuòfàn (to cook) */cooking*
Example sentence: 你喜欢做饭吗? Nǐ xǐhuan zuòfàn ma? (Do you like to cook?)			
听 tīng (to listen)		音乐 yīnyuè (music)	听音乐 tīng yīnyuè (to listen to music)

7

Example sentence:			
谁听音乐? Shéi tīng yīnyuè? (Who is listening to music?)			
上 shàng (to attend) *(LIT: on, up)*	下 xià (to get out of / off) *(LIT: off, down)*	课 kè (class)	上课/下课 shàngkè / xiàkè (to attend class / to get out of class)
Example sentence:			
他们几点上课? Tāmen jǐ diǎn shàngkè? (What time do they have class?)			
上 shàng (to attend) *(LIT: on, up)*	下 xià (to get out of / off) *(LIT: off, down)*	班 bān (work shift)	上班/下班 shàngbān / xiàbān (to start work / to get off work)
Example sentence:			
你几点下班? Nǐ jǐ diǎn xiàbān? (What time do you get off from work?)			
喝 hē (to drink)		水，茶，酒，咖啡 shuǐ, chá, jiǔ, kāfēi (water, tea, alcohol, coffee)	喝水，喝茶，喝酒，喝咖啡 hē shuǐ, hē chá, hē jiǔ, hē kāfēi (to drink water, tea, alcohol, coffee)
Example sentence:			
我们喜欢喝咖啡。 Wǒmen xǐhuan hē kāfēi. (We like to drink coffee.)			

7

Questioning

Here is how to ask what someone is doing at that monent:

他在做什么?

Tā zài* zuò shénme?

(What is he doing [right now]?)

* *"Zài" is used to express that something is happening right at that moment, much like the present continuous tense in English—we will go into further depth in a later lesson.*

 Chit-Chat Café
– The place you come to practice speaking

Module 7.1 - (7-4)

Now, let's practice all those activity verbs. Look at the below pictures and ask out loud what each person is doing, then answer as well. When you see "**YOU?**" that means you should ask "What are you doing?" and answer "I am _____." To hear each question and each answer visit 7-4. You can find the answers in **Appendix IV**.

But make it interesting

Here is the first one for you:

1.   Q: Tā zuò shénme?

     A: Tā kàn shū.

1.    2.    3.    4.

5. **YOU?** 6. 7. 8.

9. 10. 11. 12. **YOU?**

13. **YOU?** 14. 15. 16.

7

17. 18. 19. 20. **YOU?**

Word Workshop
– The place you come to learn new words and phrases

(Go to 🔘 7-5 to hear:)

OK, let's expand your vocabulary the easy way: putting together words you've already learned to form new words. Here is how it works: Each combination contains morphemes you have already learned, put together to form another meaning.

Adjectives formed with words you know

好看
hǎokàn
(good-looking, nice to look at, a good read, good to watch)

⟺

不好看
bù hǎokàn
(not good-looking, not nice to look at, not a good read, not good to watch)

or

难看
nánkàn
(not good-looking)
(LIT: difficult to look at)

好听
**hǎotīng*
(sounds good, pretty sound, nice to listen to)

⟺

不好听
bù hǎotīng
(not good sound, not pretty to hear, not nice to listen to)

or

难听
nántīng
(not good sounding)
(LIT: difficult to listen to)

* You can not say "piàoliang" for something that sounds good. You must say "hǎotīng."

好玩儿
hǎowánr
(fun)
(LIT: good, play)

⟺

不好玩儿
bù hǎowánr
(not fun)

好吃
hǎochī
(delicious, tasty)
(LIT: good, eat)

⟺

不好吃
bù hǎochī
(not delicious, not tasty)

or

难吃
nánchī
(not tasty)
(LIT: difficult to eat)

好喝
hǎohē
(delicious to drink)
(LIT: good, drink)

⟺

不好喝
bù hǎohē*
(not delicious to drink)

or

难喝
nánhē
(not tasty to drink)
(LIT: difficult to drink)

7

In Chinese, for things that you drink, you should use this expression to say whether it tastes good or not. Not the other word for delicious "hǎochī."

New Nouns

好朋友
hǎo péngyou
(good friends)

老朋友
lǎo péngyou
(old friends)

小朋友
xiǎopéngyou ⟸ xiǎohái
(kids, children)
(LIT: little, friends)

早饭
zǎofàn
(breakfast)

午饭
wǔfàn
(lunch)

晚饭
wǎnfàn
(dinner)

中国饭
Zhōngguófàn
(Chinese food)

美国饭
Měiguófàn
(American food)

法国饭
Fǎguófàn
(French food)

cān – meal, but fancier

Chit-Chat Café
– *The place you come to practice speaking*

7

Module 7.2

Answer the following questions according to your own opinions or views. You can see sample answers for this module in **Appendix IV**.

Example:

中国饭好吃吗?

Q: Zhōngguófàn hǎochī ma?

A: Zhōngguófàn hěn hǎochī.

1.   你爸爸好看吗?

Q: Nǐ bàba hǎokàn ma?

A: Wǒ de bàba bù hánkàn..

2. 美国音乐好不好听?

Q: Měiguó yīnyuè hǎo bù hǎotīng?

A: Yǒu shíhou Měiguó yīnyuè hǎotīng, yǒushíyou hen nántīng.

3. 学中文好不好玩儿?

Q: Xué Zhōngwén hǎo bù hǎowánr?

A: Xué Zhōngwen hen hǎowánr.

4. 法国饭好不好吃?

Q: Fǎguófàn hǎo bù hǎochī?

A: ~~Fǎguófàn~~ Bú zhīdao, wǒ ~~hǎo~~ mei qu le Fǎguó.

5. 咖啡难喝吗?

Q: Kāfēi nánhē ma?

Bùshì, Kāfēi hen hǎohe!

7

6. 小朋友会做饭吗?

Q: Xiǎopéngyou huì zuòfàn ma?

A: Bú huì, xiǎo péngyou bú huì zuòfàn.

7. 你的老朋友在哪儿?

Q: Nǐ de lǎo péngyou zài nǎr?

A: Wǒ de lǎo pengyou zhu zài SantaCruz.

8. 你几点吃午饭?

Q: Nǐ jǐ diǎn chī wǔfàn?

A: Wǒ chī wǔfàn shí'èr ban diǎn.

and review everything

Grammar Grove
– The place you come to learn about structure

Connecting words and phrases - Part 1

All right, so there is this word in English known as "and" it is really useful and can be used to connect nouns, verbs, phrases of all kinds, clauses and practically anything. Meanwhile, in Mandarin this universal "and" simply does not exist. So, let's get to the point: If you want to connect words and phrases, you are going to have to learn a few more connector words and concepts to express "and." In this lesson we will cover some and in the following lesson some others. Here is first an outline of all the connectors we will teach:

☐ = connectors covered in Lesson 7   ☐ = connectors covered in Lesson 8

Table of Connectors & Uses

Each box that is checked indicates that connector can connect that grammatical part.

(handwritten annotations: "no time difference, just two subjy", "something hierarchical happens at the same time (state)", "and", "also have, also", "but also", "(more actions)")

	(nothing)	hé	hái yǒu	yě	gēn	yòu...... yòu......	yìbiān...... yìbiān......
pronouns		✔	✔		✔		
nouns	✔	✔	✔		✔		
verbs	✔			✔		✔	✔
verb phrases	✔			✔		✔	✔
adjectives	✔			✔		✔	

7

Conjunction Concept #1:

The "Skip It" approach: Don't use a connector at all.

Here is a radical concept: In Chinese you can often just skip the "and" connector. Places where in English you are required to say "and" in Chinese you can often just skip. Here is how "Skip It" works:

Examples:

我爸爸妈妈去吃饭看电影。

Wǒ bàba māma qù chīfàn kàn diànyǐng.

(My father and mother are going out to eat and going to the movies.)

他不会看书不会写字。 *character*

Tā bú huì kàn shū bú huì xiězì.

(He doesn't know how to read and doesn't know how to write.)

Conjunction Concept #2:

Use a popular conjunction to express "and":

和

hé

(and)

"Hé" is commonly translated as "and;" however, it can only be used to connect pronouns, nouns and noun phrases. It may not be used to connect verbs, verb phrases and clauses, as you would be able to do with "and" in English.

Examples of how "hé" may be used:

他爸爸和妈妈都是美国人。

Tā bàba hé māma dōu shì Měiguórén.

(His father and mother are both American.)

他会说中文和英文。

Tā huì shuō Zhōngwén hé Yīngwén.

(He knows how to speak Chinese and English.)

Example of how "hé" may **not** be used:

我去他家和吃饭。

✘ Wrong: Wǒ qù tā jiā hé chīfàn.

(Wrong way to say "I go to his house and eat dinner.")

To correct this, simply use the "Skip It" approach.

我去他家吃饭。

✔ Correct   Wǒ qù tā jiā chīfàn.

(I go to his house and eat dinner.)

7

134

Conjunction Concept #3:

Use another popular connector to express "and":
You learned this connector in Lesson 5 to mean "also have (hái yǒu)." It also can mean "and."

还有

hái yǒu
(and, in addition, else, also have)
(LIT: still, have)

"Hái yǒu" is similar to "hé" in that it is used to connect nouns; however, it is not commonly used to connect pronouns. Also, like "hé," it may not be used to connect verbs and clauses. It has an additional use of expressing "and" as in the tag "And, what else?" or "And who else?".

Example of how "hái yǒu" is used like "hé":

我有一个姐姐，两个妹妹，还有一个弟弟。
Wǒ yǒu yí ge jiějie, liǎng ge mèimei, hái yǒu yí ge dìdi.
I have an older sister, two younger sisters and one younger brother.

Examples of "hái yǒu" expressing "And, (what else)...?":
Additionally "hái yǒu" may be colloquially used to express "And, what else?", or simply "And?" as shown below:

还有呢？
Hái yǒu ne?
(And [what else]?)

还有谁？
Hái yǒu shéi?
(And, who else?)

你有这个，还有什么？
Nǐ yǒu zhèige, hái yǒu shénme?
(You have this and what else?)

Conjunction Concept #4:

Use "yě (also)" to express "and":

The word "also" in Chinese can be used like the connector "and." This should be done to connect verbs and verb phrases only. Here are some examples:

他不懂中文也不懂英文。

Tā bù dǒng Zhōngwén yě bù dǒng Yīngwén.

(He doesn't understand Chinese and he doesn't understand English.)

他们要去北京学中文也要去上海玩儿。

Tāmen yào qù Běijīng xué Zhōngwén yě yào qù Shànghǎi wánr.

(They want to go to Beijing to study Chinese and they want to go to Shanghai to have fun.)

Summary:

Handy Rules of Thumb:

- When in doubt just use nothing - you'll often be right.
- When connecting pronouns at the beginning of a sentence use "hé."
- When listing things or people use "hái yǒu."

7

Chit-Chat Café
– The place you come to practice speaking

(Go to 🖸 7-6 to hear:)

Module 7.3

Hello reader, it's Rachel, the author here! You've learned so much in these seven lessons. Now I am going to tell you a bit about myself only using Chinese words and grammar you have learned. Try reading the below text in characters or *pinyin*. You should be able to understand it all. Only words you haven't learned yet will be translated into English in parenthesis. You can find a full translation on **Page 143**.

Character version:

你好。我叫梅洁如。我的英文名字是Rachel Meyer。我是中文老师，可是我不是中国人。其实(in fact)我是美国人！我会说中文、西班牙文(Spanish)、法文还有英文。我喜欢教中文和西班牙文。我不教法文，因为我的法文马马虎虎。以前我在台湾教英文。教台湾人英文很好玩儿，因为他们都是好学生。

我现在住在旧金山。以前我住在纽约。我喜欢纽约，纽约很大。旧金山比纽约小。旧金山很漂亮。纽约很有意思。在纽约我喜欢去吃饭，也喜欢看我的老朋友。在旧金山我喜欢看电影、看书、去玩儿。我也喜欢在旧金山吃中国饭。旧金山的中国饭很好吃。

我家有五个人：我爸爸、妈妈、一个姐姐、一个妹妹，还有我。我没有哥哥弟弟。我姐姐和她的先生有两个女儿。她们叫Emma和Kate。Emma九岁，Kate七岁。她们都是好孩子，很漂亮也很聪明。我妹妹和她的先生去中国领养(to adopt)了一个中国女孩。她现在三岁。她的中文名字叫宁君莉，她的英文名字叫June。我妹妹和她的先生都很快乐，June也很快乐。

7

Pinyin version:

Nǐ hǎo. Wǒ jiào Méi Jiérú. Wǒ de Yīngwén míngzi shì Rachel Meyer. Wǒ shì Zhōngwén lǎoshī, kěshì wǒ bú shì Zhōngguórén. Qíshí (in fact) wǒ shì Měiguórén! Wǒ huì shuō Zhōngwén, Xībānyáwén (Spanish), Fǎwén hái yǒu Yīngwén. Wǒ xǐhuan jiāo Zhōngwén hé Xībānyáwén. Wǒ bù jiāo Fǎwén, yīnwèi wǒ de Fǎwén mǎmahūhū. Yǐqián wǒ zài Táiwān jiāo Yīngwén. Jiāo Táiwānrén Yīngwén hěn hǎowánr, yīnwèi tāmen dōu shì hǎo xuésheng.

Wǒ xiànzài zhù zài Jiùjīnshān. Yǐqián wǒ zhù zài Niǔyuē. Wǒ xǐhuan Niǔyuē, Niǔyuē hěn dà. Jiùjīnshān bǐ Niǔyuē xiǎo.

Jiùjīnshān hěn piàoliang. Niǔyuē hěn yǒu yìsi. Zài Niǔyuē wǒ xǐhuan qù chīfàn, yě xǐhuan kàn wǒ de lǎo péngyou. Zài Jiùjīnshān wǒ xǐhuan kàn diànyǐng, kàn shū, qù wánr. Wǒ yě xǐhuan zài Jiùjīnshān chī Zhōngguófàn. Jiùjīnshān de Zhōngguófàn hěn hǎochī.

Wǒ jiā yǒu wǔ ge rén: wǒ bàba, māma, yí ge jiějie, yí ge mèimei, hái yǒu wǒ. Wǒ méiyǒu gēge dìdi. Wǒ jiějie hé tā de xiānsheng yǒu liǎng ge nǚ'ér. Tāmen jiào Emma hé Kate. Emma jiǔ suì, Kate qī suì. Tāmen dōu shì hǎo háizi, hěn piàoliang yě hěn cōngmíng. Wǒ mèimei hé tā de xiānsheng qù Zhōngguó lǐngyǎng (to adopt) le yí ge Zhōngguó nǚhái. Tā xiànzài sān suì. Tā de Zhōngwén míngzi jiào Níng Jūnlì, tā de Yīngwén míngzi jiào June. Wǒ mèimei hé tā de xiānsheng dōu hěn kuàilè, June yě hěn kuàilè.

Chit-Chat Practice 7.3

Now let's have you describe yourself in monologue form as I did above. On the below lines, write about yourself in Chinese (either *pinyin* or in characters). Here are some topics you may want to include:

- your nationality, age
- where you live
- family members & age and where they live
- your likes & dislikes
- languages you speak
- describe your children or your siblings' children
- describe one or more good friends
- tell your birthday
- tell why you are learning Chinese
- talk about your Chinese teacher (if you have one)
- tell about your boyfriend / girlfriend or husband / wife (likewise, if you have one)
- compare yourself to your siblings (who is taller?)
- compare where you live now to another city / place
- tell us if you think Chinese is difficult and more

Nǐ hǎo.

~~[crossed out]~~ Wǒ jiào Will. Xiànzài zài yíge

huánjìng zǔzhī,^(gōngzuò) kěshì ~~[crossed out]~~ xià ge yuè,

wǒ qù ~~[kāishǐ crossed out]~~ gōngzuò zài yíge fǎlǜ bàngōngshì.

Wǒ shì Měiguórén, zhù zài Jiùjīnshān.

Wǒ huì Yīngwén hěn hǎo, yě shuō yìdiǎnr

Fǎwén, Tǔěrqíwén, hé Pǔtōnghuà.

(jīngcháng) ~~[crossed out]~~ zài Jiùjīnshān, wǒ xǐhuan qù wánr

(hé péngyou), kàn shū~~[crossed out]~~, yě xué Zhōngwén.

Wǒ xǐhuan qù qí zìxíngchē yě kàn

jiē^(tóu) yìshù. Wǒ xǐhuan tīng shī ~~[crossed out]~~.

Wǒ xué Zhōngwén yīnwei wǒ yào qù

Zhōngguó ~~[crossed out]~~. ~~[crossed out]~~ (qualified) wǒ by Zhōngwén

shì hěn fúhé luójí de. Wǒ bu huì kàn,

kěshì ^(xué) shuō Zhōngwén ~~[crossed out]~~ bǐ ^(xué shuō) Fǎwén hé Tǔěrqíwén

róngyì.   Wǒ èrshíyī suì. Wǒ de shēnrì shíyī yuè shíbā (hào)

Wǒ jiā yǒu wǔge rén: ~~wǒ~~ bàba ~~māma~~,

jìmǔ, yí ge mèimei, yíge yímǔ dìdi, ~~hái~~ yǒu wǒ.

Wǒ bǐ mèimei hé yímǔ dìdi lǎo.

Wǒ de jiǎnghuà shì ~~duǎnzàn~~ (tempong) yīnwei 139

wǒ de shūxiě hěn ~~[crossed out]~~ dà!

Culture Corner
– *The place you come to learn more than just language*

不醉不归
bú zuì bù guī
"No one goes home until we're all drunk!"
Chinese saying

Now that you've learned the words "hē jiǔ (drink alcohol)," it's time to learn a bit about drinking in China. This topic will turn out to be a bit more complicated than you may have expected, and a bit more vigorous. Socially drinking in China is not for the faint of heart. Allow me to provide you with some survival skills. Keep in mind, China is changing rapidly and many of these rules may be changing, particularly in urban centers. Nevertheless, the basic rules are always good to know. Here are some of the tops:

- If you start to drink, you will be expected to continue to drink and keep pace with the whole group. There is no such thing as drinking at your own pace, or nursing a drink to just socially participate. This is an all-or-nothing affair.

- If you do not want to get involved in the complications of social drinking in China, you may opt out with the simple phrase of "Wǒ bú huì hē jiǔ." Literally this means, "I do not know how to drink alcohol." There is another expression of "suíyì", meaning roughly "to each his own" and implies you will just be drinking at your own pace. But good luck getting away with it, and certainly not a good idea for people trying to do business in China.

- If you are a woman you can get out of the drinking pressure easily with the "Wǒ bú huì hē jiǔ" expression. However, if you are a man, it will be harder to convince people. Women are generally not expected to drink alcohol, while men (particularly men on business) will be expected to keep up with the others.

- "Gānbēi" or "dry glass" is the common expression for "bottoms up." At this point you are expected to slug it back and even show the empty glass (or bowl) as a demonstration that you followed through.

- Generally, you should not sip alone from your drink, but instead always acknowledge someone with a "gānbēi" invitation or the invitation to take a sip simultaneously with someone else at the table. Then you should use "jìng nǐ" (respectfully to you)."

7

- Plum wine, rice wine and other distilled liquors such as "báijiǔ" are the traditional alcoholic beverages of China. These are very strong, some 20 to 60 percent alcohol, so drinkers beware. Beer is usually the safest bet and good beer can be found throughout China. Grape wine is often expensive and of questionable quality, but this is changing rapidly in large cities such as Shanghai or Beijing.

- When the host or another person pours tea into your glass or teacup it is polite to tap two knuckles next to the cup as a sign of humility. The two knuckles (index finger and middle finger) are meant to look like the two knees of someone kowtowing. Be particularly aware if the person pouring tea into your cup is older; you should show them extra respect by doing this. Likewise, you should be eager to fill your fellow diners' teacups. You will notice people do this often even if only a few sips have been taken.

In general your health is more important than following social protocol; don't end up like the one British businessman who died from alcohol poisoning while trying to keep up with his Chinese counterparts at a business banquet. Stick to the "I don't know how to drink alcohol" line, or even a little white lie that I have used when pressured to drink the infamous and deadly "báijiǔ": "Sorry, I can only drink beer. I have an allergy (guòmǐn) to liquor."

Advice Alcove
– The place you come to learn how to learn

In the last lesson we outlined the different types of language learners: visual, auditory and kinesthetic. Understanding which type of learner you are can help you tailor your studies to exploit your natural strengths. Here are some learning tips for each type of learner:

The Visual Learner
- Download and print free flashcards online. Write the Chinese meaning on the back and keep a stack with you to memorize in your free time.
- Go to a Chinese bookstore (can be found in any city's Chinatown) and buy flashcards, vocabulary books, and storybooks for children. You will be able to find books that have *pinyin* as well as characters. You can find children's materials online as well.

- Practice writing out imaginary dialogues using the words and phrases you have learned.
- Go to language exchange websites where you may communicate with exchange partners through IM (Instant Messenger).
- Incorporate auditory tips into your learning so you are sure to make the connection between what you see and read and what you hear.

The Auditory Learner

- Put in plenty of time listening to the audio content of Chinese Rocks.
- Download Chinese Rocks podcast lessons for your MP3 player at www.chitchatchinese.com/podcast; keep your MP3 player with you and listen to it in any downtime such as on the bus, waiting room, etc.
- Find a live or online community where you can practice or exchange language skills, such as http://www.livemocha.com.
- Make up imaginary conversations out loud in Chinese.
- Remember to include visual study time, such as textbook work, so you are sure to have a solid grammatical basis.

The Kinesthetic Learner

- Find as many opportunities to use the language as possible.
- Join an online community where you can practice your skills.
- Join a live group through www.meetup.com or elsewhere to meet other learners and native speakers.
- Talk out loud to yourself in Chinese, practicing dialogues and learned vocabulary.
- Make efforts to meet people from China with whom you could eventually practice your skills.
- Use your skills whenever possible such as in Chinese restaurants or elsewhere.
- Incorporate visual and auditory tips into your learning so that it is well-rounded.

English Translation

Module 7.3

Hello, my name is Mei Jieru. My English name is Rachel Meyer. I am a Chinese teacher, but I am not Chinese. In fact, I am American! I know how to speak Chinese, Spanish, French and English. I like to teach Chinese and Spanish. I don't teach French, because my French is only so-so. Before, I used to teach English in Taiwan. Teaching Taiwanese people English is fun, because they are all good students.

Now I live in San Francisco. Before, I used to live in New York City. I like New York. New York is big. San Francisco is small. San Francisco is very pretty. New York is very interesting. In New York I like to go out to eat and see old friends. In San Francisco I like to go to the movies, read, and go out to have fun. Also in San Francisco I like to eat Chinese food. San Francisco's Chinese food is delicious.

In my family there are five people: My father, mother, an older sister, a younger sister and myself. I don't have an older or younger brothers. My sister and her husband have two daughters. Their names are Emma and Kate. Emma is 9 years old and Kate is 7. They both are good kids, as well as beautiful and smart. My younger sister and her husband went to China to adopt a Chinese girl. She now is 3 years old. Her Chinese name is Ning Junli. Her English name is June. My younger sister and her husband are both very happy. June is happy too.

7

NOTE

LESSON 8

Pronunciation Plaza
– The place you come to practice sounds and tones

(Go to 8-1 to hear:)

Pinyin Practice

Below is a chart of the sounds we will cover in this lesson, with the initials highlighted in [light grey] and the finals highlighted in [dark grey]:

	u							
	u	ua	uo	ui	uai	uan	un	uang
z	zu		zuo	zui		zuan	zun	
c	cu		cuo	cui		cuan	cun	
s	su		suo	sui		suan	sun	
zh	zhu	zhua	zhuo	zhui	zhuai	zhuan	zhun	zhuang
ch	chu	chua	chuo	chui	chuai	chuan	chun	chuang
sh	shu	shua	shuo	shui	shuai	shuan	shun	shuang
r	ru	rua	ruo	rui		ruan	run	

Mixed Tone Practice

zú (foot)	zuò (to do)	zuì (the most)	zuàn (diamond)	zūn (to respect)
cū (thick)	cuò (mistake)	cuī (to urge)	cuàn (to scurry)	cún (to keep)
sù (speed)	suǒ (place)	suì (year of age)	suān (sour)	sūn (grandson)
zhù (to reside)	zhuā (to grab)	zhuō (table)	zhuī (to pursue)	zhuāi (to fling)

zhuǎn (to turn)	**zhǔn** (to permit)	**zhuàng** (strong)		
chū (to exit)	**chuā** (onomat.)	**chuò** (to drink)	**chuī** (to blow)	**chuǎi** (to estimate)
chuān (to wear)	**chūn** (springtime)	**chuāng** (window)		
shū (book)	**shuā** (to brush)	**shuō** (to talk)	**shuǐ** (water)	**shuài** (to lead)
shuān (bolt)	**shùn** (smooth-flowing)	**shuāng** (pair)		
rú (such as)	**ruá** (creased)	**ruò** (if)	**ruì** (auspicious)	**ruǎn** (soft)
rùn (moist)				

Sound Differentiation

The R Sound

8

Other than the umlaut in Mandarin, the initial "r" would likely win the "Mandarin's Most Menacing Sound to Produce" award. The good news is if you say it like the American "r," people will, for the most part, understand you. There are just a few words, such as Rìběn (Japan), or rìqī (date), that will leave your listener flummoxed if you don't get it right.

Nevertheless, let's try to get it right. The sound of the Mandarin "r" does not exist in English (nor our "r" in their language, hence the Chinese speakers' problem with our "r.") It is closer to the sound of "z" in "azure." You can try to produce this sound as if you are going to start to say the English "r," but pull your tongue back a bit and let it lightly touch the roof of your mouth. Many Mandarin students when they hear "rén" pronounced slowly will try to replicate it by saying "Jen" or "Zen." This is because that is exactly where your tongue should be on your palate, and it's a good attempt at replication. So, that's the idea, but if you give it a bit more of an "r" feel to it, you will have it. Now, let's try these isolated "r" morphemes:

rǎo	rǎn	ràng	ròu	rè
(to disturb)	(to dye)	(to yield)	(meat)	(hot)

rén	rēng	rì	rú	ruá
(person)	(to throw)	(day)	(such as)	(creased)

ruò	ruì	ruǎn	rùn
(if)	(sharp)	(soft)	(moist)

"R" in morpheme combinations:

dǎrǎo	ránhòu	niúròu	ruǎnruò	Ruìdiǎnrén
(to disturb)	(after)	(beef)	(weak)	(Swedish person)

rúguǒ	rèqì	rèliè	rúhé	ràokǒulìng
(if)	(steam)	(warm)	(how)	(tongue twister)

rǎorǎng	réngrán	jiàorǎng	rěnnài	ràngbù
(hustle and bustle)	(still)	(to yell)	(to endure)	(to yield)

Tone combinations

2ⁿᵈ tone + 1ˢᵗ tone

míngtiān	zhíjiē	pángbiān	píbāo	liáotiān
(tomorrow)	(direct)	(beside)	(handbag)	(to chat)

2ⁿᵈ tone + 2ⁿᵈ tone

chángcháng	cíxiáng	guójí	wúliáo	qíshí
(often)	(kindly)	(nationality)	(boring)	(in fact)

2ⁿᵈ tone + 3ʳᵈ tone

méiyǒu	yáchǐ	yóuyǒng	píjiǔ	rúguǒ
(not have)	(teeth)	(to swim)	(beer)	(if)

2ⁿᵈ tone + 4ᵗʰ tone

liánluò	xuéxiào	jiérì	juédìng	qiánmiàn
(to contact)	(school)	(festival)	(to decide)	(in front)

2ⁿᵈ tone + neutral tone

péngyou	piányi	yéye	píngzi	biéde
(friends)	(cheap)	(grandpa)	(bottle)	(other)

8

Sound Differentiation Exercise

Listen to the following sounds in 8-2 and write the correct *pinyin* spelling and tones below. See **Appendix IV** for correct answers:

1. _____   2. _____   3. _____   4. _____

5. _____   6. _____   7. _____   8. _____

9. _____   10. _____   11. _____   12. _____

13. _____   14. _____   15. _____   16. _____

17. _____   18. _____   19. _____   20. _____

Grammar Grove
– The place you come to learn about structure

Connecting words and phrases – Part 2

The following is a continuation from Lesson 7 regarding connectors in Mandarin.

☐ = connectors covered in Lesson 7   ☐ = connectors covered in Lesson 8

memorize

Table of Connectors & Uses

Each box that is checked indicates that connector can connect that grammatical part.

	(nothing)	hé	háiyǒu	yě	gēn	yòu...... yòu......	yìbiān...... yìbiān......
pronouns		✔	✔		✔		
nouns	✔	✔	✔		✔		
verbs	✔			✔		✔	✔
verb phrases	✔			✔		✔	✔
adjectives	✔			✔		✔	

Conjunction Concept #5:
Use the word "with" to connect pronouns and nouns:

跟
　　　　　　　　　　　　　　我跟我妹妹去吃饭。

gēn　　　　　　Example:　Wǒ gēn wǒ mèimei qù chīfàn.
(with, and)　　　　　　　　(My sister and I are going to eat dinner.)

Note: "gēn" is generally used with the adverb "yìqǐ" (together).

跟……一起　　　　　　　我跟我妹妹一起去吃饭。

gēn......yìqǐ　　Example:　Wǒ gēn wǒ mèimei yìqǐ qù chīfàn.
(together)　　　　　　　　(My sister and I are going to eat dinner [together]).

"gēn" should be used to link pronouns or nouns, but not verbs. It should follow this pattern:

(Noun / Pronoun) + gēn + (Noun / Pronoun) + Verb + Object

Conjunction Concept #6:

Use a sentence pattern as a connector:
Here are two common sentence patterns used to connect two adjectives or verbs. It is used to say something or someone is both one thing and another:

Sentence pattern #1:

又……又……

yòu......yòu......
(both one thing and another)

8

You should follow this grammatical structure:

Subject + yòu + Adj. / Verb + yòu + Adj. / Verb

Examples:
他又高又瘦。

Tā yòu gāo yòu shòu.
(He is both tall and thin.)

她又漂亮又聪明。

Tā yòu piàoliang yòu cōngmíng.
(She is both beautiful and intelligent.)

他又不懂英文又不懂中文。

Tā yòu bù dǒng Yīngwén yòu bù dǒng Zhōngwén.

(He neither understands English nor Chinese.)

Sentence Pattern #2:

Here is another pattern that can be used as a connector:

一边⋯⋯一边⋯⋯

yìbiān......yìbiān......

(to do something while doing something else)

This pattern should follow this structure:

Subject + yòu + Verb + Object + yòu + Verb + Object

Examples:

他一边吃饭一边看电视。

Tā yìbiān chīfàn yìbiān kàn diànshì.

(He eats dinner and watches TV [at the same time].)

我在台湾一边教英文一边学中文。

Wǒ zài Táiwān yìbiān jiāo Yīngwén yìbiān xué Zhōngwén.

(While in Taiwan I studied Chinese and taught English.)

8

Chit-Chat Café
– The place you come to practice speaking

Module 8.1

Fill in the following blanks with one of your connector words or with nothing. For the nothing option, simply write in an "X" in the blank. Choose one of the following to fill in the blank (in some cases more than one option is possible). Answers can be found in **Appendix IV**:

(nothing)	hé	háiyǒu	yě	gēn	yòu...... yòu......	yìbiān...... yìbiān......

Example:

我跟我的老师一起去吃饭。

Wǒ <u>gēn</u> wǒ de lǎoshī yìqǐ qù chīfàn.

1. 他会说法文 ~~也~~ 会说英文。

    Tā huì shuō Fǎwén ____*yě*____ huì shuō Yīngwén.

2. 你的太太 ____又____ 漂亮 ____又____ 聪明。

    Nǐ de tàitai ____*yòu*____ piàoliang ____*yòu*____ cōngmíng.

3. 我去他家吃饭 _____ 看电视。

    Wǒ qù tā jiā chīfàn ____✗____ kàn diànshì.   *Back says X, does it matter?*

4. 他在法国 _____ 工作 _____ 学法文。

    Tā zài Fǎguó ____*yìbiān*____ gōngzuò ____*yìbiān*____ xué Fǎwén.

5. 她明年要学日文、中文 _____ 德文。 *hái yǒu*

    Tā míngnián yào xué Rìwén, Zhōngwén ____~~gēn~~____ Déwén.   *gēn vs. hé, does it matter?*

6. 他 __跟__ 他的女朋友住在伦敦。

    Tā ____*gēn*____ tā de nǚpéngyou zhù zài Lúndūn.

7. 我姐姐 __跟__ 她的先生一起工作。

    Wǒ jiějie ____~~kàn~~ *gēn*____ tā de xiānsheng yìqǐ gōngzuò.

8. 我会看 _____ 会写中文。

    Wǒ huì kàn ____✗____ huì xiě Zhōngwén.

9. 小朋友上课 _____ 看书 _____写字。

    Xiǎopéngyou shàngkè ____*yìbiān*____ kàn shū ____*yìbiān*____ xiě zì.

10. 你喜欢看书、听音乐， _____ 什么？

    Nǐ xǐhuan kàn shū, tīng yīnyuè, ____~~yǒu~~____ shénme?

    hái yǒu

Word Workshop
– *The place you come to learn new words and phrases*

(Go to 8-3 to hear:)

State-of-Being Adjectives

As with other adjectives in Chinese, there is no need to use the verb "shì (to be)."
Just remember to add "hěn" before your adjective, whether you mean "very" or not,
as is the custom.

累

lèi

(tired)

Example:

Q: 你累不累?

Nǐ lèi bú lèi?

(Are you tired?)

A: 我很累。

Wǒ hěn lèi.

(I am tired.)

All other state of being adjectives follow the above grammatical pattern.

8

饿	饱	渴
è	bǎo	kě
(hungry)	(full)	(thirsty)
忙	无聊	紧张
máng	wúliáo	jǐnzhāng
(busy)	(bored)	(nervous)
舒服	不好意思	兴奋
shūfu	bù hǎoyìsi	xīngfèn
(comfortable)	(embarrassed)	(excited)
难过	高兴	
nánguò	gāoxìng	
(sad)	(happy)	
(Lit: difficult, pass)		

152

Expressions

In China it is common to greet someone with "Have you eaten until full?", instead of "How are you?". This was more common in previous times, but still in use today mostly with the elderly. Please note, the questioner does not expect you to answer honestly. If you really are hungry and state so, expect your Chinese counterpart to insist on taking you somewhere to eat something. Instead, it is best to just say you have eaten, whether you have or have not:

1 – "Have you eaten until full?"

Q: 你吃饱了吗?

Nǐ chībǎo le ma?

(Have you eaten until you are full? [common expression to greet people])

A: 我吃饱了。谢谢，你呢?

Wǒ chībǎo le. Xièxie, nǐ ne?

(I have eaten until I am full. Thank you, and you?)

2 – A polite expression: "How embarrassing!" = bù hǎoyìsi

When someone is doing something polite for you or as a favor it is common to say "how embarrassing" or "I am embarrassed." This is a way for you to state your humility as the recipient of the favor or action. This is used very commonly. For example, you are in a store and you drop something on the ground. The person you are with quickly bends down to get it for you. While he or she is doing that you can say "bù hǎoyìsi," or "how embarrassing." You have shown the person you did not expect him or her to help you and you appreciate it:

3 – A common expression: "My stomach is hungry."

"È" means "hungry" in Chinese, but it is common to say instead of "I am hungry (Wǒ è le)," to say one's stomach is hungry:

肚子 + 饿 + 了

dùzi + è + le

(stomach + hungry + le [grammatical function to be explained later])

Example:

我肚子饿了。

Wǒ dùzi è le.

(I am hungry.)

Questioning State of Being

你怎么样?

Nǐ zěnmeyàng?

(How are you doing?)

你怎么了?

Nǐ zěnme le?

(Are you alright?)

你觉得怎么样?

Nǐ juéde zěnmeyàng?

(How are you feeling?)

Or simply use the pattern you already used to ask if someone feeling a certain way:

你adj.不adj.? / 你adj.吗?

Nǐ adj. bù adj.? / Nǐ adj. ma?

Example:

你累不累? / 你累吗?

Nǐ lèi bú lèi? / Nǐ lèi ma?

(Are you tired?)

Chit-Chat Café
– The place you come to practice speaking

Module 8.2 - (8-4)

Use the below picture prompts to ask and answer questions regarding the people in the pictures. When you see the word "**YOU?**", the question should be asked about you. You may use any of the state of being questioning you have learned. Try to use a different one each time.

Example:

1. Q: Nǐmen zěnmeyàng?

    A: Wǒmen hěn lèi.

1. **YOU?**
2.
3.
4.
5. **YOU?**
6.
7.
8.
9. **YOU?**
10.
11.
12.
13.
14.
15.
16.
17.
18.
19. **YOU?**
20.

8

155

Word Workshop
– *The place you come to learn new words and phrases*

(Go to 🔘 <u>8-5</u> to hear:)

Expressing Desires
Here is a common word to express a desire:

想
xiǎng
(to think, to want)

Examples:

想做	想看	想吃	想去
xiǎng zuò	xiǎng kàn	xiǎng chī	xiǎng qù
(to want to do)	(to want to see)	(to want to eat)	(to want to go to)

Commands (Imperatives)
Stating a command in Chinese requires no change in verb form, as with all tenses (or lack there of!) You simply say the verb and object as in:

吃饭!
Chīfàn!
(Eat!)

说中文!
Shuō Zhōngwén!
(Speak Chinese!)

Suggesting
To suggest something in Chinese or to soften a command, add a "suggestion particle." This little guy, known as "ba," helps your command statement sound like a suggestion rather than an order. It is comparable in English to adding "if you'd like to" tagged on to a sentence, as in "Eat some more, if you'd like to":

吧
ba
(*"suggestion" particle*)

8

	吃吧	说吧
	chī ba	shuō ba
Literally =	(Eat!)	(Speak!)
Subtle meaning =	(Have some more to eat!)	(Go ahead and say it!)

As you can see, we need to use a few more words in English to capture the same meaning. "Ba" can also operate like "let's" in English:

Example: 我们一起去吃饭吧。

Wǒmen yìqǐ qù chīfàn ba.

(Let's go get something to eat.)

Useful Connectors

还是

你要吃中国饭还是美国饭？

háishi*   **Example:**   Nǐ yào chī Zhōngguófàn háishi Měiguófàn?

(or)   (Do you want to eat Chinese food or American food?)

* *"Háishi" is used for questions involving choice.*

或是

中国饭或是美国饭都很好。

huòshi*   **Example:**   Zhōngguófàn huòshi Měiguófàn dōu hěn hǎo.

(or)   (Chinese food or American food are both fine.)

* *"Huòshi" is used for narrative sentences.*

8

因为

我喜欢学中文，因为中文很有意思。

yīnwèi   **Example:**   Wǒ xǐhuan xué Zhōngwén, yīnwèi Zhōngwén
(because, since)   hěn yǒu yìsi.

(I like to study Chinese because Chinese is interesting.)

所以

我不会看中文，所以我不看中文书。

suǒyǐ   **Example:**   Wǒ bú huì kàn Zhōngwén, suǒyǐ wǒ bú kàn
(therefore)   Zhōngwén shū.

(I don't know how to read Chinese. Therefore I don't read Chinese books.)

Now here is a clause pattern using the above two connectors:

因为……所以……

yīnwèi......suǒyǐ......

([Since]...therefore...)

因为他是美国人，所以他会说英文。

Example: Yīnwèi tā shì Měiguórén, suǒyǐ tā huì shuō Yīngwén.

(He is American. Therefore he knows how to speak English.)

 Chit-Chat Café
– The place you come to practice speaking

Module 8.3 - (🔘 8-6) / English translation on **Page 164**
Picture this: "Yuhua" is with her boyfriend at home and wants to go out to dinner. However, her boyfriend, "Xiaolei," is tired and wants to stay home.

Yuhua:	Xiǎolěi, wǒ dùzi è le.	Yuhua:	小磊，我肚子饿了。
Xiaolei:	Ò.	Xiaolei:	哦。
Yuhua:	Nǐ zěnme le?	Yuhua:	你怎么了？
Xiaolei:	Wǒ jīntiān gōngzuò de* hěn wǎn suǒyǐ wǒ hěn lèi.	Xiaolei:	我今天工作得很晚所以我很累。
Yuhua:	Nǐ bù xiǎng qù chīfàn ma? Kěshì nǐ zǎoshang shuō wǒmen jīntiān wǎnshang gēn péngyou qù chīfàn.	Yuhua:	你不想去吃饭吗？可是你早上说我们今天晚上跟朋友去吃饭。
Xiaolei:	Shì. Kěshì xiànzài wǒ bù xiǎng qù. Wǒ xiǎng zài jiā kàn diànshì.	Xiaolei:	是。可是现在我不想去。我想在家看电视。
Yuhua:	Nà hěn wúliáo! Wǒ xiǎng qù wánr, xiǎng chīfàn kàn péngyou.	Yuhua:	那很无聊！我想去玩儿，想吃饭看朋友。

8

Xiaolei: Wǒmen míngtiān huòshi hòutiān qù ba.	Xiaolei: 我们明天或是后天去吧。
Yuhua: Yīnwèi míngtiān hòutiān wǒ gōngzuò hěn máng suǒyǐ wǒ xiǎng jīntiān qù.	Yuhua: 因为明天后天我工作很忙所以我想今天去。
Xiaolei: Kěshì zài jiā kàn diànshì hěn shūfu.	Xiaolei: 可是在家看电视很舒服。
Yuhua: Zài jiā kàn diànshì hěn wúliáo.	Yuhua: 在家看电视很无聊。
Xiaolei: Hǎo ba. Wǒ bù xiǎng ràng** nǐ bù gāoxìng. Wǒmen qù ba.	Xiaolei: 好吧。我不想让你不高兴。我们去吧。
Yuhua: Wā! Nǐ zhēn hǎo. Nǐ zhēn shì hǎo nánpéngyou. Xièxie.	Yuhua: 哇！你真好。你真是好男朋友。谢谢。
Xiaolei: Bú kèqi. Wǒmen chībǎo le yǐhòu nǐ xiǎng zuò shénme?	Xiaolei: 不客气。我们吃饱了以后你想做什么？
Yuhua: Wǒ hěn xiǎng qù kàn diànyǐng, kěshì nǐ hěn lèi, duì bú duì?	Yuhua: 我很想去看电影，可是你很累，对不对？
Xiaolei: Měiyǒu guānxi. Wǒ xiànzài bú lèi.	Xiaolei: 没有关系。我现在不累。

8

* "De (得)" indicates the manner in which the verb took place
** "Ràng (让)" = to make someone feel a certain way

Chit-Chat Practice 8.3

Answer the following questions about the above dialogue. You can find the correct answers in **Appendix IV**:

1. 玉华为什么想吃饭？
   ? Why
   Yùhuá wèishénme xiǎng chīfàn?

   (Yīnwéi tā dùzi è le.)

2. 玉华想做什么？
   Yùhuá xiǎng zuò shénme?

   Yùhuá yào chīfàn yè qù kàn diànyǐng.

3. 小磊为什么不想去吃饭？
   Xiǎolěi wèishénme bù xiǎng qù chīfàn?

   Xiǎolěi gōngzuo de hěn wǎn, tā hěn lèi.

4. 为什么小磊很累？
   Wèishénme Xiǎolěi hěn lèi?

   Tā gōngzuo de hěn wǎn.

5. 小磊想做什么？
   Xiǎolěi xiǎng zuò shénme?

   Xiǎolěi yào kàn diànshì.

6. 玉华觉得在家看电视怎么样？
   Yùhuá juéde zài jiā kàn diànshì zěnmeyàng?

   Tā juéde ~~xiǎng~~ kàn diànshì hěn wúliáo.

7. 为什么玉华不想明天或是后天去？
   Wèishénme Yùhuá bù xiǎng míngtiān huòshi hòutiān qù?

   Tā gōngzuò hěn ~~máng~~. Wǎn.

8. 小磊觉得什么很舒服?

Xiǎolěi juéde shénme hěn shūfu?

Xiǎo lěi ~~xiǎng~~ *jvéde* zài jiā kan diànshi. hěn shūfu.

9. 吃饭以后玉华想做什么?

Chīfàn yǐhòu Yùhuá xiǎng zuò shénme?

Tā yào∨ kàn diànyǐng.
      qu

Culture Corner
– The place you come to learn more than just language

Now that you have come this far with learning Mandarin you are likely to make Chinese friends and even get invited to someone's home for dinner. Cooking and entertaining guests in one's home is popular in Chinese culture and don't be surprised if you get invited by people you have just met. Before going, it is good to know certain cultural difference that will help you avoid social gaffes:

- **No shoes in the house –**
  Most (dare I say "all"?) Chinese people remove their shoes as soon as they enter their homes. Likewise the same is expected of the guest. It is also customary to put on flip-flops (拖鞋, tuōxié), which most homes have extras for the guests. These "tuōxié" are usually a kind of plastic flip-flop without the toe-divider, the kind you can slip on over your socks.

- **Arrive with a gift in hand –**
  Don't arrive empty handed. It is customary to bring something for your host. Here are some popular items to bring:
  - Fruit (oranges, pears, peaches, etc.)
  - Box of chocolates or other candies
  - Liquor or wine
  - Any special local product from where you are from

8

Do not bring anything that would be served that evening. It may be construed as saying you think your host is unable to provide the whole meal:

- NO food to be served with dinner, such as a side dish
- NO dessert of any kind to be consumed that night
- NO clocks* (on the unlikely chance you may do this) it is considered to
- wish death upon the person you give it to

The word for clock in Chinese sounds just like "the end."

Note: If you bring a present that is wrapped, do not expect your host to open it right there. Usually the gift receiver will open it after you have left.

Advice Alcove
– The place you come to learn how to learn

The Successful Language Learner

Learning languages is more comparable to learning to play a musical instrument than perhaps other academic pursuits. There is the knowledge of music theory, or the ability to read music, and then there is the ability to physically produce the music. Likewise, there can be the knowledge of how Mandarin works and then the actual ability to produce and understand the language. Like learning a musical instrument, you will not become a virtuoso overnight. You need to take lessons, study, and practice as much as you can. Think of an unscripted conversation with a native speaker as similar to an improvised musical jam session. To do that well you will need many hours of study and practice time behind you. So, who then successfully achieves this?

It is the disciplined and steady learner who keeps moving forward and does not stop. Like going to the gym several times a week to stay in shape. To learn a foreign language well, you must show up for class (or do lessons of some kind whether they are live or online); you must study and do your exercises; you must find opportunities to use the language; and, finally, you must continue to do the same thing to maintain that which you have gained. "Languages are a 'thankless mistress'" is something I have said before. Mandarin is not going to thank you for achieving an intermediate level, or any level, you need to stick around or she will simply disappear. To keep the skills you gain, just like physical exercise, you have to keep practicing to keep in shape.

Here is what I see as the phases to learning. At first the student is excited and ready to go, but then there are the later phases where discipline is required to really see your studies through to fluency:

The dating phase – You've just met Mandarin and she is wonderful and fascinating. You show up for all your dates, you think about her all the time, and you are always ready to curl up with a book about her and study. You are saying words you never thought you would and you are on the happy course to learning Mandarin.

The commitment phase – You've now spent quite a bit of time with Mandarin and she seems to be requiring more and more of your time in order to get somewhere. She now wants a commitment which means sometimes you can't go out partying with the boys or Sunday night you'll need to stay at home studying her to keep her happy.

The engagement phase – You've done all the hard work to develop a solid knowledge of Mandarin but in order to get to the next phase of true, intimate knowledge of the language, you'll need to make further commitment. This means truly welcoming her into your life. You're now living with Mandarin.

The marital phase – You now know Mandarin extremely well and have done all the hard work to keep her. Nothing can rock your knowledge, but you do need to maintain what you've got and keep it from slipping away. No need for daily dates of wining and dining, just weekly attention to make sure she remembers you (and you her).

8

English Translation

Module 8.3

Yuhua:	Xiaolei, I am hungry.
Xiaolei:	Oh.
Yuhua:	Are you alright?
Xiaolei:	Today I worked late so I am very tired.
Yuhua:	You don't want to go out to eat? But this morning you said that tonight we would go out to eat with friends.
Xiaolei:	Right, but now I don't want to go. I want to watch TV at home.
Yuhua:	That's boring! I want to go out and eat, and see friends.
Xiaolei:	Let's go tomorrow or the day after tomorrow.
Yuhua:	Tomorrow and the day after tomorrow my work is going to be very busy, so I would like to go today.
Xiaolei:	But, watching TV at home would be so cozy.
Yuhua:	Watching TV at home is boring.
Xiaolei:	All right. I don't want to make you unhappy. Let's go.
Yuhua:	Wow! You are so great. You really are a good boyfriend. Thanks!
Xiaolei:	You're welcome. After we eat what would you like to do?
Yuhua:	I'd really like to go to the movies. But you are too tired right?
Xiaolei:	That's OK. I'm not tired now.

8

Pronunciation Plaza
– The place you come to practice sounds and tones

(Go to 9-1 to hear:)

Chinese Tongue Twisters

Here are a couple more popular Chinese tongue twisters to help you practice pronunciation and tones:

Māma qí mǎ, mǎ màn, māma mà mǎ.	妈妈骑马， 马慢，妈妈骂马。

Translation:

Mother is riding the horse.
The horse is going slow, so mother scolds the horse.

Niūniu hōng niú, niú nìng, Niūniu níng niú.	妞妞轰牛， 牛拧，妞妞拧牛。

Translation:

Niuniu (kid's name) is driving the ox.
The ox is too stubborn to move, so Niuniu pinches him.

Sound Differentiation

We have now covered all the sounds in Mandarin found on your *pinyin* chart (full chart can be found at the beginning of this book). The remaining lessons will focus on reviewing the more challenging points of Mandarin pronunciation and practicing tone combinations.

"j-" vs. " zh-"

The initials "j-" and "zh-" are pronounced similarly: both like the "j" sound in "jam." The "zh-" initial also has an added retroflex sound; this means the tongue curls slightly when saying it. The other difference you should be aware of is how each initial affects the pronunciation of two final sounds: the "-i" and the "-u." Here are the rules:

* *"J-" followed by an "-i" has a long "ee" sound; "j-" followed by an "-u" has an umlauted "u" sound.*
* *"Zh-" followed by an "-i" has a retroflex short "uh" or "er" sound; "zh-" followed by an "-u" has a long "oo" sound.*

Use the above rules to note the pronunciation differences for the final "-i" and final "-u":

ji	vs.	zhi

ju*	vs.	zhu

> * **Reminder:** *The "u" is not written like so "ü," because the umlauted sound is assumed when a "j-" initial is followed by an "-u."*

Combination practice with both initials and final "-i":

zhī jì	jízhì	zhìjǐ	zhìjí	jīzhǐ
(during)	(pinnacle)	(best friend)	(extremely)	(foundation)

jīzhì	zhìjī	zhíjí	jízhǐ
(witty)	(pheasant)	(job rank)	(maxima and minima)

Combination practice with both initials and final "-u":

zhùjū	zhūjù	jūzhù	jùzhù
(to reside)	(plant spacing)	(to reside)	(monumental literary work)

Combination practice with both initials and both finals:

jíjū	jíjù	jùjí	jūjì
(community living)	(rapid)	(to gather)	(scruple)

zhīzhū	jǔzhǐ	jùzhǐ	zhīzhù
(spider)	(manner)	(polyester)	(pillar)

zhùzhǐ	zhǔjī
(address)	(machine core)

9

Tone combinations

3rd tone + 1st tone

hǎochī	bǐnggān	zuǒbiān	jiǎndān	shǒujī
(delicious)	(cookie)	(left side)	(simple)	(cellphone)

3rd tone + 2nd tone

kělián	Měiguó	nǔrén	yǐqián	xuěqiú
(pitiful)	(U.S.A.)	(woman)	(before)	(snowball)

Reminder: When you have two third tones in a row, the first one automatically changes to a second tone. So, in this next set, although you see two third tones written, you should pronounce the first one as a second tone.

3rd tone + 3rd tone

nǐ hǎo	ǒu'ěr	yǒngyuǎn	shuǐguǒ	dǔchǎng
(hello)	(rarely)	(forever)	(fruit)	(casino)

3rd tone + 4th tone

kě'ài	bǐsài	gǎnmào	kěshì	měilì
(cute)	(competition)	(a cold)	(but)	(beautiful)

3rd tone + neutral tone

jiějie	wǎnshang	yǐzi	zǎoshang	zhǔzi
(older sister)	(evening)	(chair)	(morning)	(master)

Sound Differentiation Exercise

Listen to the following **two**-character combinations in 🔊 9-2 and write the correct *pinyin* spelling and tones combinations below. See **Appendix IV** for correct answers:

1. _____ 2. _____ 3. _____ 4. _____

5. _____ 6. _____ 7. _____ 8. _____

9. _____ 10. _____ 11. _____ 12. _____

13. _____ 14. _____ 15. _____ 16. _____

17. _____ 18. _____ 19. _____ 20. _____

9

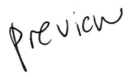 *preview*

preview

Word Workshop
– The place you come to learn new words and phrases

(Go to 🔊 9-3 to hear:)

Words describing daily activities

起床
qǐchuáng *bed*
(to get up, to get out of bed)

洗澡
xǐzǎo
wash phone/bath
(to bathe [shower or bath])

吃早饭
chī zǎofàn
(to eat breakfast)

坐公共汽车 *steam car*
zuò gōnggòng qìchē
(to ride the bus) *public*

坐火车
zuò huǒchē
(to ride the train)

开车
kāichē
(to drive a car)

去工作
qù gōngzuò
(to go to work)

上班
shàngbān
(to be at work, to be working)

electronic / *speaky*

打电话(给)
dǎ diànhuà (gěi)
(to make a telephone call [to])

play beat up

上网 *net*
shàngwǎng
(to go on the Internet)

休息
xiūxi
(to rest, to take a break)

打电脑
dǎ diànnǎo
(to work on the computer)
play a video game

开会
open kāihuì
(to have a meeting)

下班
xiàbān
(to get off work)

回家
huíjiā
(to go home)

睡觉
shuìjiào
(to go to bed, to sleep)

168

xǐng lái – to be awake

Chit-Chat Café
– The place you come to practice speaking

Module 9.1 - (9-4)

Using the following series of pictures discuss what this person does each day and at what time.

Example: 1. Tā zǎoshang qī diǎn qǐchuáng.

1.

2.

3.

4.

5.

6.

7.

8.

9.

10.

11.

12.

9

13.

14.

15.

Check your answers in **Appendix IV**.

Word Workshop
– The place you come to learn new words and phrases

(Go to 🔘 9-5 to hear:)

When

You have learned how to ask "when (**shénme shíhou**)," but have not learned how to say "when" in an indicative sentence, as in "When I eat, I also drink tea." Here is how to express that in Chinese:

的时候

de shíhou
(when [for indicative sentences])

Subject + Verb + **de shíhou**

Examples:

1. 我吃饭的时候也喝茶。
   Wǒ chīfàn de shíhou yě hē chá.
   (When I eat, I also drink tea.)

2. 我开车的时候不打电话。
   Wǒ kāichē de shíhou bù dǎ diànhuà.
   (When I drive, I do not make telephone calls.)

You translate the rest into English:

3. 我看朋友的时候很高兴。

    Wǒ kàn péngyou de shíhou hěn gāoxìng.

    When I see my friends, I am very happy.

4. 我吃晚饭的时候不看电视。

    Wǒ chī wǎnfàn de shíhou bú kàn diànshì.

    When I eat dinner, I don't watch TV.

Check your answers in **Appendix IV**.

Then

You already learned how to use "jiù" and "cái" to express "then." You can also use this word. Think of it more as an "and then" meaning:

然后

ránhòu

([and] then, after)

Example: 我早上八点吃早饭，然后去上班。

Wǒ zǎoshang bā diǎn chī zǎofàn, ránhòu qù shàngbān.

(At 8 a.m. I eat breakfast, and then I go to work.)

Words of frequency & habit

9

never	occasionally	sometimes	usually	often	always
从不	偶尔	有时候	平常	常常	总是
cóng bù	ǒu'ěr	yǒushíhou	píngcháng	chángcháng	zǒngshì

Words of frequency go precisely where any time word is placed. As a reminder here is the order:

Subject + Time + Place + Event

Example: 我平常在家吃晚饭。

Wǒ píngcháng zài jiā chī wǎnfàn.

(I usually eat dinner at home.)

Additionally, you may place the time word before the subject like so (with one exception noted below):

Time + Subject + Place + Event

Example: 平常我在家吃晚饭。

Píngcháng wǒ zài jiā chī wǎnfàn.

(Usually, I eat dinner at home.)

Note: Cóng bù (never) must come after the subject; it cannot come before.

Chit-Chat Café
– The place you come to practice speaking

Module 9.2 - (Go to 🔘 9-6)

Read the following sentences then rewrite the sentence replacing the time word with a frequency word. In other words, if the sentence says it is something the person does "every day (time word)" rewrite the sentence replacing that with "always (frequency word)." Note, there may be more than one correct answer:

Example:

她每天吃早饭然后去工作。

Time word: Tā měitiān chī zǎofàn ránhòu qù gōngzuò.

Frequency word: Tā zǒngshì chī zǎofàn ránhòu qù gōngzuò.

1. 每星期天他去看他的妈妈。

Time word: Měi Xīngqītiān tā qù kàn tā de māma.

Frequency word: *Chǎng chǎng ta tā qù kàn tā de māma.*

2.　　　　　每八年我回中国去看老朋友。

Time word:　　　Měi bā nián wǒ huí Zhōngguó qù kàn lǎo péngyou.

Frequency word:　_Ǒu'ěr wǒ huí Zhōngguó qù kàn lǎo péngyou._

3.　　　　　他每个月一次跟朋友去喝酒。

Time word:　　　Tā měi ge yuè yí cì* gēn péngyou qù hē jiǔ.

Frequency word:　_Chángcháng yí cì gēn péngyou qù hē_

* yí cì = one time　　_Ǒu'ěr_　　　　　　　　　(?) _jiǔ._

4.　　　　　他九十八岁，没有电脑所以他不会上网。

Time word:　　　Tā jiǔshíbā suì, méiyǒu diànnǎo suǒyǐ tā bú huì
　　　　　　　　shàngwǎng.

Frequency word:　_Tā méiyǒu diànnǎo, cóng bù shàngwǎng_

5.　　　　　她坐公共汽车去工作，可是星期五她开车去。

Time word:　　　Tā zuò gōnggòng qìchē qù gōngzuò, kěshì Xīngqīwǔ
　　　　　　　　tā kāichē qù.

Frequency word:　_Tā píngcháng zuò gōnggòng qìchē, kěshì yǒushí
　　　　　　　　tā kāichē qù._

6.　　　　　她每天下班以后去看她的男朋友。

Time word:　　　Tā měi tiān xiàbān yǐhòu qù kàn tā de nánpéngyou.

Frequency word:　_Zǒngshì xiàbān yǐhòu tā kàn nánpéngyou_

9

7.　　　　　他七点起床，可是不工作的时候他九点才起床。

Time word:　　　Tā qī diǎn qǐchuáng, kěshì bù gōngzuò de shíhou
　　　　　　　　tā jiǔ diǎn cái qǐchuáng.

Frequency word:　_Tā píngcháng zǎo qǐchuáng, kěshì yǒushíhou
　　　　　　　　tā cái qǐchuáng._

Check your answers in **Appendix IV**.

Chit-Chat Café
– The place you come to practice speaking

Module 9.3 - (💿 9-7) / English translation on **Page 186**
Let's read below and listen to your audio about what "Xiao Gao" does every day:

我每天早上七点起床。起床以后我洗澡，然后在家吃早饭。八点的时候我坐公共汽车去工作。我平常坐公共汽车，可是有时侯我开车去上班。开车比坐公共汽车舒服。我上班的时候常常打电话、打电脑还有上网。偶尔我去开会。每天中午休息一个小时。休息的时候我一边吃午饭一边看书或是打电话给朋友。虽然我喜欢我的工作，可是我也很喜欢休息。我的工作总是很忙，可是从不无聊。我平常五点半下班，然后回家。偶尔下班以后我跟朋友去吃饭或是看电影。平常晚上十一点的时候，我看一点儿电视就去睡觉。

Wǒ měitiān zǎoshang qī diǎn qǐchuáng. Qǐchuáng yǐhòu wǒ xǐzǎo, ránhòu zài jiā chī zǎofàn. Bā diǎn de shíhou wǒ zuò gōnggòng qìchē qù gōngzuò. Wǒ píngcháng zuò gōnggòng qìchē, kěshì yǒushíhou wǒ kāichē qù shàngbān. Kāichē bǐ zuò gōnggòng qìchē shūfu. Wǒ shàngbān de shíhou chángcháng dǎ diànhuà, dǎ diànnǎo hái yǒu shàngwǎng. Ǒu'ěr wǒ qù kāihuì. Měitiān zhōngwǔ xiūxi yí ge xiǎoshi. Xiūxi de shíhou wǒ yìbiān chī wǔfàn yìbiān kàn shū huòshi dǎ diànhuà gěi péngyou. Suīrán wǒ xǐhuan wǒ de gōngzuò, kěshì wǒ yě hěn xǐhuan xiūxi. Wǒ de gōngzuò zǒngshì hěn máng, kěshì cóng bù wúliáo. Wǒ píngcháng wǔ diǎn bàn xiàbān, ránhòu huíjiā. Ǒu'ěr xiàbān yǐhòu wǒ gēn péngyou qù chīfàn huòshi kàn diànyǐng. Píngcháng wǎnshang shíyī diǎn de shíhou, wǒ kàn yìdiǎnr diànshì jiù qù shuìjiào.

Grammar Grove
– The place you come to learn about structure

Expressing the past

The monologue you just read regarding what someone does every day could also have been written regarding something he or she did in the past or in the future. That is one of the great things about Chinese: all tenses are the same. Just add a time word, when needed, to let your listener know for sure that something already happened or will happen. There is also another way to grammatically express that something happened in the past or will happen in the future. Let's start with the past. We mentioned a word known as "le" in the previous lesson and noted that we would explain that later. Well, we did not lie. Let's start with an overview of "le":

An Introduction to "le (了)"

"Le" is grammatically referred to as a "dynamic particle," "modal particle" or "aspect particle," terms that ultimately may not aide in your understanding of its use. It is one of the most confusing grammatical points to explain. However, taken one piece at a time, it is highly digestible. First, here is the big picture regarding "le":

"Le" can be used to show an action has occurred, is beginning to occur, will occur in the future; it can be used to express the imperative and even the superlative.

Reading that you may now feel awash in the breadth of "le" and sense yourself falling into the grammatical abyss. Have no fear! You will piece "le" many uses together, taking it one facet at a time. The good news is when you encounter "le" in a sentence it will not obstruct your understanding, should you know all the other words. You may miss some subtlety, but not the whole meaning of the sentence since "le" is a particle that affects the tone or tense of a sentence but does not mean anything in and of it self.

Now, let's start with just one facet of "le" — how it is used to express the past.

"Le" to indicate the past

"Le" can be used to indicate an action was completed, or to emphasize that something took place in the past. Please take note; however, it is not necessary to indicate the past, as would be the case in English. The Chinese language typically employs time words, such as "today" or "last week," to indicate when an action took place. That said, here is how "le" can indicate the completion of an action.

"Le" is used after the verb to indicate that it happened in the past:

我吃了晚饭。

Wǒ chīle wǎnfàn.

(I ate dinner.)

他去年学了中文。

Tā qùnián xuéle Zhōngwén.

(Last year he studied Chinese.)

她去了北京。

Tā qùle Běijīng.

(She went to Beijing.)

昨天晚上他看了电视。

Zuótiān wǎnshang tā kànle diànshì.

(Last night he watched TV.)

For the activity verbs with a combination of two or more morphemes, "le" comes right after the verb and before the noun portion of the morpheme combination. Here are some examples with activity words you have already learned and new ones from this lesson:

吃饭	吃了饭
chīfàn	chīle fàn
(to eat)	(ate)
上课	上了课
shàngkè	shàngle kè
(to attend class)	(attended class)
下班	下了班
xiàbān	xiàle bān
(to get off work)	(got off work)
洗澡	洗了澡
xǐzǎo	xǐle zǎo
(to bathe [shower])	(to have bathed [showered])

9

做饭
zuòfàn
(to cook)

做了饭
zuòle fàn
(to have cooked)

睡觉 *(sleep) verb*
shuìjiào
(to sleep)

睡了觉 *(sleep/nap) noun*
shuìle jiào
(to have slept)

打电话
dǎ diànhuà
(to make a phone call)

打了电话
dǎle diànhuà
(to have made a phone call)

The Past in the Negative

To say something did not or has not happened, you can use the words "méiyǒu" (or literally "not have") plus your verb. Here is how that works:

Subject + méiyǒu + Verb

我昨天没有工作。

Wǒ zuótiān méiyǒu gōngzuò.

(I did not work yesterday.)

去年他没有去中国。

Qùnián tā méiyǒu qù Zhōngguó.

(Last year he did not go to China.)

今天我没有吃早饭。

Jīntiān wǒ méiyǒu chī zǎofàn.

(Today I did not eat breakfast.)

Expressing the future

Now that you have learned how to use "le" to indicate an action has happened, here are a couple of words you can use to indicate that something will happen in the future:

9

"Huì (会)" means "to know," as you learned in a previous lesson, but it also can mean "will." Here are some examples of how to use "huì" to express the future tense:

你明天会做什么？

Nǐ míngtiān huì zuò shénme?

(What are you going to do tomorrow?)

他明年会去中国。

Tā míngnián huì qù Zhōngguó.

(Next year he is going to go to China.)

她下个星期不会去上班。

Tā xià ge xīngqī bú huì qù shàngbān.

(Next week she is not going to go to work.)

"Huì" is not the only word in Chinese used to express the future. You have learned that "yào (要)" means "to want," but it can also mean "going to (happen)." Here is how it is used: If you want to make it clear you mean "want to" and not "going to" you should use the other word you learned to mean "to want (xiǎng 想)."

你今天晚上要做什么？

Nǐ jīntiān wǎnshang yào zuò shénme?

(What are you going to do tonight?)

今天晚上我们不要上班。

Jīntiān wǎnshang wǒmen bú yào shàngbān.

(Tonight we are not going to work.)

我的妈妈明天要打电话给我。

Wǒ de māma míngtiān yào dǎ diànhuà gěi wǒ.

(Tomorrow my mother is going to give me a call.)

More time words

时间	有时间	没(有)时间
shíjiān	yǒu shíjiān	méi(yǒu) shíjiān
(time)	(to have time)	(to not have time)

Example:

你今天晚上有没有时间跟我去看电影？

Nǐ jīntiān wǎnshang yǒu méiyǒu shíjiān gēn wǒ qù kàn diànyǐng?

(Tonight do you have time to go to the movies with me?)

对不起，我没时间。我要工作。

Duìbuqǐ, wǒ méi shíjiān. Wǒ yào gōngzuò.

(Sorry, I don't have the time. I am going to work.)

You may recognize the following root morphemes below from the words "zǎoshang (morning)" and "wǎnshang (evening)":

早	很早	不早	早一点儿
zǎo	hěn zǎo	bù zǎo	zǎo yìdiǎnr
(early)	(very early)	(not early)	(earlier)

晚	很晚	不晚	晚一点儿
wǎn	hěn wǎn	bù wǎn	wǎn yìdiǎnr
(late)	(very late)	(not late)	(later)

 Chit-Chat Café
– The place you come to practice speaking

Module 9.4 - (9-8) / English translation on **Page 186**

You heard "Xiao Gao" in the Module 9.3 discuss what he does every day. Now let's look at what he did yesterday and what he will do tomorrow as a way to compare expressing the past and future in Chinese. Notice sometimes he emphasizes the past or future using the grammatical functions we just studied above while other times he does not:

9

Past - Yesterday

昨天早上我八点半才起床。因为晚起床所以没有时间吃早饭。我平常坐公共汽车去工作，可是因为很晚所以我开车去。上班的时候我打了电脑，上了网还有开了会。没有时间休息。我很累了！八点才下班，然后回家。在家我吃了晚饭就睡觉了。

just
jiù - already

Zuótiān zǎoshang wǒ bā diǎn bàn cái qǐchuáng. Yīnwèi wǎn qǐchuáng suǒyǐ méiyǒu shíjiān chī zǎofàn. Wǒ píngcháng zuò gōnggòng qìchē qù gōngzuò, kěshì yīnwèi hěn wǎn suǒyǐ wǒ kāichē qù. Shàngbān de shíhou wǒ ~~dàle~~ *yòng??* diànnǎo, shàngle wǎng hái ~~yòu~~ kāile huì. Méiyǒu shíjiān xiūxi. Wǒ hěn lèi le! Bā diǎn cái xiàbān, ránhòu huíjiā. Zài jiā wǒ chīle wǎnfàn jiù shuìjiào le.

Future - Tomorrow

明天是星期六。我很高兴，因为星期六我不工作。我明天会晚一点儿起床，然后我会跟三个好朋友去吃午饭。我很喜欢我不工作的时间。不工作的时候我常常跟朋友去玩儿。明天下午我也要跟我女朋友去看电影。晚上我会在家一边休息一边看书。

Míngtiān shì Xīngqīliù. Wǒ hěn gāoxìng, yīnwèi Xīngqīliù wǒ bù gōngzuò. Wǒ míngtiān huì wǎn yìdiǎnr qǐchuáng, ránhòu wǒ huì gēn sān ge hǎo péngyou qù chī wǔfàn. Wǒ hěn xǐhuan wǒ bù gōngzuò de shíjiān. Bù gōngzuò de shíhou wǒ chángcháng gēn péngyou qù wánr. Míngtiān xiàwǔ wǒ yě yào gēn wǒ nǚpéngyou qù kàn diànyǐng. Wǎnshang wǒ huì zài jiā yìbiān xiūxi yìbiān kàn shū.

9 About your own life

Now talk about your own life in Chinese. First about what you do every day, then about yesterday and finally what you will do tomorrow. Use the prompts in English to write a full sentence in Chinese:

Every day - *remember to use words of frequency to discuss your daily routine*

Time you get up -
Wǒ měitiān qī diǎn bàn qǐcháng.

Shower? -

Breakfast? -

_____

Getting to work -

_____

What you do at work -

_____

Lunch? -

_____

Time get off work -

_____

Getting home -

_____

What you do at home -

_____

What time you go to bed -

_____

Yesterday - *remember to use "le" to emphasize the past*

Time you got up -

_____

Ate breakfast -

_____

Went to work -

_____

9

Took a break -

_____

What you did at work -

_____

What time you got off from work -

_____

What you did at home -

_____

Tomorrow - *Remember to use "huì" or "yào" to emphasize it is something to happen in the future*

Time you will get up -

_____

Will you take a shower? -

_____

Eat breakfast? -

_____

Go to work? -

_____

What you will do at work -

_____

Lunch? -

_____

Time you will get off work -

_____

What you will do after work -

_____

9

Time you plan to go to bed -

Culture Corner
– The place you come to learn more than just language

Beyond Words: Hand Gestures in Chinese Culture

Just as in the west we have certain hand gestures to indicate meaning, from anything as innocuous as "come here" to the vulgar, so do they too in China. Here is something prevalent that mystified me at first: Often when talking about numbers, Chinese people will also make a hand gesture. My own theory on this one is that with the many dialects in China, people would gather in markets and need to communicate about how much things cost or to haggle. The hand gestures make it clear, no matter what dialect you speak.

Mainland Chinese hand signals:

I recommend always using the "four" and "ten" signs when discussing those numbers. Some people (particularly in the south) do not say the retroflex "sh" sound so "shí diǎn (10 o'clock)" can sound much like "sì diǎn (4 o'clock)." I have found Chinese people favor using those signs as well to be clear.

Note: There are slightly different hand signals for numbers in Taiwan and Hong Kong.

Taiwan hand signals:

Hong Kong hand signals:

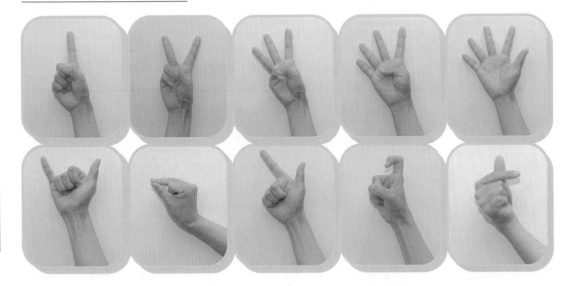

9

Advice Alcove
– The place you come to learn how to learn

自言自语
zì yán zì yǔ
"To talk to one's self"

Now that you have come this far learning Chinese structure, you should be prepared to interact in Chinese in authentic situations while meeting new acquaintances. Still at the beginner phases you may get stuck at a certain point in the conversation because the native speaker used an unfamiliar word or structure. There is one thing; however, you can be prepared for and that is what comes out of your mouth. Your most discussed topic will actually be yourself, as you explain each time who you are, where you are from, what you do and why you are learning Chinese, among other topics. To keep your conversation flowing you should practice, even rehearse as if you were an improvisational actor, for various situations in Mandarin and how you will handle them.

Talk to yourself! Imagine situations and speak out loud both parts. Ask yourself "Where are you from?"; "Why are you learning Chinese?"; "Where do you study?", etc. In my own language studies I have found this exercise invaluable. For example, before going to spend two weeks in Paris, I imagined and practiced out loud by myself all the situations I would imagine myself in, from taking a cab to ordering in a café. Likewise, you should do the same. Look up words relevant to your own life that you know will come up in conversation. Ask your teacher or a native speaker about words or structures you are unsure of. The goal is to keep the conversational flow going so your counterpart doesn't decide it's better to just speak English with you. It is the one part of authentic interaction you have control over. To that end, be well prepared for the following:

- Know how to say the country and state (or region) you are from in Chinese
- Know how to say your field of work and your specific job title
- If you work for a famous company learn the Chinese word(s) for it
- Have a quick answer to the "Why are you learning Chinese?" (I always say because I find it interesting: "Yīnwèi Zhōngwén hěn yǒu yìsi")
- Be prepared to say how long you have been learning Mandarin, where you have been learning (FYI: self-study = zìxué) and what you have found difficult
- Be prepared to discuss your spouse and children, if any, also his / her work

- Be ready to answer when asked if you would like to go to China, or if you have been, in particular where you have been or would like to go
- Be ready for any timely topics and names, such as how to say "Obama" in Chinese (Àobāmǎ)

Lastly, predict what words might come up relevant to you. For example, if you are an artist, people may ask about materials you work with; if you are student, people may want to know the specifics of what you are studying.

English Translation

Module 9.3

Every morning I get up at 7 o'clock. After I get up, I take a shower; then, I eat breakfast at home. When it's 8 o'clock, I ride the bus to go to work. I usually take the bus, but sometimes I drive to work. Driving is more comfortable than riding the bus. At work I often make phone calls, work on the computer and go online. Occasionally I go to meetings. Every day at noontime I take a break for one hour. While I am taking a break, I eat lunch and read, or I call my friends on the phone. Although I like my work, I also like my break time. My work is always very busy, but I am never bored. Usually, at 5:30 I get off work, then I go home. Occasionally, after getting off from work, I go out to eat or go to the movies with friends. Usually, when it is 11 o'clock, I watch some TV and then go to bed.

Module 9.4

Past - Yesterday

Yesterday morning I didn't get up until 8:30. Because I got up late, I didn't have time to eat breakfast. I usually ride the bus to go to work, but because I was very late, I drove (instead). While at work, I worked on the computer, went on the Internet and had a meeting. I didn't have time for a break. I was very tired! I didn't get off work until 8 o'clock, and then I went home. At home I ate dinner and then went to bed.

Future - Tomorrow

Tomorrow is Saturday. I am happy, because I won't be working. I will sleep in a bit later, then I will go out to eat with three good friends of mine. I really like not working. When I don't work I often go out with friends. Tomorrow afternoon I will also go to the movies with my girlfriend. At night I will rest and read a book at home.

 Pronunciation Plaza
— The place you come to practice sounds and tones

(Go to 10-1 to hear:)

Chinese Tongue Twister

Here is another well-known Mandarin tongue twister to help you practice pronunciation and tones:

Chī pútao bù tǔ pútaopí, bù chī pútao dào tǔ pútaopí.	吃葡萄不吐葡萄皮， 不吃葡萄倒吐葡萄皮。

Translation:
When eating grapes do not spit out the skins.
When not eating grapes, you may then spit out the skins.

Sound Differentiation

"q-" vs. "ch-"

The initials "q-" and "ch-" are pronounced similarly: both like the "ch" sound in "cherry." The "ch-" initial also has an added retroflex sound; this means the tongue curls slightly when saying it. The other difference you should be aware of is how each initial affects the pronunciation of two final sounds: the "-i" and the "-u." Here are the rules:

* "Q-" followed by "-i" has a long "ee" sound; "q-" followed by an "-u" has an umlauted u sound.
* "Ch-" followed by an "-i" has a retroflex short "uh" or "er" sound; "ch-" followed by an "-u" has a long "oo" sound.

Using the above rules to note the pronunciation differences for the final "-i" and the final "-u":

qi   vs.   chi

qu   vs.   chu

187

Combination practice with initials "q-" and "ch-" with both finals, "-i" and "-u":

qī chǐ   qǐchǐ   chūqù   qùchú   qǔchū
(7 feet long)   (start to talk)   (to exit)   (to eliminate)   (to take out something)

qùchù   qíqū   qǔqī   qǐchū
(destination)   (rugged [road])   (to take a wife)   (originally)

chūqì   qǔchǐ   qíchǔ   chūqī
(let of steam)   (tooth decay)   (miserable)   (initial stage)

Challenging Sounds

Focus on longer finals (4 letter finals): -iang, -iong, -uang

In this section we will practice the four-letter finals in *pinyin*. These can be challenging in that you need to say two vowels sounds and two ending consonant sounds. Let's look first at the two vowels sounds that will need to be pronounced:

"-ia" = should sound like "yee" + "ah"

"-io" = should sound like "yee" + "oh"

"-ua" = should sound like "woo" + "ah"

Then you will need to complete the word with the combined consonant sound of "ng," which sounds just like the English "ng" you would find in "strong" or "long." Let's look at all the morphemes that contain 4 letter finals:

niáng   liáng   jiǎng   qiáng   xiǎng
(mother)   (cool)   (award)   (strong)   (to think)

jiǒng   qióng   xióng
(embarrassed) (poor)   (bear)

zhuàng   chuāng   shuāng   guāng   kuáng   huáng
(strong)   (window)   (pair)   (light)   (crazy)   (yellow)

Combination Practice:

liángxiǎng   jiǎngzhuàng   qiángzhuàng   qiángxiàng
(army provisions)   (award)   (strong)   (strong point)

liǎng shuāng   jiǒngzhuàng   zhuàngkuàng   xióngzhuàng
(two pairs)   (embarrassing state)   (condition)   (majestic)

10

shuānghuáng	xiǎngxiàng	xiàngkuàng	liàngguāng
(theatrical duet)	(to imagine)	(picture frame)	(bright light)

Tone combinations

4th tone + 1st tone

bàituō	xiàtiān	miànbāo	rènzhēn	bàngōng
(please)	(summer)	(bread)	(diligent)	(to work)

4th tone + 2nd tone

bìngrén	diànchí	zhèngcháng	biànchéng	zìrán
(a patient)	(battery)	(normal)	(to become)	(natural)

4th tone + 3rd tone

dàolǐ	xiàyǔ	diànyǐng	guòmǐn	xiàwǔ
(reason)	(to rain)	(movie)	(allergies)	(afternoon)

4th tone + 4th tone

kuàilè	yùndòng	hòumiàn	shìjiè	fàndiàn
(happy)	(exercise)	(beind)	(the world)	(hotel)

4th tone + neutral tone

gùshi	bàba	guòqu	zuòxia	chùsheng
(story)	(father)	(past)	(to sit)	(domestic animals)

Sound Differentiation Exercise

Listen to the following **two**-character combinations in 🔘 10-2 and write the correct
pinyin spelling and tones combinations below. See **Appendix IV** for correct
answers:

1. _____ 2. _____ 3. _____ 4. _____

5. _____ 6. _____ 7. _____ 8. _____

9. _____ 10. _____ 11. _____ 12. _____

13. _____ 14. _____ 15. _____ 16. _____

17. _____ 18. _____ 19. _____ 20. _____

10

Word Workshop
— The place you come to learn new words and phrases

(Go to 🔘 10-3 to hear:)

Useful expressions & words

都
dōu
(all, entirely)

都喜欢
dōu xǐhuan
(like them all)

都没有问题
dōu méiyǒu wèntí
(no problem at all)

可以
kěyǐ
(able to, that's OK)

都可以
dōu kěyǐ
(anything is fine, either one is fine)
(LIT: all, able)

无所谓
wúsuǒwèi
(it doesn't matter (to me), I don't care)

随便
suíbiàn
(it's up to you) / whatever
(LIT: follow, convenience)

宁可
nìngkě
(would rather) this over that, but very extreme

yě bu (would rather die)

那么
nàme
(in that case, then)

走吧
zǒu ba
(let's go)

我们走吧
wǒmen zǒu ba
(let's go)

请坐
qǐng zuò
(please have a seat)

请来
qǐng lái
(please come, please bring...)

不用
búyòng
(that's not necessary, there is no need)

不用客气
búyòng kèqi
(no need to be so polite [said to make the person feel at ease, that the person can relax])

Reminder of expressions learned in earlier lessons:

请问
qǐngwèn
(excuse me, may I ask)

没有关系
méiyǒu guānxi
(that's OK, it doesn't matter)

 *Chit-Chat Café*
— *The place you come to practice speaking*

Module 10.1

Use the following situations written in English to respond correctly with a Chinese expressions taught above:

Example:

You are about to leave for the movies; you turn to your friend and say:

Zǒu ba!

10

1. You don't care which TV show you watch, so when your friend asks you what you would like to watch you say:

   Dōu kěyǐ, wúsuǒwèi, suíbiàn

2. A guest has just arrived in your home. You invite her to take a seat and say:

   Qǐng zuò.

3. A friend asks if you would like to have chicken or beef for dinner at her home. Either is all right with you so you say:

   dōu

   Wúsuǒwèi, jīròu huoshi niúròu kěyǐ.

4. You need to ask a stranger something. The first thing that should come out of your mouth is:

   Qǐngwèn ...

5. Your friend wants to know if you prefer eating at home or going out. You want to leave it up to her to decide. You say:

   Dōu kěyǐ, suíbiàn.

6. Your friend asks you which of two shirts you like. You like them both and say:

   Dōu xǐhuan.

7. Someone is being very polite to you and thanking you profusely; you want him or her to know he or she can relax:

   Bù hǎoyìsi, búyòng kèqi.

8. Your friend thanks you profusely for doing her a favor. You feel it is no problem at all and say:

   Dōu méiyǒu wèntí.

9. You think it's late and you and your friends should all get going. You say:

   Hěn wǎn! Wǒmen zǒu ba!

   le → to indicate now

10

10. Your friend apologizes about something and you want to tell him that is all right, it doesn't matter to you. You say:

Méiyǒu guānxi, dōu méiyǒu wèntí.

Check your answers in **Appendix IV**.

 Word Workshop
– The place you come to learn new words and phrases

(Go to 🔘 10-4 to hear:)

Restaurant words

饭馆
fànguǎn
(restaurant)

位
wèi → seat
(polite measure word for counting people)

客人　　　　　　　一位客人　　　　　　你们几位?
kèrén　　　　　　　yí wèi kèrén　　　　Nǐmen jǐ wèi?
(guest, customer)　(one guest, one customer)　(How many of you are there?)

小姐 zài Měiguo　　　　zài zhong　先生
xiǎojiě* _xiǎomèi._　　　　xiānsheng*
(miss)　　　　　　　　　　　　(mister)
polite way to address a waitress or waiter in a restaurant

开　　　　　　关　　　　　　开门　　　　　　关门
kāi　　　　　　guān　　　　　kāimén*　only for doors　guānmén*
(to open)　　　(to close)　　　(open)　　　　　　　　(close)
turn on　　　turn off　　　_(LIT: open, door)　(LIT: close, door)_
　　　　　　　　　　　　　　　　for establishments

菜　　　　　　中国菜　　　　　美国菜
cài　　　　　　Zhōngguócài　　Měiguócài
(dish, food)　　(Chinese food)　(American food)
vegetable

193

北京菜
Běijīngcài
(Beijing food)

四川菜
Sìchuāncài
(Szechuanese food)

click

点菜
diǎncài
(to order food)

菜单 →sheet/single
càidān
(menu)

buy

请来菜单 *except*
qǐng lái càidān *Chinese don't say this*
(Please bring a menu.)

买单
mǎidān *Cantonese phrase,*
(the bill [in a restaurant])

jié zhàng on Mainland
end of the bill

 ## *Chit-Chat Café*
– The place you come to practice speaking

Module 10.2 - (10-5) / English translation on **Page 213**
Picture this: Lisa is hungry and she and her friend, Yingying, decide to go get something to eat. Here is the first part of a three-part dialogue.

Part 1

Lisa:	Wǒ dùzi è le.	Lisa:	我肚子饿了。
Yingying:	Zhēn de ma? Nàme, wǒmen qù chīfàn ba.	Yingying:	真的吗？那么，我们去吃饭吧。
Lisa:	Hǎo a. Nǐ xiǎng chī shénme?	Lisa:	好啊。你想吃什么？
Yingying:	Dōu kěyǐ. Suíbiàn.	Yingying:	都可以。随便。
Lisa:	Wǒ yě wúsuǒwèi.	Lisa:	我也无所谓。
Yingying:	Nǐ xiǎng chī Zhōngguócài háishi Měiguócài?	Yingying:	你想吃中国菜还是美国菜？

10

[handwritten: I haven't eaten Chinese food]

Lisa: *[handwritten: xie]*	Zhōngguócài. Wǒ hěn jiǔ méiyǒu chī Zhōngguócài le.	Lisa:	中国菜。我很久没有吃中国菜了。
Yingying:	Nǐ juéde Běijīngcài hǎo bù hǎochī?	Yingying:	你觉得北京菜好不好吃？
Lisa:	Hěn hǎochī.	Lisa:	很好吃。
Yingying:	Nàme, wǒmen qù "Běijīng kǎoyā diàn (Peking Duck House)", hǎo ma?	Yingying:	那么，我们去"北京烤鸭店 (Peking Duck House)"，好吗？
Lisa:	Hǎo a, wǒ hěn xǐhuan nàr. Kěshì, tāmen jǐ diǎn guānmén?	Lisa:	好啊，我很喜欢那儿。可是，他们几点关门？
Yingying:	Hěn wǎn, shíyī diǎn cái *[handwritten: until/still]* guān.	Yingying:	很晚，十一点才关。
Lisa:	Hěn hǎo. Zǒu ba!	Lisa:	很好。走吧！
Yingying:	Zǒu ba!	Yingying:	走吧！
(zài fànguǎn)		(在饭馆)	
Waitress:	Qǐngwèn, nǐmen jǐ wèi?	Waitress:	请问，你们几位？
Lisa:	Wǒmen liǎng wèi.	Lisa:	我们两位。
Waitress:	Zhèr hǎo ma?	Waitress:	这儿好吗？
Yingying:	Hěn hǎo. Xièxie.	Yingying:	很好。谢谢。
Waitress:	Bú kèqi.	Waitress:	不客气。
Yingying:	Xiǎojiě, qǐng lái càidān.	Yingying:	小姐，请来菜单。
Waitress:	Méiyǒu wèntí.	Waitress:	没有问题。
(to be continued...)		(to be continued...)	

10

Chit-Chat Practice 10.1

Create a similar dialogue of your own. Use the prompts in English below to create sentences in Chinese for this couple who is discussing going out to eat. The first one is done for you. You can find the answers in **Appendix IV**.

1.

(Woman says she is hungry.)

Wǒ dùzi è le.

2.

(Man asks if she would like to eat at home or in a restaurant.)

Nǐ yào chī zài jiā haishi fànguǎn?

3.

(Woman says she doesn't care.)

Wúsuǒwèi,

4.

(Man says he prefers to eat in a restaurant tonight.)

Wǒ nìngkě qu fànguan zhèige wǎnshng
(yěbu)

5.

(Woman says that's good and asks if he'd like Szechuanese food.)

Hen hǎo. Ni yao Sìchuancai ma?
          chī

6.

(Man says "It's up to you.")

Suibian.

7.

(Woman says "OK. Let's go to a Szechuanese food restaurant.")

Name, zoo ba Si chuancai
de fànguǎn. Bù
              去

10

8.

(Man says "Let's go.")

Zŏu ba.

At the restaurant:

9.

(Waitress says "Excuse me, how many of you are there?")

Qĭngwèn, nĭmen jĭ wèi?

10.

(Man says "There are two of us.")

Yŏu èr wèi kèrén.

11.

(Waitress asks them to "Please sit down.")

Qĭng zuò.

12.

(Man and Woman say "Thank you.")

Xiè xiè.

13.

(Waitress says "You're welcome.")

Bù kèqì.

14.

(Man asks for a menu.)

Yào yíge càidān ba.

Word Workshop
– *The place you come to learn new words and phrases*

(Go to 🔘 10-6 to hear:)

Beverages

fruit → roomally non-alcoholic (usually soda)

饮料
yǐnliào
(beverage[s])

茶
chá
(tea)

水
shuǐ
(water)

fruit ↓

果汁
guǒzhī
(fruit juice)

juice/ sauce

bubbled western →

汽水
qìshuǐ
(soda)

water

咖啡
kāfēi
(coffee)

酒
jiǔ
(alcohol)

啤酒
píjiǔ
(~~liquor~~ beer)

葡萄酒
pútáojiǔ
(wine)

grape

hóngjiǔ (red wine)

米酒
mǐjiǔ
(rice wine)

huángjiǔ (yellow wine)

Food

肉
ròu
(meat)

牛
niú
(cow)

牛肉
niúròu
(beef)

bái jiǔ (not white wine!)

bái pú táo jiǔ (white wine)

猪
zhū
(pig)

猪肉
zhūròu
(pork)

鸡
jī
(chicken)
(the animal)

鸡肉
jīròu
(chicken)
(the meat)

鸭
yā
(duck)
(the animal)

鸭肉
yāròu
(duck)
(the meat)

鱼
yú
(fish)
(both live and as a dish)

豆腐
dòufu*
(tofu)

[handwritten: uh more like getting really touchy feeling]

* *Amusing Note:* "to eat tofu" has the double meaning of flirting with someone, as in "*Tā chī tā de dòufu.* (He is flirting with her)" or "*Tā xǐhuan* [handwritten: harassment] *chī nǚháizi de dòufu.* (He likes to flirt with women)."

蔬菜
shūcài
(vegetables)
[handwritten: sùcài]

汤
tāng
(soup)
[handwritten: vegetarian (veggie dish)]

Note: Three things about "tāng": Watch your tone since "táng = sugar." Don't do as I did and think you are ordering a bowl of soup in a restaurant and instead get a bowl of sugar. The other note about "tāng" is Chinese people say "drink soup (hē tāng)" not "eat soup" as we do in English. The last thing about "tāng" is typically Chinese people have soup at the end of the meal, not at the beginning.

饭
fàn*
(rice, meal)

10

* *Interesting Note: There are five words for "rice" in Chinese to distinguish its various states: rice on the plant (dào 稻), picked rice (mǐ 米), uncooked brown rice (cāomǐ 糙米), uncooked white rice (báimǐ 白米) and finally cooked white rice (báifàn 白饭).*

面
miàn
(noodles)
[handwritten: stir fry]

炒面
chǎomiàn
(chow mein [fried noodles])

炒饭
chǎofàn
(fried rice)

饺子
jiǎozi
(dumpling[s])

Also see www.chitchatchinese.com/dishes for a list of popular dishes in Chinese and for more food words, including tips on how to order in Chinese.

Words about eating & drinking

筷子
kuàizi
(chopsticks)

用筷子
yòng kuàizi
(to use chopsticks)

叉子
chāzi
(fork)

请/请客
qǐng / qǐngkè *(guest)*
(to treat someone, to pay for someone else)

请坐
qǐng zuò
(please sit down, please have a seat)

Say ba instead of qǐng to be more authentic

马上
mǎshàng
(immediately)
(LIT: horse, on)

回来
huílái
(come back)
(LIT: return, come)

我马上回来。
Wǒ mǎshàng huílái.
(I'll be right back.)

干杯
gānbēi*
(bottoms up, cheers)

* *Careful! Sometimes this is invoked in a lighthearted way as in "cheers" or "drink up." However, sometimes the person really means "bottoms up" and will expect you to empty your glass.*

10

慢慢吃
mànman chī *(→ Slowly)*
(bon appetite, enjoy your meal)
(LIT: slowly, slowly eat)

mànman shuo

来吃饭吧!
Lái chīfàn ba!
("Come and eat!," "Go ahead and start eating!")

辣
là
(spicy)

你吃辣吗?
Nǐ chī là ma?
(Do you eat spicy food?)

吃素
chīsù
(vegetarian)

你吃素吗?
Nǐ chīsù ma?
(Are you vegetarian?)

很多
hěn duō
(very many)

太多 le
tài duō
(too many)

gue — expensive

再
zài
(again, once more, another)

再点
zài diǎn
(order more)

再来
zài lái
(bring more)

再喝
zài hē
(drink more)

Asking questions

这是什么?
Zhè shì shénme?
(What is this?)

那是什么?
Nà shì shénme?
(What is that?)

_____ 中文怎么说?
_____ Zhōngwén zěnme shuō?
(How do you say _____ in Chinese?)

10

这个叫什么?
Zhèige jiào shénme?
(What is this called?)

201

Grammar Grove
– The place you come to learn about structure

It's time to revisit a concept we introduced in an earlier lesson: measure words. You have learned the most popular one: "ge (个)." You'll remember that measure words are used much like we use classifiers in English, such as "a loaf of bread," "a can of soda" or "a glass of milk." Let's look at a few new ones as they relate to words introduced in this lesson:

盘
pán
(a dish, measure word for dishes of food)

一盘菜
yì pán cài
(a dish of food)

杯
bēi
(a glass, cup, measure word for beverages [those served in glasses or cups])

两杯茶
liǎng bēi chá
(two cups of tea)

瓶
píng
(a bottle, measure word for beverages [served in bottles])

三瓶啤酒
sān píng píjiǔ
(three bottles of beer)

bíng píjiǔ
(ice beer)
[cold]

碗
wǎn
(a bowl, measure word for things served in a bowl)

两碗饭
liǎng wǎn fàn
(two bowls of rice)

位
wèi
(polite measure word for people)

五位老师
wǔ wèi lǎoshī
(five teachers)

Wěi?
Hello on phone

条
tiáo
(measure word for long thin things [e.g. rivers, snakes, roads, fish])

一条鱼
yì tiáo yú
(a fish, one fish)

10

Module 10.3 - (🔘 10-7) / English translation on **Page 214**
Picture this: This next dialogue is a continuation of the previous one with Lisa and Yingying in a Chinese restaurant.

Part 2

Waitress:	Zhè shì nǐmen de càidān. Nǐmen xiǎng hē shénme?	Waitress:	这是你们的菜单。你们想喝什么？
Yingying:	Wǒ xiǎng hē chá.	Yingying:	我想喝茶。
Lisa:	Wǒ yě shì. Yíngying, nǐ xiǎng bù xiǎng hē píjiǔ?	Lisa:	我也是。莹莹，你想不想喝啤酒？
Yingying:	Hǎo a. ~~Xiǎojiě~~ Fuyan, qǐng nǐ yě lái yì píng píjiǔ.	Yingying:	好啊。小姐，请你也来一瓶啤酒。
Waitress:	Nǐmen yào hē Měiguó píjiǔ háishi Zhōngguó de Qīngdǎo Píjiǔ (*Tsingtao Beer*)?	Waitress:	你们要喝美国啤酒还是中国的青岛啤酒 (*Tsingtao Beer*)?
Yingying:	~~Qǐng~~ Yào lái yì píng Qīngdǎo Píjiǔ.	Yingying:	请来一瓶青岛啤酒。
Waitress:	Hǎo. Wǒ mǎshàng huílái.	Waitress:	好。我马上回来。
Yingying:	Lisa, nǐ xiǎng chī shénme?	Yingying:	Lisa，你想吃什么？
Lisa:	Wǒ bù zhīdao. Wǒ xiǎng chī jīròu kěshì wǒ kàn bù dǒng càidān.	Lisa:	我不知道。我想吃鸡肉可是我看不懂菜单。

10

Yingying:	Ò, nǐ xǐhuan chī là ma?	Yingying:	哦，你喜欢吃辣吗？
Lisa:	Wǒ hěn xǐhuan.	Lisa:	我很喜欢。
Yingying:	Hǎo, wǒmen diǎn "gōngbǎo jīdīng," nà hěn hǎochī. Yīngwén jiào "Kung Pao chicken," hǎo bù hǎo?	Yingying:	好，我们点 "宫保鸡丁"，那很好吃。英文叫 "Kung Pao chicken"，好不好？
Lisa:	Hǎo a. Wǒ hěn xǐhuan chī gōngbǎo jīdīng. Wǒmen diǎn nèige ba.	Lisa:	好啊。我很喜欢吃宫保鸡丁。我们点那个吧。
Yingying:	Nǐ xiǎng bù xiǎng chī jiǎozi?	Yingying:	你想不想吃饺子？
Lisa:	Jiǎozi yǒu zhūròu, duì bú duì?	Lisa:	饺子有猪肉，对不对？
Yingying:	Duì.	Yingying:	对。
Lisa:	Duìbuqǐ, wǒ bù chī zhūròu.	Lisa:	对不起，我不吃猪肉。
Yingying:	Kěshì nǐ bù chīsù, duì bú duì?	Yingying:	可是你不吃素，对不对？
Lisa:	Duì, wǒ bù chīsù. Wǒ chī jīròu, niúròu, yú, yě chī yāròu. Kěshì wǒ bù xìhuan chī zhūròu, suǒyǐ _yìbàn_ ~~píngcháng~~ bù chī.	Lisa:	对。我不吃素。我吃鸡肉、牛肉、鱼，也吃鸭肉。可是我不喜欢吃猪肉，所以平常不吃。
Yingying:	Nǐ xǐ bù xǐhuan chǎomiàn?	Yingying:	你喜不喜欢炒面？
Lisa:	Wǒ hěn xǐhuan.	Lisa:	我很喜欢。
Yingying:	Hǎo, wǒ diǎn yì pán chǎomiàn. Nǐ xiǎng bù xiǎng hē tāng?	Yingying:	好，我点一盘炒面。你想不想喝汤？

10

Lisa:	Hǎo a. Wǒ hěn xǐhuan "hot and sour soup," Zhōngwén zěnme shuō?	Lisa:	好啊。我很喜欢"hot and sour soup"，中文怎么说？
Yingying:	Zhōngwén shì suānlàtāng. Wǒmen diǎn yì wǎn suānlàtāng.	Yingying:	中文是酸辣汤。我们点一碗酸辣汤。
Waitress:	Nǐmen xiǎng chī shénme?	Waitress:	你们想吃什么？
Yingying:	Wǒmen yào gōngbǎo jīdīng, chǎomiàn, hái yǒu suānlàtāng.	Yingying:	我们要宫保鸡丁、炒面，还有酸辣汤。
Waitress:	Méiyǒu wèntí. Wǒ mǎshàng huílái.	Waitress:	没有问题。我马上回来。
Yingying:	Xièxie.	Yingying:	谢谢。
Waitress:	Bú kèqi.	Waitress:	不客气。

Chit-Chat Practice 10.3

Answer these questions about the dialogue. You can find the answers in **Appendix IV**.

1.   Lisa 和莹莹想喝什么？

   Q: Lisa hé Yíngying xiǎng hē shénme?

   A: Lisa hé Yíngying xiǎng hē chá.

2.   他们点了美国啤酒还是中国啤酒？

   Q: Tāmen diǎnle Měiguó píjiǔ háishi Zhōngguó píjiǔ?

   A: Tāmen diǎnle Zhōngguó píjiǔ.

3.   Lisa 想吃什么？

   Q: Lisa xiǎng chī shénme?

   A: Lisa xiǎng chī jīrou keshi

4. Lisa 吃辣吗?

    Q: Lisa chī là ma?

    A: Méi cuò, Lisa chī là.

5. Lisa 为什么不想吃饺子?

    Q: Lisa wèishénme bù xiǎng chī jiǎozi?

    A: Lisa bù xiǎng chī jiǎozi yinwei ~~tā~~
    tā bu chī zhūròu.

6. 中文怎么说 "chow mein"?

    Q: Zhōngwén zěnme shuō "chow mein"?

    A: Zhōngwén shuō chǎo miàn.

7. Lisa 和莹莹点了什么菜?

    Q: Lisa hé Yíngying diǎnle shénme cài?

    A: Tāmen diǎnle gōngbǎo jīdīng chǎomiàn,
    hái yǒu suānlàtāng.

8. 他们点了什么汤?

    Q: Tāmen diǎnle shénme tāng?

    A: Tāmen diǎnle suānlàtāng.

Chit-Chat Café
– *The place you come to practice speaking*

Module 10.4 - (10-8) / English translation on **Page 215**

Part 3

Waitress: Zhè shì nǐmen de cài.	Waitress: 这是你们的菜。
Yingying Xièxie. & Lisa:	Yingying 谢谢。 & Lisa:

Yingying:	Lisa, wǒmen lái gānbēi ba.	Yingying:	Lisa，我们来干杯吧。
Lisa:	Gānbēi.	Lisa:	干杯。
Yingying:	Lái chīfàn ba.	Yingying:	来吃饭吧。
Lisa:	Kěshì, Yíngying, duìbuqǐ, wǒ bú huì yòng kuàizi.	Lisa:	可是，莹莹，对不起，我不会用筷子。
Yingying:	Méiyǒu guānxi. Xiǎojiě, qǐng lái chāzi.	Yingying:	没有关系。小姐，请来叉子。
Lisa:	Xièxie nǐ.	Lisa:	谢谢你。
Yingying:	Búyòng kèqi.	Yingying:	不用客气。
(Waitress brings fork.)		*(Waitress brings fork.)*	
Lisa:	Hǎo, wǒmen lái chīfàn ba.	Lisa:	好，我们来吃饭吧。
Yingying:	Gōngbǎo jīdīng hǎo bù hǎochī?	Yingying:	宫保鸡丁好不好吃？
Lisa:	Hěn hǎochī.	Lisa:	很好吃。
Yingying:	Là bú là?	Yingying:	辣不辣？
Lisa:	Yǒu yìdiǎnr là, kěshì wǒ xǐhuan.	Lisa:	有一点儿辣，可是我喜欢。
Yingying:	Mànman chī. Wǒmen yǒu hěn duō cài.	Yingying:	慢慢吃。我们有很多菜。
Lisa:	Yíngying, nǐ zài hē yì bēi píjiǔ ba.	Lisa:	莹莹，你再喝一杯啤酒吧。
Yingying:	Hǎo, nǐ yào zài diǎn cài ma?	Yingying:	好，你要再点菜吗？
Lisa:	Búyòng, cài tài duō le.	Lisa:	不用，菜太多了。
Yingying:	Méi guānxi, jīntiān wǒ qǐngkè.	Yingying:	没关系，今天我请客。

10

Lisa:	Kěshì nǐ shàng ge xīngqī qǐngkè. Jīntiān wǒ yào qǐngkè.	Lisa:	可是你上个星期请客。今天我要请客。
Yingying:	Hǎo ba, xià ge xīngqī wǒ qǐng nǐ.	Yingying:	好吧，下个星期我请你。
Lisa:	Nǐ chībǎo le ma?	Lisa:	你吃饱了吗？
Yingying:	Chībǎo le, nǐ ne?	Yingying:	吃饱了，你呢？
Lisa:	Wǒ yě chībǎo le.	Lisa:	我也吃饱了。
Yingying:	Xiǎojiě, mǎidān.	Yingying:	小姐，买单。
(They pay the bill.)		*(They pay the bill.)*	
Lisa:	Wǒmen zǒu ba.	Lisa:	我们走吧。
Yingying:	Zǒu ba.	Yingying:	走吧。

Chit-Chat Practice 10.4

Create your own dialogue in Chinese of two friends visiting a restaurant. Follow the English prompts to create questions and answers (answers in **Appendix IV**.)

Entering restaurant -

Nǐmen jǐ wèi?

1. Waitress: _Nǐ hǎo._ 开始吃饭了吗

   (how many people?)

2. You: _Nǐ hǎo. Wǒmen liǎng wèi._

   (two people)

3. Waitress: _Qǐng zuò._

   (have a seat)

4. You & Friend: _Xièxie._

   (thanks)

At table getting drink order -

1. Waitress: _Nǐ xiǎng hē shenme?_

   (drink?)

208

2. You: Wǒ xiǎng ~~xiǎng~~ yào guǒzhī
(juice)

3. Friend: Wǒ ~~xiǎng~~ yào yī bēi pútáojiǔ.
(wine)

At table getting food order -

1. Waitress: Nǐ xiǎng chīshíme?
(eat?)

2. You: Wǒ diǎn ~~cài~~ chǎomiàn hái yǒu suānlàtāng.
(chow mein, hot and sour soup)

3. Friend: Wǒ ~~xiǎng~~ yào gōngbǎo jīdīng gēn chǎofàn.
(Kung Pao chicken and fried rice)

Talking with friend about food -
Suggested topics: telling the person to enjoy their meal; asking if they like their food;
if it is spicy; if they should order more; if they should order
something else to drink.

1. You: Qǐng . . .
(bon appetite / enjoy your meal)

2. Friend: Mànman chī.
(enjoy your meal [eat slowly])

3. You: Gōngbǎo jīdīng là ma?
(is the Kung Pao chicken spicy?)

4. Friend: Yìdiǎr là, ~~zěnmeyàng~~ zěnmeyàng chǎomiàn?
(a little spicy; how is chow mein?)

5. You: Hǎo, ~~yòngdiàncài~~ ~~tài?~~ yào zài diǎn?
(good; you want to order more?)

6. Friend: ~~Bù kěn~~ Búyòng, tài zuō.
(not necessary, too much)

10

209

7. You: *also* Wǒ *hái* ~~yào~~ *yào* yī bēi pú táo jiǔ.
(I also want a glass of wine.)

8. Friend: Fú wù yuán, *qǐng lái* yī bēi pú táo jiǔ ba.
(waitress, please bring a glass of wine)

9. You: Xiè xie, nǐ ~~me xiǎng~~ *yě xiǎng* ~~yào~~ *yào yào* yī bēi ma?
(thanks, you also want a glass?)

10. Friend: Bú yòng.
(that's not necessary)

11. You: Fú wùyuán, qǐng lái liǎng wǎn fàn.
(miss, please also bring two bowls of rice)

Finishing up meal -

1. Friend: Nǐ chī bǎo le ma?
(are you full?)

2. You: Wǒ chī bǎo le; fú wùyuán, qǐng lái jiǔ *zhàng.*
(I am full; waitress, please bring the bill)

3. Friend: Wǒ qǐngkè.
(I'm treating)

4. You: Nǎ lǐ, nǎ lǐ... wǔ ~~diǎn~~ *fēn zhōng* yǐqián...
(thanks, let's go)
Xiè xie, zǒu ba.

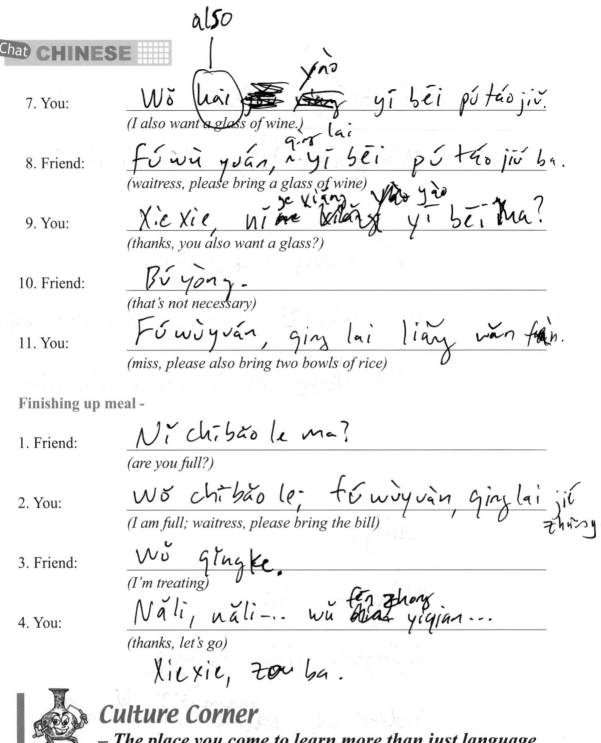

10 Culture Corner
– The place you come to learn more than just language

Dining Etiquette in China

Eating out is the single most popular social event to be found in Chinese culture. As you begin to meet more Chinese people you will find yourself the recipient of many a dinner invitation. Wonderful as these invitations are, they also abound with face--losing opportunities. To avoid the major missteps, here are the "Do's" and "Don'ts" of dining out:

Do!

- Do arrive on time. Chinese people tend to be very punctual and usually arrive right on time, or even early. There is no such thing as being "fashionably late" in Chinese culture.

- Do arrive hungry and make a good show of eating a lot. Taking small portions and pacing yourself is a good idea.

- Do continuously help pour tea for others. You will notice your friends doing this for you even when just a small amount of tea is gone.

- Do lift up your rice bowl or soup bowl if you like. It is all right to sip from the soup bowl lip or to scoop food or rice into your mouth from the bowl.

- Do compliment your host on his or her choice of dishes.

- Do be ready to try some things you thought you would never put in your mouth. It's part of the adventure!

Don't!

- Don't play with your chopsticks. Avoid the temptation to channel your inner drummer. Do not play with them in any way. Likewise, you should not gesticulate with chopsticks in your hand or point to people or things with your chopsticks. Additionally, you should never rest your chopsticks vertically sticking into your rice bowl or food. This is considered to resemble incense in a funerary urn and is considered bad luck. When not using your chopsticks they should be placed on the table or over the top of your bowl side-by-side in an even fashion.

- Don't start eating until your host has started or your host has insisted more than once that you begin first.

- Don't take the entire amount you intend to eat as the dish passes you the first time. You should take small portions repeatedly over the course of the meal.

- Don't drink any alcoholic beverage on your own, or sip casually when you feel like it. Either drink when someone toasts you or the whole table, or pick someone to toast and take a sip then.

Advice Alcove
– The place you come to learn how to learn

Tips for Ordering Chinese Food

One of the first responses I get when Americans learn that I speak Chinese is "You must be good to go to a Chinese restaurant with!" Actually, that isn't necessarily true. It depends on what menu I happen to pick up and which dishes that menu contains that have become familiar to my pallet. True mastery of the Chinese menu may allude even the native speaker. Here is why: There are thousands of regional dishes all with their own names; the names are poetic or historically based and cannot be taken at their face value; the dish name often does not even contain any of the ingredients of the dish. Here are some examples of popular Chinese dishes:

狮子头 shīzitóu = Lion's Head

蚂蚁上树 mǎyǐ shàng shù = Ants Going Up a Tree

口水鸡 kǒushuǐ jī = Drooling Chicken

PETA need not worry: the first dish contains no lion's meat (in fact it made of large pork meatballs.) Nor should the less adventurous eater fear: the second dish does not contain ants (it's a delicious noodle dish.) And, lastly, you will not be delivered a chicken with spittle coming out of its mouth for the last dish. That said, what is a non-native speaker to do in a Chinese restaurant. Here are my tips:

Going to a restaurant with a Chinese friend

Bring a paper and pen, or small notebook for future use. Tell your friends the kind of foods and flavors you like and ask for their suggestions. Write down any dishes you like and their Chinese names. You should keep this with you each trip to a Chinese restaurant.

Going to a restaurant on your own

This is a far more complicated task. Likely you will have a Chinese-only menu, or menu with incomprehensible English translations. Here are some tips for this scenario:

- Tell your waiter or waitress the kind of food you would like to eat and ask for his or her suggestion. Start with the type of meat or vegetable (e.g. Wǒ yào chī jīròu. = I want to eat chicken,) then restrictions (e.g. Wǒ bù chī là. = I don't eat spicy food.) The wait staff is usually happy to provide suggestions and may even have experience with what seems to be popular with Western guests.

10

- Eye the dishes on other tables. If you see something you like, point to it and say "Wǒ yào chī nèige.", or "I want to eat that."

- Do your research ahead of time. Go here and find dishes you like or would like to try. The dishes are written in pinyin and even have photos. Write the names out and create your own cheat sheet to put in your wallet and have handy: http://www.howtoorderchinesefood.com/

English Translation

Module 10.2

Part 1

Lisa:	I am hungry.
Yingying:	Really? Then, let's go out to eat.
Lisa:	All right. What do you want to eat?
Yingying:	Anything is fine. It's up to you.
Lisa:	It also doesn't matter to me.
Yingying:	Do you want to eat Chinese food or American food?
Lisa:	Chinese food. It's been a long time since I've had Chinese food.
Yingying:	Do you think Beijing-style food is good?
Lisa:	Delicious.
Yingying:	Then, let's go to "Peking Duck House," all right?
Lisa:	Sure. I really like that place. But, what time do they close?
Yingying:	Really late, they don't close until 11 p.m.
Lisa:	Great, let's go!
Yingying:	Let's go!

(At the restaurant)

Waitress:	Excuse me, how many people are you?
Lisa:	We are two.
Waitress:	How is here?
Yingying:	Great. Thanks.

10

| Yingying: | Miss, please bring us the menu. |
| Waitress: | No problem. |

(to be continued...)

Module 10.3

Part 2

Waitress:	Here is your menu. What would you like to drink?
Yingying:	I want to drink tea.
Lisa:	Me too. Yingying, do you want to drink beer?
Yingying:	Sure. Miss, please also bring a bottle of beer.
Waitress:	Would you like to drink American beer or the Chinese beer "Tsingtao"?.
Yingying:	Please bring a bottle of Tsingtao Beer.
Waitress:	All right. I'll be right back.
Yingying:	Lisa, what do you want to eat?
Lisa:	I don't know. I want to eat chicken, but I can't read the menu.
Yingying:	Oh, do you like to eat spicy (food)?
Lisa:	I like it a lot.
Yingying:	All right, let's order Gong Bao chicken. That is delicious. In English it's called "Kung Pao chicken." Is that OK?
Lisa:	Sure. I really like Kung Pao chicken. Let's order that.
Yingying:	Do you want to eat dumplings?
Lisa:	Dumplings have pork, right?
Yingying:	Right.
Lisa:	I'm sorry. I don't eat pork.
Yingying:	But you're not a vegetarian, right?
Lisa:	Right. I am not a vegetarian. I eat chicken, beef, fish and also duck. But, I don't like pork so I don't usually eat it.
Yingying:	Do you like fried noodles?
Lisa:	I like it a lot.

10

Yingying:	OK, I'll order one order of fried noodles. Do you want to have soup?
Lisa:	Sure. I really like "hot and sour soup." How do you say that in Chinese?
Yingying:	In Chinese it is "suan la tang." Let's order a bowl of hot and sour soup.
Waitress:	What do you want to eat?
Yingying:	We want Kung Pao chicken, fried noodles, and hot and sour soup.
Waitress:	No problem. I will be right back.
Yingying:	Thank you.
Waitress:	You're welcome.

Module 10.4

Part 3

Waitress:	Here are your dishes.
Yingying & Lisa:	Thanks.
Yingying:	Lisa, let's cheers.
Lisa:	Cheers.
Yingying:	Let's eat.
Lisa:	But, Yingying, I'm sorry, I don't know how to use chopsticks.
Yingying:	That's OK. Miss, please bring a fork.
Lisa:	Thank you.
Yingying:	You're welcome.

(Waitress brings fork.)

Lisa:	All right, let's eat.
Yingying:	How is the Kung Pao chicken?
Lisa:	Delicious.
Yingying:	Is it spicy?
Lisa:	It's a little hot, but I like it.
Yingying:	Enjoy your meal. We have plenty of food.

10

Lisa:	Yingying, have another glass of beer.
Yingying:	All right. Do you want to order more food?
Lisa:	There's no need. There are already too many dishes.
Yingying:	That's OK, today I am treating.
Lisa:	But, last week you treated. Today I want to treat (you).
Yingying:	All right, next week I'll treat you.
Lisa:	Are you full?
Yingying:	Yes, I am. And you?
Lisa:	I am full too.
Yingying:	Miss, the check.

(They pay the bill.)

Lisa:	Let's go.
Yingying:	Let's go.

10

LESSON 11

Pronunciation Plaza
– *The place you come to practice sounds and tones*

(Go to 🔘 11-1 to hear:)

Pronunciation Practice and Poetry

This is probably China's most famous poem. Most people in Mainland China and Taiwan know this poem by heart. If you memorize it as well, your Chinese friends will be quite impressed:

静夜思 床前明月光， 疑是地上霜， 举头望明月， 低头思故乡。	Jìng Yè Sī Chuáng qián míng yuè guāng, Yí shì dì shàng shuāng, Jǔ tóu wàng míng yuè, Dī tóu sī gùxiāng.

Translation:
Tranquil Evening Reflection - By Li Bai (701-762 A.D.)

Before my bed moonbeams cast a glow,
As if frost were covering the floor,
I lift my head and gaze at the brilliant moon,
Then lower my head reflecting on my hometown.

Sound Differentiation

x- vs. sh-

The initials "x-" and "sh-" are pronounced similarly: both like the "sh" sound in "ship." The "sh-" initial also has an added retroflex sound; this means the tongue curls slightly when saying it. The other difference you should be aware of is how each initial affects the pronunciation of two final sounds: the "-i" and the "-u." Here are the rules:

* *"x-" followed by "-i" has a long "ee" sound; "x-" followed by "-u" has an umlauted "u" sound.*

* *"sh-" followed by an "-i" has a retroflex short "uh" or "er" sound; "shu-" followed "-u" has a long "oo" sound.*

Use the above rules note the pronunciation differences for the final "-i" and the final "-u":

xi   vs.   shi

xu*   vs.   shu

* *Again, no need to write this "u" as "ü," since the umlauted sound is implied.*

Combination practice with final "-i":

xīshì   shīxǐ   xīshí   xǐshì
(Western style)   (to baptize)   (to suck)   (happy occassion)

shíxí   shìxí
(field work)   (hereditary)

Combination practice with final "-u":

xùshù   xùshū   shūxù
(ordinal number)   (literary sequel)   (preface of a book)

Combination practice with both "x-" and "sh-" initials with both "-i" and "-u" finals:

xīshū   shúxī   xīshù   shíxù
(sparse)   (to be familiar)   (all)   (time course)

xùshì   shíshū   shūshì   shúshí
(narrative)   (seasonal vegetables) (cozy)   (cooked food)

Chinese Intonation & Avoiding Becoming a Tone Robot:

One of the more challenging points of Chinese pronunciation is saying each individual tone accurately, while not sounding like a "tone robot." A tone robot may get each tone right, but does not capture the natural cadence and intonation of

Mandarin and ends up sounding like, well, a robot. The same thing can happen with learners of English. Take someone pronouncing each word carefully and accurately in this sentence, pausing after each word: "I-am-going-to-go-to-the-store." The person would sound robotic and odd. Most native speakers would say something closer to "I'm gonna go t'the store." Likewise, in Mandarin you should try to accurately replicate each tone without becoming a slave to the precise tone number. This means listening to how native speakers speak and trying to replicate the natural cadence. You may hear some tones said slowly for emphasis and others lightly as they slip through the sentence.

In this exercise, your goal is to say each particular tone accurately, yet capture the natural intonation and cadence of a native Mandarin speaker.

Language Cadence Exercise - (💿 11-2)

Listen to the following sentences and repeat each one concentrating on copying the cadence of the native Mandarin speaker.

1. 你想吃什么？
   Nǐ xiǎng chī shénme?

2. 我们星期五去看电影吧。
   Wǒmen xīngqīwǔ qù kàn diànyǐng ba.

3. 你们为什么来中国？
   Nǐmen wèishénme lái Zhōngguó?

4. 他不是我的男朋友。
   Tā bú shì wǒ de nánpéngyou.

5. 你坐公共汽车去上班吗？
   Nǐ zuò gōnggòng qìchē qù shàngbān ma?

6. 他明天几点去学校上课？
   Tā míngtiān jǐ diǎn qù xuéxiào shàngkè?

7. 你有没有兄弟姐妹？
   Nǐ yǒu méiyǒu xiōng-dì-jiě-mèi?

8. 中文难学可是很好玩儿。
   Zhōngwén nán xué kěshì hěn hǎowánr.

9. 他的先生是美国人。
   Tā de xiānsheng shì Měiguórén.

10. 我没有女儿，我有一个儿子。
    Wǒ méiyǒu nǚ'ér, wǒ yǒu yí ge érzi.

Word Workshop
– The place you come to learn new words and phrases

(Go to 🔘 11-3 to hear:)

Colors

颜色
yánsè
(color)

这是什么颜色?
Zhè shì shénme yánsè?
(What color is this?)

什么颜色的 _____?
Shénme yánsè de _____?
(What color of [something] ?)

bái de – white an

白色 báisè		黑色 hēisè		灰色 huīsè	
红色 hóngsè		粉红色 fěnhóngsè		黄色 huángsè	
橙色 chéngsè		蓝色 lánsè		绿色 lǜsè	
紫色 zǐsè		咖啡色 kāfēisè			

11

Clothes

衣服
yīfu
(clothes)

穿
chuān
(to wear)

穿衣服
chuān yīfu
(to wear clothes)

穿上
chuānshàng
(to put [a piece of clothing] on)

戴
dài
accessories
(to wear [caps, gloves, glasses, etc.])

脱下
tuōxià
(to take off [a piece of clothing])

 衬衫 *shirt*
chènshān

 裤子
kùzi

 短裤子 ~~duǎn kùzi~~
duǎn kùzi

 裙子
qúnzi

 鞋子
xiézi

 夹克
jiākè

外套 *outershirt*
wàitào

 帽子
màozi

手套
shǒutào

内裤
nèikù

 袜子
wàzi

 连衣裙
liányīqún

Measure words for clothes

件
jiàn*
(measure word for events, items and clothes)
* used for the following clothes: shirts, jackets, overcoats, skirts, and dresses

条
tiáo*
(measure word for long thin things [e.g. rivers, roads, ribbons, certain clothes])
* used for pants, shorts and underwear

双
shuāng*
(a pair of, double, measure word for things that come in pairs)
* used for shoes, socks and gloves

11

顶
dǐng
(top, apex, crown of the head, measure word for hats)

Grammar Grove
– The place you come to learn about structure

New use of "de (的)"

You have learned "de" as a word that follows a pronoun or noun to make it possessive. As in "wǒ de" = my, or "lǎoshī de" = the teacher's. "De" is also a word (or "associative particle," to be more precise) you will need to put between adjectives and the nouns they describe.

So, in a declarative sentence you would say:

她很漂亮。
Tā hěn piàoliang.
(She is pretty.)

However, in a descriptive sentence you will need a "de" between the adjective and the noun it describes:

她是一个很漂亮的人。
Tā shì yí ge hěn piàoliang de (rén)   *can eliminate but must keep de*
(She is a pretty person.)

Here are examples using the vocabulary you just learned:

红色的衬衫
hóngsè de chènshān = a red shirt

黑色的裤子
hēisè de kùzi = black pants

蓝色的鞋子
lánsè de xiézi = blue shoes

Here are some more examples using vocabulary from earlier lessons:

不好的人
bù hǎo de rén = a bad person

大问题
dà wèntí = a big problem

很有意思的书
hěn yǒu yìsi de shū = an interesting book

好看的电影
hǎokàn de diànyǐng = a good film

不好听的音乐
bù hǎotīng de yīnyuè = unpleasant music

聪明的学生
cōngmíng de xuésheng = an intelligent student

Notes:
- Occasionally "de" may be omitted in common, established adjective-noun pairs to improve sentence flow.
- If the noun was mentioned previously, it may be omitted in a later clause or sentence, such as "Wǒ xǐhuan hēisè de xiézi, kěshì wǒ bù xǐhuan báisè de (I like black shoes, but I do not like white ones.)."

Chit-Chat Café
– The place you come to practice speaking

Module 11.1 - (11-4)
Use the picture prompts below to ask and answer related questions. The first one is done for you in the example:

Example:

1. Q: **Zhè shì shénme?** (What is this?)
    A: **Zhè shì yí jiàn hóngsè de liányīqún.** (This is a red dress.)

1.

2.

3.

4.

5.

6.

7.

8.

9.

10.

11.

12.

13.

14.

15.

16.

17.

18.

19.

20.

11

Check your answers in **Appendix IV**.

Module 11.2 - (11-5)

Xiaomei is very picky when it comes to clothes. She likes certain pieces of clothing in one color, but does not like to wear them in other colors. Use the below picture prompts to form sentences regarding Xiaomei's likes and dislikes. The first one is done for you in the example:

Example:

1. 小美很喜欢穿绿色的夹克，可是她不喜欢穿紫色的。
   Xiǎoměi hěn xǐhuan chuān lǜsè de jiākè, kěshì tā bù xǐhuan chuān zǐsè de.
   (Xiaomei really likes green jackets, but doesn't like purples ones.)

1.

2.

3.

4.

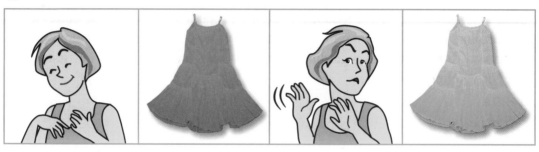

5.

6.

Check your answers in **Appendix IV**.

 Word Workshop
– The place you come to learn new words and phrases

(Go to 🔘 11-6 to hear:)

Money & Prices

多
duō
(many, much)

很多
hěn duō
(very many, very much)

少
shǎo
(few, little)

很少
hěn shǎo
(very few, very little)

多少
duōshao
(how much, how many)
(LIT: many, few)

多少钱
duōshao qián
(how much money, how much [is it])
(LIT: many, few, money)

块
kuài
(a dollar)
or yuan

毛
máo
(a dime [1/10 of a kuài])

分
fēn
(a cent [1/100 of a kuài])

钟
fēn zhong –
minute (quantity of time)

also minute/part/verb to separate
fēn shou – breakup

Saying Amounts of Money:

When saying the price of something, you start by saying how many "kuài (dollars)," then how many "máo (dimes)," next the number of "fēn (cents)," and, finally the word "qián (money)." In colloquial speech, however, people commonly omit "qián" and "fēn."

renminbi – People's money
měi jīn – american gold
ōu yuán – euro

kuài # máo # fēn + qián (optional)

Examples:

$1.54 =

一块五毛四分
yí kuài wǔ máo sì fēn

$47.61 =

四十七块六毛一分
sìshíqī kuài liù máo yì fēn

$13.99 =

十三块九毛九
shísān kuài jiǔ máo jiǔ

Chit-Chat Café
– The place you come to practice speaking

Module 11.3 - (🔊 11-7)

Use the picture prompts below to ask how much each item is. Answer in full sentences, using the correct measure word for each piece of clothing and the correct amount based on the tag shown (Answers in **Appendix IV**):

Example:

1.   Q: Zhèi jiàn qúnzi duōshao qián?
     A: Zhèi jiàn qúnzi èrshíwǔ kuài wǔ máo.

1.	2.	3.	4.
$ 25.50	$ 75.60	$ 45.25	$ 12.35

5.	6.	7.	8.
$ 11.19	$ 2.12	$ 5.00	$ 121.75

9.

$ 3.67

10.

$ 32.35

11.

$ 8.25

12.

$ 1.37

228

13. $ 10.98
14. $ 26.45
15. $ 38.22
16. $ 15.23
17. $ 19.44
18. $ 9.95
19. $ 67.88
20. $ 2.20

Check your answers in **Appendix IV**.

Grammar Grove
– The place you come to learn about structure

Modifiers

Here are some more commonly used words to modify tone or meaning in Mandarin:

1.
adj. + 一点 / 一点儿
adj. + yìdiǎn / yìdiǎnr
(a bit more [adj.])

You've learned yìdiǎnr (一点儿) to mean "a little" or "a bit." Now, if you use those same words before an adjective you can modify its meaning to say it is "a bit more" of what ever the particular adjective means:

大一点	小一点	晚一点	多一点
dà yìdiǎn	xiǎo yìdiǎn	wǎn yìdiǎn	duō yìdiǎn
(a bit larger)	(a bit smaller)	(a bit later)	(a bit more)

好一点	难一点	高一点	贵一点
hǎo yìdiǎn	nán yìdiǎn	gāo yìdiǎn	guì yìdiǎn
(a bit better)	(a bit more difficult)	(a bit taller)	(a bit more expensive)

When this expression has "yǒu" in front, it has a similar but different meaning:

有一点 / 有一点儿 + adj.
yǒu yìdiǎn / yǒu yìdiǎnr + adj.
(to be rather..., to be somewhat..., to be a bit...)

有一点儿难	有一点儿无聊	有一点儿早
yǒu yìdiǎnr nán	yǒu yìdiǎnr wúliáo	yǒu yìdiǎnr zǎo
(rather difficult)	(somewhat boring)	(a bit early)

2.

一下	V. + 一下
yíxià	V. + yíxià
(all of a sudden, in an instant)	(give sth. a go, do sth. a bit)
	(LIT: one, down)

"Yíxià" is used after a verb to soften the tone and encourage someone to give something a try, or to do something just for a bit or, more literally, just for "an instant."

看一下	坐一下	问一下
kàn yíxià	zuò yíxià	wèn yíxià
(have a look)	(have a seat [for a bit])	(ask sth. [quickly])

听一下	穿一下
tīng yíxià	chuān yíxià
(have a listen)	(try something on)

3.

11

When you say a verb and then the number one (yī) and that same verb again you've softened the tone to encourage the person to do it a while or to give it a try. In mock English it would be like this:

"look one look" = give it a look
"try one try" = give it a try

Here is the construction for Mandarin:

V. 一 V.
V. yī V.
(give sth. a try, do sth. for a moment)

试一试	看一看	问一问
shì yí shì	kàn yí kàn	wèn yí wèn
(give sth. a try)	(have a look)	(ask [not long])
想一想	学一学	逛一逛
xiǎng yì xiǎng	xué yì xué	guàng yí guàng
(think it over)	(study for a bit)	(stroll around a bit)

 Word Workshop
– *The place you come to learn new words and phrases*

(Go to 🄲 11-8 to hear:)

Shopping

买
mǎi*
(to buy)

卖
mài*
(to sell)

* *That's right, same sound, different tone! This is an occasion you will have to get the tone right to be understood.*

太
tài ⊢ adj ⊢ le   (to make more balanced)
(too [much], extremely)

贵
guì
(expensive)

便宜
piányi
(cheap, inexpensive)

商店
shāngdiàn
(store, shop)

家
jiā*

(measure word for stores, restaurants & businesses)

* same character as "family" or "home"

一家商店
yì jiā shāngdiàn

(a store)

逛
guàng

(to stroll)

逛街
guàngjiē

(to window-shop)

欢迎光临
huānyíng guānglín*

(welcome, you honor us with your presence)

(LIT: welcome, bright, arrival)

* This is what you will hear any time you enter a business establishment, said by all or some of the staff.

[handwritten: If j wlt want to say welcome]

不错
búcuò

(not bad, pretty good)

(LIT: not, mistake)

还可以
hái kěyǐ*

(it's OK, it's alright, it's fine)

(LIT: still, able to)

* said with the sense that something might not be up to your expectations or is not ideal

流行
liúxíng

(popular, fashionable)

(LIT: to flow, current)

您
nín*

(you [formal])

* This is used in formal situations, such as in business introductions, by staff in stores or restaurants to customers, patients to doctors, or to other higher-ranking individuals (e.g. your boss, respected elders, your professors, etc.)

11

试
shì
(to try)

来
lái
(to come)

进去
jìnqù
(to go in)
(LIT: enter, go)

看看
kànkan
(to have a look)

 Chit-Chat Café
– The place you come to practice speaking

Module 11.4 - (11-9) / English translation on **Page 248**

Picture this: Jenny is out shopping and goes into a medium-sized store to see if she can find a shirt and a pair of pants to buy for an upcoming event she plans to attend.

Clerk: **Huānyíng guānglín!**	Clerk: 欢迎光临！
Jenny: **Xiǎojiě, qǐngwèn nǐmen zhèi jiā shāngdiàn mài bú mài chènshān?**	Jenny: 小姐，请问你们这家商店卖不卖衬衫？
Clerk: **Yǒu, wǒmen zhèr yǒu hěn duō.**	Clerk: 有，我们这儿有很多。
Jenny: **Nǐmen yǒu méiyǒu Yìdàlì de chènshān?**	Jenny: 你们有没有意大利的衬衫？
Clerk: **Yǒu, zhè jiù shì yí jiàn hěn piàoliang de Yìdàlì chènshān.**	Clerk: 有，这就是一件很漂亮的意大利衬衫。
Jenny: **Duōshao qián?**	Jenny: 多少钱？
Clerk: **Liǎngbǎi liùshí kuài, nín xǐhuan ma?**	Clerk: 两百六十块，您喜欢吗？

11

Jenny: Wǒ hěn xǐhuan, kěshì tài guì le. Nǐ yǒu méiyǒu piányi yìdiǎnr de?	Jenny: 我很喜欢，可是太贵了。你有没有便宜一点儿的？
Clerk: Zhèi jiàn bú shì Yìdàlì de, kěshì háishì hěn piàoliang, yě bú guì.	Clerk: 这件不是意大利的，可是还是很漂亮，也不贵。
Jenny: Zhèi jiàn búcuò. Kěshì tài xiǎo. Nǐ yǒu méiyǒu dà yìdiǎnr de?	Jenny: 这件不错。可是太小。 你有没有大一点儿的？
Clerk: Yǒu, nín kěyǐ shì yí shì zhèi jiàn.	Clerk: 有，您可以试一试这件。
Jenny: Hǎo. Wǒ yě xiǎng mǎi yì tiáo kùzi.	Jenny: 好。我也想买一条裤子。
Clerk: Hǎo. Lái, wǒmen zhèr yǒu hěn duō nǚháizi de kùzi. Nín xiǎng mǎi shénme yánsè de?	Clerk: 好。来，我们这儿有很多女孩子的裤子。您想买什么颜色的？
Jenny: Dōu kěyǐ.	Jenny: 都可以。
Clerk: Zhèi tiáo hēisè de kùzi hěn liúxíng. Hěn duō rén lái mǎi.	Clerk: 这条黑色的裤子很流行。很多人来买。
Jenny: Zhèi tiáo búcuò. Duōshao qián?	Jenny: 这条不错。多少钱？
Clerk: Zhèi tiáo yìbǎi wǔshí'èr kuài.	Clerk: 这条一百五十二块。
Jenny: Nà hái kěyǐ. Wǒ xiǎng shì yíxià.	Jenny: 那还可以。我想试一下。
Clerk: Hǎo. Nín chuānshàng kànkan zěnmeyàng.	Clerk: 好。您穿上看看怎么样。
(Jenny comes out of dressing room.)	*(Jenny comes out of dressing room.)*

11

(handwritten, top) more formal

Clerk: (Nín) juéde zěnmeyàng?	Clerk: 您觉得怎么样？
Jenny: Búcuò, wǒ xǐhuan. Kěshì wǒ juéde kùzi tài dà. Yǒu méiyǒu xiǎo yìdiǎnr de?	Jenny: 不错，我喜欢。可是我觉得裤子太大。有没有小一点儿的？
Clerk: Yǒu, nín shì yí shì zhèi tiáo.	Clerk: 有，您试一试这条。
(Jenny comes out again.)	*(Jenny comes out again.)*
Jenny: Zhèi tiáo hěn hǎo, yě hěn shūfu. Xièxie.	Jenny: 这条很好，也很舒服。谢谢。
Clerk: Bú kèqi.	Clerk: 不客气。

Chit-Chat Practice 11.4

Answer these questions about the dialogue. You can find the answers in **Appendix IV**.

1. 那家商店有没有意大利的衬衫？
   Nèi jiā shāngdiàn yǒu méiyǒu Yìdàlì de chènshān?

   Nèi jiā shāngdiàn yǒu Yìdàlì de chènshān.

2. 那件意大利的衬衫贵不贵？
   Nèi jiàn Yìdàlì de chènshān guì bú guì?

   Nèi jiàn Yìdàlì de chènshān hen guì.

3. 那件意大利的衬衫多少钱？
   Nèi jiàn Yìdàlì de chènshān duōshao qián?

   Nèi jiàn Yìdàlì de chènshān shì liǎngbǎi liùshí kuì

4. Jenny 觉得那件衬衫怎么样？
   Jenny juéde nèi jiàn chènshān zěnmeyàng?

   Jenny juéde nèi jiàn chènshān tài guì.

11

5. 商店卖不卖女孩子的裤子?
   Shāngdiàn mài bú mài nǚháizi de kùzi?

   Shāng diàn mài nǚháizi de kùzi.

6. Jenny想买什么颜色的裤子?
   Jenny xiǎng mǎi shénme yánsè de kùzi?

   Jenny shuō dōu kěyǐ.

7. 那条黑色的裤子多少钱?
   Nèi tiáo hēisè de kùzi duōshao qián?

   Nèi tiáo kùzi shì yìbǎi wǔshí'èr kuài.

8. Jenny觉得那条裤子怎么样?
   Jenny juéde nèi tiáo kùzi zěnmeyàng?

   Tā xǐhuan, juéde hěn shūfú.

Word Workshop
– The place you come to learn new words and phrases

(Go to 11-10 to hear:)

The telephone & making plans

打电话给 sb. / give to
dǎ diànhuà gěi sb.
(to give [somebody] a call)
(*LIT: hit, telephone, give*)

喂? / 喂!
Wéi? / Wèi!
(Hello? [on telephone] / "Hey!")

_____ 在吗?	他/她在。
_____ zài ma?	Tā / Tā zài.
(Is _____ there?)	(He / She is here.)

请问，您哪位？
Qǐngwèn, nín něi wèi?
("May I ask who is calling?")
(LIT: excuse me, you [polite], which, individual)

You've learned "zàijiàn" to mean goodbye, which transliterates as the words "again + see." Now, you can use a similar construction to indicate when you will see the person next, just as we would say in English "see you next week" or "see you on Monday." Here is how it works:

time + 见
time + jiàn
(time + to see)

下个星期见
xià ge xīngqī jiàn
(see you next week)

明天见
míngtiān jiàn
(see you tomorrow)

三点半见
sān diǎn bàn jiàn
(see you at 3:30)

等
děng
(to wait)

等一下
děng yíxià
(wait a moment)

请等一下
qǐng děng yíxià
(wait a moment, please)

等一下见
děng yíxià jiàn
(see you in a moment)

你的电话
Nǐ de diànhuà.
(It's for you. / Telephone for you.)
(LIT: your, phone)

我就是
Wǒ jiù shì.
(It's me.)

见面
jiànmiàn
(to meet [up])
(LIT: see, face)

11

237

接
jiē
(to pick someone up [at a place]) *also used for answer phone*
(LIT: connect)

可以
kěyǐ
(able, that's OK, that's fine)

可以，没有问题。
Kěyǐ, méiyǒu wèntí.
(Sure, no problem.)
(LIT: able, not have, problem)

可以吗?
Kěyǐ ma?
("Is that alright?", "Is that OK?")
(LIT: able + ?)

行	不行	行不行?
xíng	bù xíng	Xíng bù xíng?
(possible, can work)	(not possible, can't work)	("Is that possible?"; "Could that work?")

你说对了。
Nǐ shuōduì le.   *Nǐ ano shuō duò le.*
("You're right."; "What you are saying is correct.")
(LIT: you, say, correct + particle "le")   *You are wrong.*

看看
kànkan
(have a look, see what sth. looks like)
(LIT: look, look)

借钱
jièqián*
(borrow money, ~~lend money~~)
* ~~Yes, that is the same word for both borrowing and lending.~~

11

太谢谢你了。
Tài xièxie nǐ le.
(Thanks so much.)
(LIT: too, thank you + particle "le")

不用客气。
Búyòng kèqi.
("You are very welcome."; "You are most welcome.")
(LIT: not, use, politeness)

别的
biéde
(other)

good word
something else

对啊
duì a
(that's right; you've got it right)
(LIT: correct + exclamation "a")

哇
wā
(Wow!)

Grammar Grove
– The place you come to learn about structure

Expressing "-ing" in Chinese

Although we have largely stressed that there are no tenses in Mandarin, there are ways to emphasize states of being with words you have learned, such as "le" for completed actions, or "huì" and "yào" for future actions. Now, here is a way to express something is being done right now (much like the English gerund, or the "ing" after a verb):

在 + verb
zài + verb
(doing something, [verb]ing, emphasizing sth. is being done right now)

在看书
zài kàn shū
(reading a book [right now])

在吃饭
zài chīfàn
(eating [right now])

在学中文
zài xué Zhōngwén
(studying Chinese [right at this moment])

你在做什么？
Nǐ zài zuò shénme?
(What are you doing? [right now])

 *Chit-Chat Café*
– The place you come to practice speaking

Module 11.5 - (11-11) / English translation on **Page 249**

Picture this: "Dijia" is calling her friend "Jieru" to see what she is up to and if she would like to go out window shopping. Jieru's roommate answers the phone.

Roommate:	Wéi?	Roommate:	喂？
Dijia:	Wéi, Jiérú zài ma?	Dijia:	喂，洁如在吗？
Roommate:	Zài, qǐngwèn nín něi wèi?	Roommate:	在，请问您哪位？
Jieru:	Wǒ shì Díjiā.	Jieru:	我是迪佳。
Roommate:	Qǐng děng yíxià. Jiérú, nǐ de diànhuà.	Roommate:	请等一下。洁如，你的电话。
Jieru:	Wéi?	Jieru:	喂？
Dijia:	Wéi, Jiérú? Wǒ shì Díjiā.	Dijia:	喂，洁如？我是迪佳。
Jieru:	Nǐ hǎo ma?	Jieru:	你好吗？
Dijia:	Búcuò, nǐ zài zuò shénme?	Dijia:	不错，你在做什么？
Jieru:	Wǒ zài kàn diànshì. Nǐ ne?	Jieru:	我在看电视。你呢？

Dijia:	Wǒ xiǎng qù guàngjiē. Nǐ xiǎng bù xiǎng qù?	Dijia:	我想去逛街。你想不想去？
Jieru:	Hǎo. Wǒmen jǐ diǎn jiànmiàn?	Jieru:	好。我们几点见面？
Dijia:	Liǎng diǎn bàn zěnmeyàng?	Dijia:	两点半怎么样？
Jieru:	Hǎo, wǒmen zài nǎr jiànmiàn?	Jieru:	好，我们在哪儿见面？
Dijia:	Zài nǐ jiā. Wǒ qù jiē nǐ, hǎo bù hǎo?	Dijia:	在你家。我去接你，好不好？
Jieru:	Hǎo, xièxie.	Jieru:	好，谢谢。
Dijia:	Bú kèqi. Děng yíxià jiàn.	Dijia:	不客气。等一下见。
Jieru:	Hǎo, liǎng diǎn bàn jiàn?	Jieru:	好，两点半见。
(while window-shopping)		*(while window-shopping)*	
Dijia:	Zhèi jiā shāngdiàn hěn búcuò. Nǐ xǐhuan ma?	Dijia:	这家商店很不错。你喜欢吗？
Jieru:	Wǒ hěn xǐhuan. Wǒmen jìnqù guàng yí guàng. Hǎo ma?	Jieru:	我很喜欢。我们进去逛一逛。好吗？
Dijia:	Hǎo.	Dijia:	好。
Jieru:	Díjiā, zhèi jiàn chènshān hěn hǎokàn.	Jieru:	迪佳，这件衬衫很好看。
Dijia:	Duì a, yánsè hěn piàoliang. Nǐ qù shì yí shì.	Dijia:	对啊，颜色很漂亮。你去试一试。
Jieru:	Bù xíng. Wǒ xiànzài méiyǒu qián.	Jieru:	不行。我现在没有钱。
Dijia:	Méi guānxi, nǐ kàn, zhèi jiàn bú guì.	Dijia:	没关系，你看，这件不贵。

Jieru: Ò, zhēn de. Zhèi jiàn zhēn piányi! Wǒ qù shì yíxià, kànkan zěnmeyàng.	Jieru: 哦，真的。这件真便宜！我去试一下，看看怎么样。
(comes out of dressing room)	*(comes out of dressing room)*
Dijia: Wā, zhēn de hěn piàoliang. Nǐ xiǎng bù xiǎng mǎi?	Dijia: 哇，真的很漂亮。你想不想买？
Jieru: Wǒ xiǎng mǎi, kěshì wǒ xiǎng *best* wǒ zuì hǎo děng xià ge xīngqī.	Jieru: 我想买，可是我想我最好等下个星期。
Dijia: Wèishénme?	Dijia: 为什么？
Jieru: Xià ge xīngqī wǒ huì yǒu duō yì diǎnr qián. *Wo hui you xie qián*	Jieru: 下个星期我会有多一点儿钱。
Dijia: Méi guānxi, wǒ kěyǐ jiè nǐ qián.	Dijia: 没关系，我可以借你钱。
Jieru: Kěyǐ ma? Tài xièxie nǐ le.	Jieru: 可以吗？太谢谢你了。
Dijia: Búyòng kèqi.	Dijia: 不用客气。
Jieru: Nǐ ne? Nǐ xiǎng bù xiǎng mǎi shénme?	Jieru: 你呢？你想不想买什么？
Dijia: Wǒ xiǎng mǎi yí jiàn wàitào.	Dijia: 我想买一件外套。
Jieru: Zhèi jiā bú mài wàitào, wǒmen qù bié de shāngdiàn.	Jieru: 这家不卖外套，我们去别的商店。
Dijia: Macy's yǒu hěn duō wàitào. Wǒmen qù nàr ba.	Dijia: Macy's 有很多外套。我们去那儿吧。
Jieru: Hǎo a. Zǒu ba.	Jieru: 好啊。走吧。
Dijia: Zǒu ba.	Dijia: 走吧。

11

Chit-Chat Practice 11.5

Role Play

Your Chinese friend calls you to see if you would like to go shopping. Fill in the following dialogue with appropriate answers following the English prompts. The first two are completed for you. For example answers see **Appendix IV**.

Example:

喂？

1. You: Wéi? _____

喂， (your name) 在吗？

Friend: Wéi, (your name) zài ma?

我就是。

2. You: Wǒ jiù shì. _____

怎么样？ 你好吗？

Friend: Zěnmeyàng? Nǐ hǎo ma?

3. You: ~~Hǎi Dhǎo~~ Běi shǎo, nǐ ne? _____
          (very good; and you?)

我也很好。 你在做什么？

Friend: Wǒ yě hěn hǎo. Nǐ zài zuò shénme?

4. You: Wǒ dúshū. Hěn wúliáo! _____
          (reading a book; I am bored)

你想不想跟我一起去逛街？

Friend: Nǐ xiǎng bù xiǎng gēn wǒ yìqǐ qù guàngjiē?

5. You: Hǎo, jǐ diǎn jiàn miàn? _____
          (great; what time will we meet?)

三点怎么样？

Friend: Sān diǎn zěnmeyàng? wǒmen

6. You: Méiyǒu wèntí; ~~wǒ~~ zài nǎli jiànmiàn? _____
          (that's fine; where will we meet?)

11

243

/

我去你家接你。好不好?

Friend: Wǒ qù nǐ jiā jiē nǐ, hǎo bù hǎo?

7. You: *Hǎo, sān diǎn bàn jiàn.*
(great; I'll see you at 3 o'clock)

(while you and your friend are out shopping)

这件连衣裙好不好看?

Friend: Zhèi jiàn liányīqún hǎo bù hǎokàn?

8. You: *Zhèi jiàn liányīqún hěn ~~hǎokàn~~ piàoliàng nǐ xiǎng mǎi bu mǎi?*
(that one is really pretty; do you want to buy it?)

我很想买,可是我没有钱。

Friend: Wǒ hěn xiǎng mǎi, kěshì wǒ méiyǒu qián.

9. You: *Méiyǒu guānxi, wǒ kěyǐ jiè gěi nǐ qián.*
(no problem; I can lend you money)

太谢谢你了。你想不想买什么?

Friend: Tài xièxie nǐ le. Nǐ xiǎng bù xiǎng mǎi shénme?

10. You: *Wǒ yào mǎi yī ~~shū~~ tiáo de kùzi.*
(I want to buy a pair of pants)

这条你喜不喜欢?

Friend: Zhèi tiáo nǐ xǐ bù xǐhuan?

11. You: *Wǒ bú xǐhuan na yánsé, wǒ yào mǎi hēisè de kùzi*
(I don't like that color; I want to buy black pants)

这家商店的裤子不多。我们去别的商店逛一逛,
好吗?

Friend: Zhèi jiā shāngdiàn de kùzi bù duō. Wǒmen qù bié de shāngdiàn guàng yí guàng, hǎo ma?

12. You: *Hǎo, zǒu ba.*
(OK, let's go)

11

244

Colors and their Cultural Meaning in China

There are a few colors with strong associations in Chinese culture, and here some you should be aware of:

White

The color white is associated with death and mourning. People generally dress in white for funerals. White does not connote "purity" or "cleanliness" as it does in the West.

Red

Red is considered a joyful and lucky color. It is the color associated with weddings. Traditionally the bride wears a red gown and the groom red pants. The reception room is usually decorated in red with red linens, lanterns and other red objects. It is the color of the envelope for lucky money given at Chinese New Year and given to the bride and groom at weddings.

Yellow

Purple is to traditional Western royalty as yellow is to imperial China. In ancient China the emperor was the only person allowed to wear yellow or to decorate his dwelling (the palace, as it were) in yellow. Now, yellow can be worn by all, but it still holds an imperial association. Yellow is also generally associated with money (gold) and is paired with red for extra good luck (as you will see on lucky money envelopes).

11

The "Do's" and "Don'ts" of colors:

- **Do** give money in a red envelope as a present at New Year's or at weddings
- **Do** wear white (or black) to a funeral
- **Do** write sayings of good luck on red paper
- **Do** give money in a white envelope at a funeral (báibāo)
- **Do** wear red underwear when gambling (it will bring you good luck!)

- **Don't** wear anything red to a funeral (it will look like you are celebrating)
- **Don't** give any money gifts in a white envelope at any celebration
- **Don't** give yellow roses to your Chinese boyfriend or girlfriend (it means you want to break up)
- **Don't** write your name with a red pen (it will bring you bad luck)
- **Don't** wear a green hat if you are a man (it means your lover is cheating on you)

Advice Alcove
– The place you come to learn how to learn

Overcoming Obstacles: Part 1

If you've made it this far, you likely no longer need advice on studying. You clearly have the skills and determination to see your studies through. At this point you have basic Mandarin conversational skills and may even be putting your skills to the test out in the real world. Using your language skills in real life is the key to improving and retaining what you have learned. That said, you might still encounter a few roadblocks on your linguistic journey. Here are some common barriers to practicing Mandarin and ways around them:

The Fast Speaker Obstacle

Learners of any language are going to encounter the speaker who is not used to speaking to non-native speakers. They may run off rapid-fire speech, throwing in slang and expressions, leaving you in the linguistic dust. Here are some expressions you can use to handle this situation:

对不起，我听不懂。

Duìbuqǐ, wǒ tīng bù dǒng.
(Sorry, I don't understand.)

请你再说一次。

Qǐng nǐ zài shuō yí cì.
(Please, say that again.)

11

请你说慢一点儿。

Qǐng nǐ shuō màn yìdiǎnr.

(Please talk a little bit slower.)

_____ 是什么意思?

_____ shì shénme yìsi?

(What does _____ mean?)

The English Pirate

There is a secret term used among foreigners living in China or Taiwan that refers to the type of local who seeks you out just to practice their English. This person is known as the dreaded "English pirate (determined to gain the booty of free English practice)." This might be wonderful for an American alone abroad and uninterested in learning Chinese. However, if you came specifically to learn Mandarin, this becomes a huge barrier to actually getting to practice your skills. You may start the conversation in Chinese, and no matter what you do your counterpart will only reply in English. This is discouraging and may make you feel the person thinks your Chinese is not good enough for a conversation. But, rest assured, no matter what level you reach in Chinese, you will continually encounter this. Sometimes the person may not be a pirate, but simply be unaccustomed to seeing a foreigner speak their language. Other locals may feel they are being polite and more welcoming by speaking your language. Either way, the situation is not going to help you with your Mandarin skills. Here are some ways around this issue:

- Ask the person politely if they don't mind speaking in Chinese and explain that you are trying to learn:

  请你跟我说中文。我想练习。可以吗?

  Qǐng nǐ gēn wǒ shuō Zhōngwén. Wǒ xiǎng liànxí. Kěyǐ ma?

  (Please speak to me in Chinese. I would like to practice. Is that all right?)

- Seek out older people to speak with in Mandarin. They often have the time and patience to chat with learners (and often don't know English).

- Identify the people who are comfortable and willing to speak with you in Mandarin and develop these relationships.

Ironically, one of the best places to practice Mandarin is right here in the U.S., in any Chinatown in any major city. People are more than happy to speak to you in Mandarin (almost everyone speaks some). They get plenty of practice with English and are thrilled to take a break.

Stay tuned for Part 2 in Lesson 12 next!

11

English Translation

Module 11.4

Clerk:	Welcome!
Jenny:	Excuse me miss, does this store sell shirts?
Clerk:	Yes, we have many here.
Jenny:	Do you have Italian shirts?
Clerk:	Yes, this one is a beautiful Italian shirt.
Jenny:	How much is that?
Clerk:	$260. Do you like it?
Jenny:	I really like it, but it's too expensive. Do you have ones a bit cheaper?
Clerk:	This one isn't Italian, but it's still very pretty, and it's not expensive.
Jenny:	That one isn't bad. But it's too small. Do you have one that is a bit larger?
Clerk:	Yes, you can try this one.
Jenny:	All right. I also want to buy a pair of pants.
Clerk:	OK, come (this way), here we have many woman's pants. What color (pants) were you thinking of buying?
Jenny:	Anything is fine. I don't care.
Clerk:	This pair of black pants is very popular. Many people come to buy it.
Jenny:	That pair isn't bad. How much is it?
Clerk:	This pair is $152 dollars.
Jenny:	That's pretty good. I'd like to try it on.
Clerk:	OK. Put it on and see what it's like.
(Jenny comes out of dressing room)	
Clerk:	What do you think?
Jenny:	No bad. I like it. But I think the pants are too big. Do you have ones a bit smaller?
Clerk:	Yes, try this pair.

(Jenny comes out again)

Jenny:	This pair is really good. It's also very comfortable. Thanks.
Clerk:	You're welcome.

Module 11.5

Module 11.5

Roommate:	Hello?
Dijia:	Hello, is Jieru there?
Roommate:	Yes. May I ask who is calling?
Dijia:	This is Dijia.
Roommate:	Please wait a moment. Jieru, telephone for you.
Jieru:	Hello?
Dijia:	Hello, Jieru? This is Dijia.
Jieru:	Hello. How is it going?
Dijia:	Not bad. What are you doing?
Jieru:	I am watching TV. How about you?
Dijia:	I want to go window shopping. Do you want to come?
Jieru:	OK. When should we meet?
Dijia:	How about 2:30?
Jieru:	OK. Where should we meet?
Dijia:	At your home. I'll come pick you up. All right?
Jieru:	OK. Thanks.
Dijia:	You're welcome. See you soon.
Jieru:	OK. See you at 2:30.

(while window shopping)

Dijia:	This store is very good. Do you like it?
Jieru:	I like it a lot. Let's go in and stroll around a bit. OK?
Dijia:	OK.
Jieru:	Dijia, this shirt is really nice (good looking).

11

Jieru:	I can't (not possible). I don't have any money.
Dijia:	That's OK. Look, this one is not expensive.
Jieru:	Oh, you're right. This one is inexpensive! I'm going to try it on and see what it's like.

(comes out of dressing room)

Dijia:	Wow, really beautiful. Do you want to buy it?
Jieru:	I want to buy it, but I think I'd better wait until next week.
Dijia:	Why?
Jieru:	Next week I will have a bit more money.
Dijia:	That's OK. I can lend you money.
Jieru:	Can you? Thank you so much.
Dijia:	You're very welcome.
Jieru:	How about you? Do you want to buy something?
Dijia:	I want to buy an overcoat.
Jieru:	This store doesn't sell overcoats. Let's go to another store. Macy's has many overcoats. Let's go there.
Dijia:	All right. Let's go.
Jieru:	Let's go.

11

Pronunciation Plaza
– The place you come to practice sounds and tones

(Go to 🔘 12-1 to hear:)

Tones in Songs

Similar to the way tones are subject to change in the flow of nature speech, even more liberty is taken with tones sung in songs. You may hear some tones ignored, or changed to create a more flowing tune. Here is one of China's most famous folk songs. It's a good one to memorize, since everyone is familiar with this tune and it is bound to come up:

好一朵美丽的茉莉花	Hǎo yì duǒ měilì de mòlìhuā
好一朵美丽的茉莉花	Hǎo yì duǒ měilì de mòlìhuā
芬芳美丽满枝桠	Fēnfāng měilì mǎn zhī yā
又香又白人人夸	Yòu xiāng yòu bái rén rén kuā
让我来将你摘下	Ràng wǒ lái jiāng nǐ zhāixià
送给别人家	Sòng gěi biéren jiā
茉莉花呀茉莉花	Mòlìhuā ya mòlìhuā

Translation:

So many beautiful jasmine flowers!
So many beautiful jasmine flowers!
Perfumed and lovely vines,
"so fragrant and white" people cheer.
Allow me to pluck you carefully;
And give you to others to enjoy.
Jasmine flower, oh, jasmine flower!

Your Last Pronunciation Section! - (12-2)

Dear Learner,

This is your last pronunciation section for *Chit-Chat Chinese*. We have covered all the sounds from your *pinyin* chart, all the tones and all possible tone combinations; we have focused and worked on the finer points of the more difficult sounds of Mandarin and, finally, we have looked at the cadence of the language in natural speech and in songs. You are probably in pretty good shape. Now, here is my last piece of advice: Try to <u>really</u> nail the most common words that you will use.

You are inevitably going to be saying "Měiguó" and "Měiguórén" one million times. You are without a doubt going to be talking about "xué Zhōngwén" and where you do it. These are your gateway words that will let your listener know whether you have a command of the language or not. If you are able to (more or less) nail these, you have given your listener confidence that they can continue in Mandarin and have just made "breaking the ice" that much easier. Besides universally common words and phrases, you should also work on pronouncing accurately words and phrases common to your life: your profession, hobbies, interests, habits, etc.

Here is a list of universally common words you should try to nail. I have left blank spots for you to add words specific to your life that you know you will need to say accurately. I recommend listening to the audio, and then working with a native speaker (be it a Chinese tutor, language exchange partner, friend or spouse) and really get these words and the words you add right.

Words to "Nail"

Word 1
Měiguó — Notice this 3rd and 2nd tone combination. The 3rd tone dips down and flows into the lower 2nd tone, without stopping.

Example: 我住在美国。

Wǒ zhù zài Měiguó.

Word 2
Zhōngguó — Make sure you say "zhōng" as a nice, clear first tone. Also be sure that "retroflexive" sound of the initial "zh-" is there, so it doesn't sound like you are pronouncing it as an English "j" (making it sound like "jong.")

Example: 我喜欢中国。

Wǒ xǐhuan Zhōngguó.

Word 3

Zhōngwén — Again, make sure your "zh-" doesn't sound like an English "j," and that you are saying a clear first tone for "zhōng."

Example: 我会说一点儿中文。

Wǒ huì shuō yìdiǎnr Zhōngwén.

Word 4

jiào — With this word many Western speakers fail to include the "i" sound, and make it sound more like "jao" or "zhao." Remember to get each vowel sound in there, as in "j-ee-aow."

Example: 你叫什么名字?

Nǐ jiào shénme míngzi?

Word 5

Nǐ hǎo — In this word you will need to nail your 2nd and 3rd tone combination. Your "nǐ" should rise up and then, when you pronounce "hǎo," dip deeply to capture the 3rd tone.

Example: 你好。我叫Bob。

Nǐ hǎo. Wǒ jiào Bob.

Word 6

xièxie — Make sure to get in each vowel sound for both the "i" and "e" so it sounds like "sh-ee-yea." You should also take note that the second "xie" is a neutral tone.

Example: 很谢谢你。

Hěn xièxie nǐ.

Word 7

rén — This initial "r-" is tough. Listen to the audio and work on trying replicate what you hear. The tongue should lightly touch the roof of your mouth (unlike the English "r.")

12

253

Example: 你是中国人吗？

Nǐ shì Zhōngguórén ma?

Word 8

xué — Don't forget any "u" that follows an intial "x-" should have an umlauted sound.

Example: 你在哪儿学中文？

Nǐ zài nǎr xué Zhōngwén?

Word 9

yào — There is a temptation for English speakers to soften this 4th tone, so it doesn't sound like a rude command - as in, "I want that!". Unfortunately, if you do this, it can come off sounding like a 3rd tone, which means "to bite," or "I bite that." As counter intuitive as it may feel to say "want" with a sharp 4th tone, it is the way you will have to say it for it to be correct.

Example: 我要吃鸡肉。

Wǒ yào chī jīròu.

Word 10

búyòng kèqi — If you are polite, you will be saying this often. To get this one right, remember that "bù" becomes a 2nd tone when followed by a 4th tone. "Kè" is a 4th tone and "qi" is neutral.

Example: 请不用客气。

Qǐng búyòng kèqi

Your specific words:

_____

_____

_____

_____

_____

12

Word Workshop

– The place you come to learn new words and phrases

(Go to 🔘 12-3 to hear:)

Transportation

Friendly Reminder of transportation words you've already learned:

汽车
qìchē
(car)

开车
kāichē
(to drive a car)

火车
huǒchē
(train)

坐火车
zuò huǒchē
(to take a train, to ride a train)

公共汽车
gōnggòng qìchē
(bus)

坐公共汽车
zuò gōnggòng qìchē
(to ride a bus)

New words:

自行车
zìxíngchē
(bicycle)

骑自行车
qí zìxíngchē
(to ride a bicycle)

出租车
chūzūchē
(taxi)

坐出租车
zuò chūzūchē ←   *out rent chart*
(to ride a taxi)

摩托车
mótuōchē
(motorcycle)

骑摩托车
qí mótuōchē   *or kai passenger would say*
(to ride a motorcycle)   *zuo*

船
chuán
(boat)

坐船
zuò chuán
(to ride on a boat, to take a boat)

12

飞机　　　　坐飞机　　*kāi*
fēijī　　　　zuò fēijī
(airplane)　　(to ride an airplane, to take a plane)

地铁　　　　坐地铁
dìtiě　　　　zuò dìtiě
(subway, metro)　　(to ride the subway, to ride the metro)

走　　　　　走路
zǒu　　　　zǒulù
(to walk)　　(to walk [on the road])

Supplementary Vocabulary

位子　　　　坐下　　　　休息
wèizi　　　　zuòxià　　　xiūxi
(seat)　　　(to sit down)　　(to rest, to take a break)

到 ____(place)____ 去　　　　Example: 我要到中国去。
dào ____(place)____ qù　　　　Wǒ yào dào Zhōngguó qù.
(to go [somewhere])　　　　　(I want to go to China.)

从 ____(place)____ 到 ____(place)____
cóng ____(place)____ dào ____(place)____
(from [place] to [place])

从 ____(place / country)____ 来的　　Example: 我从美国来的。
cóng (place / country) lái de　　　　Wǒ cóng Měiguó lái de.
(to come from [a place / country])　　(I am from the U.S.)

你从哪儿来的？
Nǐ cóng nǎr lái de?
(Where are you from?)

过去　　　　　　　　　危险
guòqù　　　　　　　　wēixiǎn
(to get somewhere, to pass by)　　(dangerous)

麻烦
máfan
(troublesome, "a pain")

无聊
wúliáo
(boring)

方便
fāngbiàn
(convenient)

郊外
jiāowài
(suburbs, outskirts [of a city])

安静
ānjìng
(peaceful, quiet)

 Grammar Grove
– The place you come to learn about structure

Expressing Habits

You've learned the word "huì" to describe actions that will occur in the future much like the way we use "will" in English. Likewise, "huì" can mean "would" for the past and describe habits or things someone would do in the past. Further, you may use it to describe habits in the present.

会
huì
(will, would, [used to described habits], to know)

他平常早上不会吃早饭。

Tā píngcháng zǎoshang bú huì chī zǎofàn.

(In the morning he usually doesn't eat breakfast.)

我以前去工作会坐公共汽车，可是现在我开车去。

Wǒ yǐqián qù gōngzuò huì zuò gōnggòng qìchē, kěshì xiànzài wǒ kāichē qù.

(Before I used to take the bus to work, but now I drive there.)

12

257

你每天会打电话给你妈妈吗？

Nǐ měitiān huì dǎ diànhuà gěi nǐ māma ma?
(Do you call your mother every day?)

我上大学的时候会骑自行车去学校。

Wǒ shàng dàxué de shíhou huì qí zìxíngchē qù xuéxiào.
(When I was in college I used to ride a bike to school.)

Chit-Chat Café
– The place you come to practice speaking

Module 12.1 - (🔘 12-4) / English translation on **Page 282**
Let's practice the transportation words you've learned and new grammatical structures by reading about the author's (my) life. Here is a monologue about my previous and present habits regarding transportation:

　　我住在旧金山的时候每天坐公共汽车去工作，有的时候也会走路或是骑自行车过去。现在我不住旧金山，我住在旧金山的郊外，所以我每天开车一个小时到旧金山去。偶尔我累的时候会坐火车。以前我住旧金山的时候坐公共汽车去工作很方便，现在要开车有一点儿麻烦，可是没有关系，因为我开车的时候可以听音乐或是打电话给我朋友们，所以不会觉得很无聊。五年前我住在纽约的时候每天都坐地铁去上班。我觉得那真麻烦！从我Brooklyn的家到Manhattan去工作要四十五分钟。平常因为人很多所以没有位子，如果有位子我会坐下，一边休息一边看书，可是我还是觉得坐地铁很不方便。我住纽约的时候也常常坐出租车，每次在饭馆跟朋友们吃饭以后我们会坐出租车回家。在旧金山我偶尔也会坐出租车。旧金山的出租车比纽约贵，所以我在旧金山不常坐。以前我住台湾的时候我会骑摩托车去工作。骑摩托车很方便也很好玩儿，可是有一点儿危险，所以现在我不常骑摩托车。我在台湾的时候，有的时候会坐船从台湾到香港。我很喜欢坐船，坐船又安静又舒服。我不太喜欢坐飞机，我觉得坐飞机很不舒服，可是很方便。

Wǒ zhù zài Jiùjīnshān de shíhou měitiān zuò gōnggòng qìchē qù gōngzuò, yǒude shíhou yě huì zǒulù huòshi qí zìxíngchē guòqù. Xiànzài wǒ bú zhù Jiùjīnshān, wǒ zhù zài Jiùjīnshān de jiāowài, suǒyǐ wǒ měitiān kāichē yí ge xiǎoshí dào Jiùjīnshān qù. Ǒu'ěr wǒ lèi de shíhou huì zuò huǒchē. Yǐqián wǒ zhù Jiùjīnshān de shíhou zuò gōnggòng qìchē qù gōngzuò hěn fāngbiàn, xiànzài yào kāichē yǒu yìdiǎnr máfan, kěshì méiyǒu guānxi, yīnwèi wǒ kāichē de shíhou kěyǐ tīng yīnyuè huòshi dǎ diànhuà gěi wǒ péngyoumen, suǒyǐ bú huì juéde hěn wúliáo. Wǔ nián qián wǒ zhù zài Niǔyuē de shíhou měitiān dōu zuò dìtiě qù shàngbān. Wǒ juéde nà zhēn máfan! Cóng wǒ Brooklyn de jiā dào Manhattan qù gōngzuò yào sìshíwǔ fēnzhōng. Píngcháng yīnwèi rén hěn duō suǒyǐ méiyǒu wèizi, rúguǒ yǒu wèizi wǒ huì zuòxià, yìbiān xiūxi yìbiān kàn shū, kěshì wǒ háishi juéde zuò dìtiě hěn bù fāngbiàn. Wǒ zhù Niǔyuē de shíhou yě chángcháng zuò chūzūchē, měi cì zài fànguǎn gēn péngyoumen chīfàn yǐhòu wǒmen huì zuò chūzūchē huíjiā. Zài Jiùjīnshān wǒ ǒu'ěr yě huì zuò chūzūchē. Jiùjīnshān de chūzūchē bǐ Niǔyuē guì, suǒyǐ wǒ zài Jiùjīnshān bù cháng zuò. Yǐqián wǒ zhù Táiwān de shíhou wǒ huì qí mótuōchē qù gōngzuò. Qí mótuōchē hěn fāngbiàn yě hěn hǎowánr, kěshì yǒu yìdiǎnr wēixiǎn, suǒyǐ xiànzài wǒ bù cháng qí mótuōchē. Wǒ zài Táiwān de shíhou, yǒude shíhou huì zuò chuán cóng Táiwān dào Xiānggǎng. Wǒ hěn xǐhuan zuò chuán, zuò chuán yòu ānjìng yòu shūfu. Wǒ bú tài xǐhuan zuò fēijī, wǒ juéde zuò fēijī hěn bù shūfu, kěshì hěn fāngbiàn.

12

Chit-Chat Practice 12.1

Answer the following questions about the above monologue. You can find the correct answers in **Appendix IV**:

1. Q: 她住在旧金山的时候怎么去工作？
   Tā zhù zài Jiùjīnshān de shíhou zěnme qù gōngzuò?

   A: Tā zhù zài Jiùjīnshān de shíhou píngchang zuò gōnggòng qìchē

2. Q: 她觉得坐旧金山的公共汽车方便吗？
   Tā juéde zuò Jiùjīnshān de gōnggòng qìchē fāngbiàn ma?

   A: Tā juéde zuò Jiùjīnshān de gōnggòng qìchē hěn fāngbian.

3. Q: 她为什么不觉得开车很无聊？
   Tā wèishénme bù juéde kāichē hěn wúliáo?

   A: Yīnwei tā kěyǐ tīng yīnyue huoshi da diànhua gěi pengyoumen.

4. Q: 她在纽约坐地铁方不方便？为什么？
   Tā zài Niǔyuē zuò dìtiě fāng bù fāngbiàn? Wèishénme?

   A: Bù fāngbiàn, cáng Brooklyn dào Manhattan hěn jiǔ. ?

5. Q: 地铁有位子的时候她会做什么？
   Dìtiě yǒu wèizi de shíhou tā huì zuò shénme?

   A: Dìtiě yǒu wèizi de shíhou tā zuò kan shū.

6. Q: 她跟朋友们在纽约的饭馆吃饭以后怎么回家？
   Tā gēn péngyoumen zài Niǔyuē de fànguǎn chīfàn yǐhòu zěnme huíjiā?

   A: Tā gēn tā de pengyoumen zuò chūzūchē.

7. Q: 为什么她在旧金山的时候不常坐出租车?
   Wèishénme tā zài Jiùjīnshān de shíhou bù cháng zuò chūzūchē?

   A: Zai Jiùjīnshān zuò chūzūchē hěn guì.

8. Q: 她觉得骑摩托车怎么样?
   Tā juéde qí mótuōchē zěnmeyàng?

   A: Wǒ zhǐ zuò mótuōchē, cóng bù qí *yǒu* Yidiǎr wēixiǎr zài Jian... zuò yǒu zuò zài. Jiǎnpūzhài.

9. Q: 她为什么喜欢坐船?
   Tā wèishénme xǐhuan zuò chuán?

   A: Zuò chuán yòu ānjìng yòu shūfu.

10. Q: 她觉得坐飞机怎么样?
    Tā juéde zuò fēijī zěnmeyàng?

    A: Tā bù xǐhuan, kěshì tā *juéde* ~~xiǎng~~ hěn fāngbiàn.

Word Workshop
– The place you come to learn new words and phrases

(Go to 🔘 12-5 to hear:)

libian – inside
waibian – outside

Directional Words

往
wǎng
(to, toward)

side
yi(bian) yibian
(at the same time)

左	左拐	往左拐
zuǒ	zuǒ guǎi	wǎng zuǒ guǎi
(left)	(turn left)	(turn to the left)

12

261

右
yòu
(right)

右拐
yòu guǎi
(turn right)

往右拐
wǎng yòu guǎi
(turn to the right)

直
zhí
(straight)

直走
zhí zǒu
(go straight)/*keep going*
(LIT: straight, walk)

附近 /*yuan* *far*
fùjìn
(nearby, in the vicinity)

_____ (place) 的附近
_____ (place) de fùjìn
(nearby [someplace], in the vicinity of [a place])

请问，到 _____ (place) 怎么走？
Qǐngwèn, dào _____ (place) zěnme zǒu?
(Excuse me, how to you get to [place]?)

上车
shàngchē
(get on / into [train, plane, bus, etc.])

下车
xiàchē
(get off / out of [train, plane, bus, etc.])

Supplementary Vocabulary

太好了!
Tài hǎo le!
("That's great!")
(LIT: too, good, "le")

好好儿
~~hǎohāor~~
(well)

告诉
gàosu
(to tell, to inform)
Here is an expression used when someone is leaving and saying goodbye. It should

be said by the person staying, to the person who is leaving. It literally means "depart slowly," and is meant to express the person's desire that the other person not depart so soon:

慢走

mànzǒu
("Take care!"; "Goodbye!"; "Take it easy!")
(LIT: slowly, walk)

地方

dìfang — *not singular*
(a place)

故宫 → *like old, but more "lost", long ago, don't use it*
Gùgōng
(The Forbidden City, The palace Museum, former Chinese imperial palace)

天安门 ← *door/gate*
Tiān'ānmén
(Tiananmen Square)   *Guǎngchǎng — Square*
(LIT: heavenly, peaceful, gate)

Grammar Grove
– The place you come to learn about structure

An introduction to a new "de"

You already know one "de" to express possession, as in "wǒ de (mine)." The character for that "de" is this: 的. The new "de" you are going to learn is pronounced exactly the same, and is a neutral tone as well, but is written differently and has a different grammatical function. Here is how this new "de" is written:

得

de

(a descriptive complement used to indicate the manner, result or potential of a verb)

12

This new "de" (得), when placed after a verb, creates an adverbial phrase or clause. Just as we need to add an "ly" to the adjective in an English adverbial sentence (e.g. walk quickly, speak slowly), you will need to place this "de" between the verb and the adjective in Chinese:

verb + de (得) + adjective

Example verb pairings:

说得

shuō de
(the manner in which something is spoken)

学得

xué de
(the manner in which something is studied or learned)

走得

zǒu de
(the manner in which one walks)

Example sentences:

他走得很慢。

Tā zǒu de hěn màn.
(He walks slowly.)

他的中文说得很好。

Tā de Zhōngwén shuō de hěn hǎo.
(He speaks Chinese very well.)

老师很好，所以学生们学得很快。

Lǎoshī hěn hǎo, suǒyǐ xuéshengmen xué de hěn kuài.
(The teacher is good; therefore, the students learn quickly).

A new use of "le (了)"

You've learned one use of "le" so far, that to express something that was completed in the past. And, now for a new usage: "Le" can also be used to express the present perfect, as in "I <u>have been</u> there;" "I <u>have studied</u> for 2 years," etc. In other words, it can be used to express something begun in the past and continuing until the present. "Le" should be placed after the time word or time-question word (e.g. how long, when, since when, etc.)

Declarative sentence:

Subject + (location) + action + time word + le (了).

Interrogative sentence:

Subject + (location) + action + time-questions word + le (了)?

Examples:

我在这儿工作三年了。

Wǒ zài zhèr gōngzuò sān nián le.

(I <u>have</u> worked here for 3 years.)

你中文学多久了?

Nǐ Zhōngwén xué duō jiǔ le?

(How long <u>have</u> you studied Chinese?)

他不吃肉五年了。

Tā bù chī ròu wǔ nián le.

(He <u>hasn't</u> eaten meat in five years.)

你住美国多久了?

Nǐ zhù Měiguó duō jiǔ le?

(How long <u>have</u> you lived in the U.S.?)

12

Chit-Chat Café
– The place you come to practice speaking

Module 12.2 - (🔘 12-6) / English translation on Page 283

Picture this: Judy is in Beijing doing an immersion program. She meets a man on the bus, named Jian'an and asks him how to get to the Forbidden City.

Jian'an:	Excuse me, are you American?	Jian'an:	Excuse me, are you American?
Judy:	Yes, I am. Wǒ huì shuō Zhōngwén.	Judy:	Yes, I am. 我会说中文。
Jian'an:	Tài hǎo le! Nǐ zài nǎr xué Zhōngwén?	Jian'an:	太好了！你在哪儿学中文？
Judy:	Wǒ zài Běijīng Dàxué xué.	Judy:	我在北京大学学。
Jian'an:	Nǐ xué duō jiǔ le?	Jian'an:	你学多久了？
Judy:	Wǒ xué yì nián le.	Judy:	我学一年了。
Jian'an:	Nǐ shuō de hěn hǎo.	Jian'an:	你说得很好。
Judy:	Nǎli nǎli.	Judy:	哪里哪里。
Jian'an:	Zhēn de. Nǐ de Zhōngwén bǐ wǒ de Yīngwén hǎo. Wǒ xuéle sì nián de Yīngwén, kěshì xué de bù hǎo. Shàngkè de shíhou lǎoshī yě chángcháng gēn wǒmen shuō Zhōngwén. Suǒyǐ wǒ huì kàn Yīngwén, kěshì zhǐ huì shuō yìdiǎnr.	Jian'an:	真的。你的中文比我的英文好。我学了四年的英文，可是学得不好。上课的时候老师也常常跟我们说中文。所以我会看英文，可是只会说一点儿。
Judy:	Wǒ yǐqián zài Měiguó xué Zhōngwén yě xué de bù	Judy:	我以前在美国学中文也学得不好。老师教

hǎo. Lǎoshī jiāo de hěn hǎo, kěshì wǒ méiyǒu shíjiān hǎohāor xué. Xiànzài zài Běijīng wǒ měitiān zǎoshang shàngkè sì ge xiǎoshí, suǒyǐ xiànzài xué de kuài yìdiǎnr.	得很好，可是我没有时间好好儿学。现在在北京我每天早上上课四个小时，所以现在学得快一点儿。
Jian'an: Nǐ juéde Zhōngwén nán bù nán xué?	Jian'an: 你觉得中文难不难学？
Judy: Zhōngwén yǒu yìdiǎnr nán, kěshì wǒ hěn xǐhuan xué.	Judy: 中文有一点儿难，可是我很喜欢学。
Jian'an: Nǐ xiànzài qù shàngkè ma?	Jian'an: 你现在去上课吗？
Judy: Bú shì, wǒ xiànzài qù wánr, qù guàngjiē. Wǒ yě xiǎng qù Gùgōng, kěshì wǒ bù zhīdao zěnme zǒu.	Judy: 不是，我现在去玩儿，去逛街。我也想去故宫，可是我不知道怎么走。
Jian'an: Méiyǒu wèntí. Nǐ gēn wǒ yìqǐ, xiàchē wǒ huì gàosu nǐ zěnme zǒu.	Jian'an: 没有问题。你跟我一起，下车我会告诉你怎么走。
Judy: Tài xièxie nǐ le.	Judy: 太谢谢你了。
Jian'an: Búyòng kèqi. Wǒ zài Gùgōng de fùjìn xiàchē. Wǒ gōngzuò de dìfang jiù zài Gùgōng de fùjìn, suǒyǐ hěn fāngbiàn.	Jian'an: 不用客气。我在故宫的附近下车。我工作的地方就在故宫的附近，所以很方便。

12

Judy:	Nǐ xiànzài qù gōngzuò ma?	Judy:	你现在去工作吗？
Jian'an:	Duì, wǒ xiàwǔ hé wǎnshang shàngbān.	Jian'an:	对，我下午和晚上上班。
Judy:	Wǒmen zài nǎr xiàchē?	Judy:	我们在哪儿下车？
Jian'an:	Zhèr jiù shì. Wǒmen xiàchē ba.	Jian'an:	这儿就是。我们下车吧。
	(They get off the bus.)		*(They get off the bus.)*
Judy:	Hǎo, xiànzài dào Gùgōng zěnme zǒu?	Judy:	好，现在到故宫怎么走？
Jian'an:	Nǐ wǎng qián zǒu, zài Tiān'ānmén wǎng yòu guǎi. Gùgōng jiù zài nàr.	Jian'an:	你往前走，在天安门往右拐。故宫就在那儿。
Judy:	Xièxie nǐ.	Judy:	谢谢你。
Jian'an:	Búyòng kèqi. Nǐ mànzǒu.	Jian'an:	不用客气。你慢走。

Chit-Chat Practice 12.2

Answer the following questions about the above dialogue. Answer in complete sentences with as much detail as possible. You can find example answers in **Appendix IV**:

1. Q: Judy 在哪儿学中文？
   Judy zài nǎr xué Zhōngwén?

   A: ~~Her~~ zài Běijīng Dìxué xué.

2. Q: 她学多久了？
   Tā xué duō jiǔ le?

   A: Tā xué yì nián le.

3. Q: 她以前为什么没有学得很好?

Tā yǐqián wèishénme méiyǒu xué de hěn hǎo?

A: Tā méiyǒu xué de hěn hǎo yīnwei tā méiyǒu shíjīn.

4. Q: 她现在在北京学得怎么样?

Tā xiànzài zài Běijīng xué de zěnmeyàng?

A: Zài Běijīng, tā xué miàn~ sì ge xiǎoshí.

5. Q: 建安学了四年的英文, 可是他为什么还是说得不好?

?. (still) Jiàn'ān xuéle sì nián de Yīngwén, kěshì tā wèishénme háishi shuō de bù hǎo?

A: Zài Yīngwén kè de shíhou, tā de lǎoshī yě cháng~ b.kdexveshy chángcháng shuō Zhōngwen.

6. Q: 建安的英文比Judy的中文好吗?

Jiàn'ān de Yīngwén bǐ Judy de Zhōngwén hǎo ma?

A: Judy de Zhōngwen bǐ Jiàn'ān de Yīngwén hǎo.

7. Q: Judy想去哪儿?

Judy xiǎng qù nǎr?

A: Judy xiǎng ~~~~~ qù Gùgōng.

8. Q: 建安工作的地方在哪儿?

Jiàn'ān gōngzuò de dìfang zài nǎr?

A: Jiàn'ān gōngzuò de dìfang fùjìn Gùgōng

9. Q: 建安什么时候工作?

Jiàn'ān shénme shíhou gōngzuò?

A: Jiàn'ān xiàwǔ he wǎnshg ~~gōngzuò~~ shàngbān.

10. Q: 他们为什么一起下车?

Tāmen wèishénme yìqǐ xiàchē?

A: Yīnwèi Jiàn'ān de gōngzuò *zài* fùjìn Gùgōng, *de fùjìn*, *le* Judy qù Gùgōng. qù.

11. Q: Judy到故宫要怎么走?

Judy dào Gùgōng yào zěnme zǒu?

A: Tā wǎng qián zǒu, zài Tiān'ān mén wǎng yòu guǎi.

Word Workshop
– The place you come to learn new words and phrases

(Go to 🔘 12-7 to hear:)

Work & Professions

公司	家	一家公司
gōngsī	jiā	yì jiā gōngsī
(company)	(measure word for company)	a company

to deal with →

办公室
bàngōngshì
(office)

生意人
shēngyirén
(business man / woman)

律师
lǜshī
(lawyer)

教授 *to give*
jiàoshòu
(professor)

医生　　　　　　中医　　　　　　　西医
yīshēng　　　　　zhōngyī　　　　　　xīyī
(doctor)　　　　　(Chinese doctor)　　(Western doctor)

护士
hùshi
(nurse)

艺术家　　　　　作家　　　　　　　音乐家　(rock n' roll)
art yìshùjiā　　　 zuòjiā　　　　　　yīnyuèjiā　yaogun
(artist)　　　　　(author, writer)　　(musician)　gaxing
　　　　　　　　　　　　　　　　　　　　　　　(singer)
司机　　　　　　　　　　　　　　　shuō chun
sījī　Shīfù (Sir)but not　　　　　(hip hop)
(driver [taxi, truck, etc])　for leaders)　　　star

演员　　　　　　运动员　　　　　　服务员
yǎnyuán　　　　　yùndòngyuán　　　　fúwùyuán
(actor / actress)　(athlete)　　　　　(waiter / waitress)

农民
nóngmín
(farmer)

会计师　kuàjì is accountant
kuàijìshī　CPA
(accountant)

你做什么工作?
Nǐ zuò shénme gōngzuò?
(What kind of work do you do?)

If your profession is not shown above, you can use this online English-Chinese
dictionary to look it up: www.mdbg.net

12

Chit-Chat Café
– *The place you come to practice speaking*

Module 12.3 - (12-8)

Use the picture prompts below to ask what each person does in the picture. Here is the first one:

Example:

1. Q: Tā zuò shénme gōngzuò? (What does he / she do?)

   A: Tā shì lǎoshī. (She is a teacher.)

13. 　　14. 　　15. 　　16.

Check your answers in **Appendix IV**.

 Word Workshop

　　– *The place you come to learn new words and phrases*

(Go to 🔘 12-9 to hear:)

Formally Asking and Telling Names

- When meeting someone more formally, there is a politer way to ask the person's name than just "Nǐ jiào shénme míngzi?". You should ask the person (literally) for their "noble surname." Here is how to do that:

请问您贵姓?

Qǐngwèn nín guì xìng?

(Excuse me, may I ask your last name?)

(LIT: excuse me, your, noble, surname)

- Then, when answering the above question, you should offer both your last name (surname) and given name, like so:

我姓 ___(surname)___ 叫 ___(given name)___

Wǒ xìng ___(surname)___ jiào ___(given name)___

(My last name is [surname], and my first name is [given name].)

(LIT: my, surname, _____, called, _____)

- The next thing in Chinese that is then assessed is what are the actual characters in your name. So, the person will then ask you "which one?":

哪一个 ___(character)___ ?

Nǎ yí ge ___(character)___ ?

(Which one [character]?)

12

- Since there are many homophones (words that sound alike) in Chinese, the new acquaintance will want to know which of the characters the person has for his or her name. For example, if the person says his or her last name is "Wang," the questioner will ask "Which Wang is it?". Here is how to do that:

哪一个王?

Nǎ yí ge Wáng?

(Which "Wang" is it?)

- The person being questioned then clarifies either by describing which character it is or by using a finger to mime writing the character on his or her hand. Here is what normally is said for people with the surname "Wang," the one that means king (keep in mind that there are other surnames pronounced "wang" that have other meanings):

三横的王

Sān héng de Wáng

(The "wang" with 3 horizontal lines in it)

(Note that Wang is written like so : 王)

- If you do not have a Chinese name, you may just use your English first and last name. Here is how I answer this question both for my English name and my Chinese name.

- Telling my English name:

我姓Meyer，叫Rachel。

Wǒ xìng Meyer, jiào Rachel.

(My last name is Meyer and my first Rachel.)

- Telling my Chinese name (with explanations of what characters it contains):

我中文姓梅叫洁如。梅花的梅，清洁的洁，如果的如。

Wǒ Zhōngwén xìng Méi jiào Jiérú. Méihuā de méi, qīngjié de jié, rúguǒ de rú.

(My Chinese surname is "Mei" and give name "Jieru." It's the "mei" from "plum blossom," the "jie" from "purity" and the "ru" from "if.")

- If you do get a Chinese name, the questioner will usually ask where you got it or who gave it to you:

取名字
qǔ míngzi
(to get a name, to be given a name)

谁取了你的中文名字?
Shéi qǔle nǐ de Zhōngwén míngzi?
(Who gave you your Chinese name?)

Supplementary Vocabulary

我很高兴认识你/您。
Wǒ hěn gāoxìng rènshi nǐ / nín.
(I am very happy to meet you [or formal "you"].)

请问，这个位子是空的吗?
Qǐngwèn, zhèige wèizi shì kōng de ma?
(Excuse me, is this seat empty?)

是的
shìde
(yes, that's right)

 ***Chit-Chat Café***
– The place you come to practice speaking

Module 12.4 - (12-10) / English translation on **Page 284**
Picture this: Margaret lives in China and is in Beijing getting on a bus when she meets Meiying.

Margaret: Qǐngwèn, zhèige wèizi shì kōng de ma?	Margaret: 请问，这个位子是空的吗?
Meiying: Shìde. Qǐng zuò.	Meiying: 是的。请坐。
Margaret: Xièxie. Qǐngwèn nín guì xìng?	Margaret: 谢谢。请问您贵姓?

Meiying: Wǒ xìng Wáng, jiào Méiyīng.	Meiying: 我姓王，叫梅英。
Margaret: Něige Wáng?	Margaret: 哪个王？
Meiying: Sān héng de Wáng, méihuā de méi, Yīngguó de yīng. Nín guì xìng?	Meiying: 三横的王，梅花的梅，英国的英。您贵姓？
Margaret: Wǒ xìng Gaines, jiào Margaret. Wǒ Zhōngwén xìng Gāo jiào Měizhōng.	Margaret: 我姓Gaines，叫Margaret。我中文姓高叫美中。
Meiying: Něige Gāo?	Meiying: 哪个高？
Margaret: Gāo ǎi de gāo, Měiguó de měi, Zhōngguó de zhōng.	Margaret: 高矮的高，美国的美，中国的中。
Meiying: Hěn gāoxìng rènshi nǐ.	Meiying: 很高兴认识你。
Margaret: Wǒ yě hěn gāoxìng rènshi nǐ.	Margaret: 我也很高兴认识你。
Meiying: Nǐ lái Zhōngguó duō jiǔ le?	Meiying: 你来中国多久了？
Margaret: Yì nián le.	Margaret: 一年了。
Meiying: Nǐ lái xué Zhōngwén ma?	Meiying: 你来学中文吗？
Margaret: Wǒ lái gōngzuò, kěshì wǒ yě xué Zhōngwén. Wǒ yìbiān xué yìbiān gōngzuò. Wǒ zǎoshang xué xiàwǔ gōngzuò.	Margaret: 我来工作，可是我也学中文。我一边学一边工作。我早上学下午工作。
Meiying: Nǐ zuò shénme gōngzuò?	Meiying: 你做什么工作？
Margaret: Wǒ shì shēngyirén. Nǐ ne? Nǐ zuò shénme gōngzuò?	Margaret: 我是生意人。你呢？你做什么工作？
Meiying: Wǒ shì lǜshī. Nǐ de gōngsī shì Měiguó gōngsī	Meiying: 我是律师。你的公司是美国公司还是中国

12

háishi Zhōngguó gōngsī?	公司？
Margaret: Shì yì jiā Měiguó gōngsī.	Margaret: 是一家美国公司。
Meiying: Nǐ de jiārén gēn nǐ yìqǐ lái ma?	Meiying: 你的家人跟你一起来吗？
Margaret: Duì, wǒ de xiānsheng hé liǎng ge háizi yě lái le.	Margaret: 对，我的先生和两个孩子也来了。
Meiying: Nǐ de háizimen yě huì shuō Zhōngwén ma?	Meiying: 你的孩子们也会说中文吗？
Margaret: Huì. Tāmen shuō de bǐ wǒ hǎo. Kěshì wǒ xiānsheng zhǐ huì shuō yìdiǎnr.	Margaret: 会。他们说得比我好。可是我先生只会说一点儿。
Meiying: Nǐ de háizimen jǐ suì?	Meiying: 你的孩子们几岁？
Margaret: Wǒ nǚ'ér liù suì, érzi sì suì.	Margaret: 我女儿六岁，儿子四岁。
Meiying: Ò, tāmen hěn xiǎo suǒyǐ xué de hěn kuài.	Meiying: 哦，他们很小所以学得很快。
Margaret: Duì, tāmen yě shàng Zhōngguó xuéxiào, suǒyǐ xué de hěn kuài. Nǐ yǒu méi yǒu háizi?	Margaret: 对，他们也上中国学校，所以学得很快。你有没有孩子？
Meiying: Yǒu, yí ge érzi. Tā yǐjīng èrshíbā suì le.	Meiying: 有，一个儿子。他已经二十八岁了。
Margaret: Tā zuò shénme gōngzuò?	Margaret: 他做什么工作？
Meiying: Tā shì yīshēng.	Meiying: 他是医生。
Margaret: Zhōngyī háishi xīyī?	Margaret: 中医还是西医？
Meiying: Tā shì xīyī, kěshì tā yě xué zhōngyī.	Meiying: 他是西医，可是他也学中医。
Margaret: Hěn yǒu yìsi.	Margaret: 很有意思。

12

277

Chit-Chat Practice 12.4

Pretend you are an American from Los Angeles in China doing a summer language program at Beijing University (Běijīng Dàxué). It is the end of the summer and you have been in China for 2 months. Including your American studies, you have been studying Chinese for a total of 3 years. You are a 29-year-old actress, have no children, and you don't find learning Chinese difficult. Now answer the following questions.

1. Q: 请问，您贵姓？
   Qǐngwèn, nín guì xìng?

   A: Wǒ míngz Xìng Hilton jiào Paris.

2. Q: 你有没有中文名字？
   Nǐ yǒu méiyǒu Zhōngwén míngzi?

   A: Méi Yǒu, wǒ míngzi jiào Hǎokan jiào Piàoliang.

3. Q: 你来中国工作吗？
   Nǐ lái Zhōngguó gōngzuò ma?

   A: Bú duì Měi duì, wǒ lái xue Zhōngwen.

4. Q: 你在哪儿学中文？
   Nǐ zài nǎr xué Zhōngwén?

   A: Zài Běijīng Dàxué.

5. Q: 你来中国多久了？
   Nǐ lái Zhōngguó duō jiǔ le?

   A: Wǒ zài Zhōngguó liǎng yue le.

6. Q: 你学中文多久了？
   Nǐ xué Zhōngwén duō jiǔ le?

   A: Wǒ xué Zhōngwén sān niánle.

7. Q: 你住在美国哪儿?

   Nǐ zhù zài Měiguó nǎr?

   A: Wǒ zhù zài Luòshānjī.

8. Q: 你在美国做什么工作?

   Nǐ zài Měiguó zuò shénme gōngzuò?

   A: Wǒ jiu shi tuì huǒ yǎn yuán.

9. Q: 你几岁?

   Nǐ jǐ suì?

   A: Wǒ yǒu èrshíjiǔ nian.

10. Q: 你有没有孩子?

    Ní yǒu méiyǒu háizi?

    A: Méi yǒu huìzi... keshi wǒ hen lǚxíng.

11. Q: 中文难不难学?

    Zhōngwén nán bù nán xué?

    A: Zhōngwén hěn róngyi!

Check your answers in **Appendix IV**.

Culture Corner
– The place you come to learn more than just language

The "Wrong" Trap

While living in Taiwan and traveling through China a popular topic of conversation for us "out-of-country people (wàiguórén)," or foreigners, was how we were experiencing Chinese culture. There was a frequent exchange of anecdotes about our daily encounters and observations, both out of an interest and out of a need to sort through the cross-cultural challenges we were going through. Going through my own cross-cultural journey was an amazing experience that broadened my mind and

12

changed my worldview. Some challenges were overwhelming, and others difficult to understand or accept. However, overall it was an enjoyable and fulfilling experience.

At the time, I also would bump into the type of foreigner who was not having such a great time in this process. Their response was often to pass a value judgment on what they saw happening, typically coming to the conclusion that "It's just wrong." I heard this word many times from foreigners, describing situations that just did not make sense to them, coming to the conclusion that therefore it was "wrong." This is what I call "The Wrong Trap"; as soon as one begins to see a culture different from one's own through a prism of "right and wrong," one then will cease to be able to understand and learn. And, even worse yet, the person will miss all the fun.

The shock, the challenge is the fun part. I never cease to learn something new or be surprised by something I would not have expected in Chinese culture and its many facets. Take my last trip to China: I was in the countryside of Jiangxi Province with my sister and brother-in-law, accompanying them on the trip to adopt their daughter. My sister was back in the hotel room taking care of her newly adopted daughter, while I, along with several adoptive parents, took a trip to see the orphanage. Approaching the front gates I could feel butterflies in my stomach with anxious nerves to see where my niece had been cared for the 7 months before I met her. Emotions were rising in me as a plump, elderly woman with a big smile opened the gate and warmly waved. Then, without warning, our van was engulfed in the sound of gunfire from all angles. We all ducked for cover, trembling until we lifted our heads up to see through the smoke the friendly smile of the elderly lady who had clearly just thrown a round of firecrackers at our van. We all laughed at how startled we had become, and I explained to a few others that firecrackers are considered welcoming and thought to scare away evil spirits. After calming down and taking a tour of the orphanage, we piled back into the van and waved goodbye to the smiling woman, the picture of joviality. Waving goodbye, again without notice, the sneaky granny threw another round of fire at us making us all leap up in our seats. This time we laughed even harder. Then, I turned to my brother-in-law and said: "This is what I love about Chinese culture, just when I think I've got it figured out, it surprises me again." In order to enjoy learning about any culture different from our own it's important to have a sense of humor, remain open-minded and to stay away from "The Wrong Trap."

Overcoming Obstacles: Part 2

In the last Advice Alcove we discussed overcoming barriers, such as dealing with the fast talker and dealing with people who prefer to practice their English than to speak Chinese. Here are some other obstacles you may run into and how to get by them:

"Their English is Better Than My Chinese" Obstacle

People all over the world start learning English at a young age. Likely, the majority of educated Chinese people you run into have studied English much longer and more intensively than you have studied Mandarin. This means that even if you are not sailing in pirate waters, you may reach a point in your conversation or in friendship where speaking English just makes more sense. Of course, try to keep as many conversations you can in Chinese, but if it reaches a point where your insistence is getting in the way of you accomplishing something or getting to know someone, you may find you prefer to switch to English. If this happens, don't beat yourself up; just put your energy into creating more natural opportunities, where sticking to Chinese makes sense. Again, older people and children are great. Usually neither has an interest in working on their English and both likely have the time and patience. If you pick a sleek bar in Shanghai as your spot, you will find a lot of well-educated Chinese people and foreigners with whom you will probably end up speaking English. Seek out the people who will speak with you in Chinese. If you find a noodle shop whose owner likes to converse with you in Chinese, make that your daily lunch spot. If you are studying from outside China, seek virtual friendships over the Internet where you can join forums and meet people you can chat with in Chinese. The good news is this problem is mostly present in the beginning stages of learning. Once your speaking is at a solid intermediate level, you will find most people will naturally stick to Chinese.

The "No Time" Obstacle

If you are trying to learn Mandarin as a professional adult, you may not have the time to dedicate to your studies, or to do an immersion program in China. I have heard many times from Americans "you can't really learn unless you live there." And, it's simply not true. People accomplish the same feat all over the world with English, never having lived outside their country. I have seen the same accomplishment from Americans who have never lived in China: They do their lessons, they study with frequency, they use auxiliary materials to widen their skills, but, most importantly,

they make speaking Chinese a part of their regular life. They make friendships with language exchange partners, they go to language groups they find online, they frequent restaurants with staff who speak to them in Chinese, they volunteer their time to non-profits who help elderly Chinese immigrants, and many other creative ways you can incorporate speaking Chinese into your life.

Congratulations on your motivation and dedication to making it this far! As they say in Chinese: "ADD OIL!(jiāyóu)," or "GO FOR IT!"

加油！
jiāyóu

English Translation

Module 12.1

When I lived in San Francisco I took the bus to work every day. Sometimes I also would walk or ride a bike there. Now I don't live in San Francisco. I live in the suburbs of San Francisco, therefore every day I drive one hour to San Francisco. Occasionally, when I am tired, I will take the train. Before, when I lived in San Francisco, taking the bus was very convenient. Now, driving is bit of a pain. But, it's not a big deal, because when I drive I also can listen to music or call my friends on the phone, so I don't feel bored. Five years ago when I lived in New York City, every day I took the subway to work. I thought that was a real pain! From my Brooklyn home to get to work in Manhattan took 45 minutes. Usually, because there were many people there were no seats. If there was a seat, I would sit down, and rest while reading a book. However, I still think riding the subway is very inconvenient. When I lived in New York City, I also often took taxis. Every time after eating with friends in a restaurant, we would take taxis home. In San Francisco I occasionally also will take a taxi. San Francisco's taxis are more expensive than New York City's, so in San Francisco I don't often take them. Before, when I lived in Taiwan I would ride a motorcycle to work. Riding motorcycles is convenient and also fun, but are a bit dangerous. Therefore, now I don't often ride a motorcycle. When I was in Taiwan, sometimes I would ride a boat from Taiwan to Hong Kong. I really liked riding a boat. Riding was peaceful and comfortable. I don't like taking airplanes very much. I think taking airplanes is very uncomfortable, but it is very convenient.

Module 12.2

Jian'an:	Excuse me, are you American?
Judy:	Yes, I am. I know how to speak Mandarin.
Jian'an:	That's great. Where did you learn Mandarin?
Judy:	I am studying it at Beijing University.
Jian'an:	How long have you been studying it?
Judy:	I have been studying it for one year.
Jian'an:	You speak Mandarin very well.
Judy:	Not really.
Jian'an:	Really. Your Mandarin is better than my English. I studied English for 4 years, but I did't learn it well. During class the teacher would often speak in Chinese. So, I know how to read English, but I only know how to speak a little.
Judy:	Before, When I was studying Mandarin in the U.S., I wasn't learning well. The teacher taught very well, but I didn't have time to study. Now, in Beijing every morning I go to class for four hours, so now I am learning a bit faster.
Jian'an:	Do you think Mandarin is difficult to learn?
Judy:	Mandarin is a bit difficult to learn, but I like learning it a lot.
Jian'an:	Are you going to class right now?
Judy:	No, now I am going out to have fun, to go window-shopping. I also want to go see the Forbidden City, but I don't know how to get there.
Jian'an:	It's no problem. Get off the bus with me and I will tell you how to get there.
Judy:	Thank you very much.
Jian'an:	You're very welcome. I am getting off near the Forbidden City. My work place is right near the Forbidden City, so it is very convenient.
Judy:	Are you going to work now?
Jian'an:	Yes, I work in the afternoons and evenings.
Judy:	Where do we get off?
Jian'an:	Here it is. Let's get off.

(They go off the bus.)

12

Judy:	OK, now how do I get to the Forbidden City?
Jian'an:	You go straight ahead, at Tiananmen Square turn right. The Forbidden City is right there.
Judy:	Thank you.
Jian'an:	You're welcome. Take it easy.

Module 12.4

Margaret:	Excuse me, is this seat free?
Meiying:	Yes, it is. Please have a seat.
Margaret:	Thanks. Excuse me, may I ask your last name?
Meiying:	My last name is Wang and my first name is Meiying.
Margaret:	Which "wang"?
Meiying:	The "wang" with three horizontal lines in it; the "mei" of "plum blossom"; and the "ying" of "England." And, your surname?
Margaret:	My last name is Gaines and my first name is Margaret. My Chinese surname is "Gao" and "Meizhong" is my first name.
Meiying:	Which "gao"?
Margaret:	"Gao" as in "tall and short"; "mei" as in "America"; and "zhong" as in "China."
Meiying:	I am very happy to meet you.
Margaret:	I am also very happy to meet you.
Meiying:	How long have you been in China?
Margaret:	For a year.
Meiying:	Did you come to study Chinese?
Margaret:	I came for work, but I also study Chinese. I both study and work. In the morning I attend class and in the afternoon I work.
Meiying:	What work do you do?
Margaret:	I am a businesswoman. How about you? What work do you do?
Meiying:	I am a lawyer. Is your company an American company or a Chinese company?
Margaret:	It's an American company.
Meiying:	Did your family come with you?

12

Margaret:	Yes, my husband and my two children also came.
Meiying:	Do your children also know how to speak Chinese?
Margaret:	Yes. They speak better than me. But my husband only speaks a little.
Meiying:	How old are your children?
Margaret:	My daughter is six, and my son is four.
Meiying:	Oh, they are very small, so they will learn fast.
Margaret:	Right. They also go to a Chinese school, so they are learning quickly. Do you have children?
Meiying:	Yes, one son. He is already 28 years old.
Margaret:	What work does he do?
Meiying:	He is a doctor.
Meiying:	Is he a doctor of Chinese medicine or Western medicine?
Margaret:	He is a doctor of Western medicine, but he has also studied Chinese medicine.
Meiying:	That's so interesting.

12

NOTE

I. *Pinyin* Chart

	a					o			e					i										u									ü			
	a	ai	ao	an	ang	o	ong	ou	e	ei	en	eng	er	i	ia	iao	ie	iu	ian	iang	in	ing	iong	u	ua	uo	ui	uai	uan	un	uang	ueng	ü	üe	üan	ün
	a	ai	ao	an	ang	o		ou	e		en	eng	er	yi	ya	yao	ye	you	yan	yang	yin	ying	yong	wu	wa	wo	wei	wai	wan	wen	wang	weng	yu	yue	yuan	yun
b	ba	bai	bao	ban	bang	bo				bei	ben	beng		bi		biao	bie		bian		bin	bing		bu												
p	pa	pai	pao	pan	pang	po		pou		pei	pen	peng		pi		piao	pie		pian		pin	ping		pu												
m	ma	mai	mao	man	mang	mo		mou		mei	men	meng		mi		miao	mie	miu	mian		min	ming		mu												
f	fa			fan	fang	fo		fou		fei	fen	feng												fu												
d	da	dai	dao	dan	dang		dong	dou	de	dei	den	deng		di	dia	diao	die	diu	dian			ding		du		duo	dui		duan	dun						
t	ta	tai	tao	tan	tang		tong	tou	te	tei		teng		ti		tiao	tie		tian			ting		tu		tuo	tui		tuan	tun						
n	na	nai	nao	nan	nang		nong	nou	ne	nei	nen	neng		ni		niao	nie	niu	nian	niang	nin	ning		nu		nuo			nuan	nun			nü	nüe		
l	la	lai	lao	lan	lang		long	lou	le	lei		leng		li	lia	liao	lie	liu	lian	liang	lin	ling		lu		luo			luan	lun			lü	lüe		
z	za	zai	zao	zan	zang		zong	zou	ze	zei	zen	zeng		zi										zu		zuo	zui		zuan	zun						
c	ca	cai	cao	can	cang		cong	cou	ce		cen	ceng		ci										cu		cuo	cui		cuan	cun						
s	sa	sai	sao	san	sang		song	sou	se		sen	seng		si										su		suo	sui		suan	sun						
zh	zha	zhai	zhao	zhan	zhang		zhong	zhou	zhe	zhei	zhen	zheng		zhi										zhu	zhua	zhuo	zhui	zhuai	zhuan	zhun	zhuang					
ch	cha	chai	chao	chan	chang		chong	chou	che		chen	cheng		chi										chu	chua	chuo	chui	chuai	chuan	chun	chuang					
sh	sha	shai	shao	shan	shang			shou	she	shei	shen	sheng		shi										shu	shua	shuo	shui	shuai	shuan	shun	shuang					
r			rao	ran	rang		rong	rou	re		ren	reng		ri										ru	rua	ruo	rui		ruan	run						
j														ji	jia	jiao	jie	jiu	jian	jiang	jin	jing	jiong										ju	jue	juan	jun
q														qi	qia	qiao	qie	qiu	qian	qiang	qin	qing	qiong										qu	que	quan	qun
x														xi	xia	xiao	xie	xiu	xian	xiang	xin	xing	xiong										xu	xue	xuan	xun
g	ga	gai	gao	gan	gang		gong	gou	ge	gei	gen	geng												gu	gua	guo	gui	guai	guan	gun	guang					
k	ka	kai	kao	kan	kang		kong	kou	ke	kei	ken	keng												ku	kua	kuo	kui	kuai	kuan	kun	kuang					
h	ha	hai	hao	han	hang		hong	hou	he	hei	hen	heng												hu	hua	huo	hui	huai	huan	hun	huang					

Go to 🔊 0-1 to hear:

II. Vocabulary Index

(*Pinyin*-English)

Pinyin	Characters	English	Lesson
ǎi	矮	short	3
ānjìng	安静	peaceful, quiet	12
bā	八	8	5
Bālí	巴黎	Paris	4
Bāyuè	八月	August	6
bàba	爸爸	father	5
bàba māma	爸爸妈妈	parents	5
ba	吧	*"suggestion" particle*	8
báisè	白色	white	11
bān	班	work shift	7
bàn	半	half	6
bàngōngshì	办公室	office	12
bǎo	饱	full	8
bēi	杯	a glass, cup, M.W. for beverages (those served in glasses or cups)	10
Běijīng	北京	Beijing	4
Běijīngcài	北京菜	Beijing food	10
bèn	笨	stupid	3
biéde	别的	other	11
búcuò	不错	not bad, pretty good	11
bú kèqi	不客气	you're welcome	1
búyòng	不用	that's not necessary, there is no need	10
búyòng kèqi	不用客气	"You are very welcome."; "You are most welcome."	10, 11
bù	不	not	1
bù hǎo	不好	not good	1

bù hǎoyìsi	不好意思	embarrassed	8
bù xíng	不行	not possible, can't work	11
cài	菜	dish, food	10
càidān	菜单	menu	10
chāzi	叉子	fork	10
chá	茶	tea	7, 10
chángcháng	常常	often	9
chǎofàn	炒饭	fried rice	10
chǎomiàn	炒面	chow mein (fried noodles)	10
chènshān	衬衫	shirt	11
chéngsè	橙色	orange	11
chī	吃	to eat	7
chīfàn	吃饭	to eat	8, 9
chīsù	吃素	vegetarian	10
chī zǎofàn	吃早饭	to eat breakfast	9
chǒu	丑	ugly	3
chūzūchē	出租车	taxi	12
chuān	穿	to wear	11
chuānshàng	穿上	to put (a piece of clothing) on	11
chuān yīfu	穿衣服	to wear clothes	11
chuán	船	boat	12
cōngmíng	聪明	intelligent	3
cóng bù	从不	never	9
cóng (place) dào (place)	从(place)到(place)	from (place) to (place)	12
cóng (place) lái de	从(place)来的	to come from (a place / country)	12
dǎ diànhuà (gěi)	打电话(给)	to make a telephone call (to)	9, 11
dǎ diànnǎo	打电脑	to work on the computer	9
dà	大	big	3
dài	戴	to wear (caps, gloves, glasses, etc.)	11

dào (place) qù	到(place)去	to go (somewhere)	12
Déguó	德国	Germany	1
Déguórén	德国人	German (person)	1
Déwén	德文	German (language)	1
de	得	a descriptive complement used to indicate the manner, result or potential of a verb	12
_____ de fùjìn	_____的附近	nearby (someplace), in the vicinity of (a place)	12
de shíhou	的时候	when (for indicative sentence)	9
děng	等	to wait	11
děng yíxià	等一下	wait a moment	11
dìdi	弟弟	younger brother	5
dìfang	地方	a place	12
dìtiě	地铁	subway, metro	12
diǎn	点	o'clock	6
diǎncài	点菜	to order food	10
diànshì	电视	television	7
diànyǐng	电影	movie	7
dǐng	顶	top, apex, crown of the head, M.W. for hats	11
dòufu	豆腐	tofu	10
Dōngjīng	东京	Tokyo	4
dǒng	懂	understand	1
dōu	都	all, both, entirely	5, 10
dōu kěyǐ	都可以	anything is fine, either one is fine	10
duǎn kùzi	短裤子	shorts	11
duì	对	correct / right	4
duì a	对啊	that's right; you've got it right	11
duìbuqǐ	对不起	sorry	4
duō	多	many, much	11
duōshao	多少	how much, how many	11

duōshao qián	多少钱	how much money, how much (is it)	11
érzi	儿子	son	5
èr	二	2	5
è	饿	hungry	8
èrshí	二十	20	5
èrshíbā	二十八	28	5
èrshí'èr	二十二	22	5
èrshíjiǔ	二十九	29	5
èrshíliù	二十六	26	5
èrshíqī	二十七	27	5
èrshísān	二十三	23	5
èrshísì	二十四	24	5
èrshíwǔ	二十五	25	5
èrshíyī	二十一	21	5
Èryuè	二月	February	6
Fǎguó	法国	France	1
Fǎguófàn	法国饭	French food	7
Fǎguórén	法国人	French (person)	1
Fǎwén	法文	French (language)	1
fàn	饭	rice, meal	7, 10
fànguǎn	饭馆	restaurant	10
fāngbiàn	方便	convenient	12
fēijī	飞机	airplane	12
fēn	分	minute(s)	6
fēn	分	a cent (1/100 of a kuài)	11
fěnhóngsè	粉红色	pink	11
fúwùyuán	服务员	waiter / waitress	12
fùjìn	附近	nearby, in the vicinity	12
gānbēi	干杯	bottoms up, cheers	10
gāo	高	tall / high	3

gāoxìng	高兴	happy	8
gàosu	告诉	to tell, to inform	12
gēge	哥哥	older brother	5
ge	个	M.W. for saying the number of things	5
gēn	跟	with, and	8
gēn……yìqǐ	跟……一起	together	8
gōnggòng qìchē	公共汽车	bus	12
gōngsī	公司	company	12
Gùgōng	故宫	The Forbidden City, The palace Museum, former Chinese imperial palace	12
guān	关	to close	10
guānmén	关门	close (for establishments)	10
guānxi	关系	relations, connections, to matter	5
guàng	逛	to stroll	11
guàngjiē	逛街	to window-shop	11
guì	贵	expensive	11
guǒzhī	果汁	fruit juice	10
guòqù	过去	to get somewhere, to pass by	12
hái kěyǐ	还可以	it's OK, it's alright, it's fine	11
háishi	还是	or	8
hái yǒu	还有	also have, there also is, and	5, 7
háizi	孩子	child	5
hǎo	好	good	1
hǎochī	好吃	delicious, tasty	7
hǎohē	好喝	delicious to drink	7
hǎokàn	好看	good-looking, nice to look at, a good read, good to watch	3, 7
hǎo péngyou	好朋友	good friends	7
hǎotīng	好听	sounds good, pretty sound, nice to listen to	7

hǎowánr	好玩儿	fun	7
hào	号	number, date	6
hē	喝	to drink	7
hé	和	and	7
hēisè	黑色	black	11
hěn duō	很多	very many, very much	10, 11
hěn hǎo	很好	very good	1
hěn shǎo	很少	very few, very little	11
hóngsè	红色	red	11
hùshi	护士	nurse	12
huānyíng guānglín	欢迎光临	welcome, you honor us with your presence	11
huángsè	黄色	yellow	11
huīsè	灰色	gray	11
huíjiā	回家	to go home	9
huílái	回来	come back	10
huì	会	to know (a skill)	2, 12
huǒchē	火车	train	12
huòshi	或是	or	8
jī	鸡	chicken (animal)	10
jīròu	鸡肉	chicken (meat)	10
jǐ	几	How many?	5
Jǐ diǎn?	几点？	What time?	6
Jǐ ge?	几个？	How many (of something)?	5
Jǐ ge xīngqī?	几个星期？	How many weeks?	6
Jǐ ge yuè?	几个月？	How many months?	6
Jǐ hào?	几号？	What day (of the month)?	6
Jǐ suì?	几岁？	How many years old?	5
Jǐ yuè?	几月？	What month?	6
jiā	家	family, home	5
jiā	家	M.W. for stores, restaurants & businesses	11, 12

jiākè	夹克	jacket	11
jiārén	家人	family member	5
jiàn	件	M.W. for events, items and clothes	11
jiànmiàn	见面	to meet (up)	11
jiāo	教	to teach	2
jiāowài	郊外	suburbs, outskirts (of a city)	12
jiǎozi	饺子	dumpling(s)	10
jiàoshòu	教授	professor	12
jiē	接	to pick someone up (at a place)	11
jiějie	姐姐	older sister	5
jiè qián	借钱	borrow money, lend money	11
jīntiān	今天	today	6
jǐnzhāng	紧张	nervous	8
jìnqù	进去	to go in	11
jiǔ	九	9	5
jiǔ	酒	alcohol	7, 10
Jiǔyuè	九月	September	6
Jiùjīnshān	旧金山	San Francisco	4
jiù shì	就是	happens to be (emphasizes that something is precisely or exactly what is stated)	6
kāfēi	咖啡	coffee	7, 10
kāfēisè	咖啡色	brown	11
kāi	开	to open	10
kāichē	开车	to drive a car	9, 12
kāihuì	开会	to have a meeting	9
kāimén	开门	open (for establishments)	10
kàn	看	to see, to read, to look at, to watch	2, 7
kànkan	看看	to have a look	11
kàn shū	看书	to read a book	7

kě	渴	thirsty	8
kěshì	可是	but	4
kěyǐ	可以	able to, that's OK, that's fine	10, 11
kè	课	class	7
kèrén	客人	guest, customer	10
kùzi	裤子	pants	11
kuài	块	a dollar	11
kuàijìshī	会计师	accountant	12
kuàilè	快乐	happy	3
kuàizi	筷子	chopsticks	10
là	辣	spicy	10
lái	来	to come	11
lánsè	蓝色	blue	11
lǎo pényou	老朋友	old friends	7
lǎoshī	老师	teacher	1
lèi	累	tired	8
liányīqún	连衣裙	dress	11
liǎng diǎn	两点	2 o'clock	6
líng	零	0	5
liúxíng	流行	popular, fashionable	11
liù	六	6	5
Liùyuè	六月	June	6
lǜsè	绿色	green	11
lǜshī	律师	lawyer	12
Lúndūn	伦敦	London	4
Luòshānjī	洛杉矶	Los Angeles	4
māma	妈妈	mother	5
máfan	麻烦	troublesome, "a pain"	12
mǎmahūhū	马马虎虎	so so	1
mǎshàng	马上	immediately	10
mǎi	买	to buy	11

măidān	买单	the bill (in a restautant)	10
mài	卖	to sell	11
mànman chī	慢慢吃	bon appetite, enjoy your meal	10
mànzǒu	慢走	"Take care!"; "Goodbye", "Take it easy!"	12
máng	忙	busy	8
máo	毛	a dime (1/10 of a kuài)	11
màozi	帽子	hat	11
méi guānxi	没关系	that's OK, it doesn't matter	4
méiyǒu	没有	to not have	5
méiyǒu guānxi	没有关系	it doesn't matter, it's OK	5, 10
méiyǒu wèntí	没有问题	no problem	11
méiyǒu yìsi	没有意思	not interesting, boring	5
měi	美	beautiful	3
Měiguó	美国	the U.S.A.	1
Měiguócài	美国菜	American food	10
Měiguófàn	美国饭	American food	7
Měiguórén	美国人	American	1
mèimei	妹妹	younger sister	5
mǐjiǔ	米酒	rice wine	10
miàn	面	noodles	10
míngtiān	明天	tomorrow	6
mótuōchē	摩托车	motorcycle	12
nǎ	哪	which	4
nǎli / nǎr	哪里/哪儿	where	4
nǎli nǎli	哪里哪里	not so, not so	1
Nǎ yì nián?	哪一年？	What year?	6
nàli / nàr	那里/哪儿	there	4
nàme	那么	in that case, then	10
nán	难	difficult	3
nán	男	male	5

nánchī	难吃	not tasty	7
nánguò	难过	sad	3, 8
nánháizi	男孩子	boy	5
nánhē	难喝	not tasty to drink	7
nánkàn	难看	unattractive	3, 7
nánpényou	男朋友	boyfriend	5
nántīng	难听	not good sounding	7
nèikù	内裤	underwear	11
nǐ	你	you	1
nǐ de	你的	your	1
nǐ hǎo	你好	hello	1
nǐmen	你们	you all	1
nǐmen de	你们的	your (plural)	1
nián	年	year	6
nín	您	you (formal)	11
nìngkě	宁可	would rather	10
niú	牛	cow	10
niúròu	牛肉	beef	10
Niǔyuē	纽约	New York	4
nóngmín	农民	farmer	12
nǚ	女	female	5
nǚ'ér	女儿	daughter	5
nǚháizi	女孩子	girl	5
nǚpéngyou	女朋友	girlfriend	5
ǒu'ěr	偶尔	occasionally	9
pán	盘	a dish, M.W. for dishes of food	10
pàng	胖	fat	3
péngyou	朋友	friend(s)	5, 7
píjiǔ	啤酒	beer	10
piányi	便宜	cheap, inexpensive	11

piàoliang	漂亮	beautiful	3
píng	瓶	a bottle, M.W. for beverages (served in bottles)	10
píngcháng	平常	usually	9
pútáojiǔ	葡萄酒	wine	10
qī	七	7	5
Qīyuè	七月	July	6
qǐchuáng	起床	to get up, to get out of bed	9
qìchē	汽车	car	12
qìshuǐ	汽水	soda	10
qǐng	请	to treat someone, to pay for someone else	10
qǐngkè	请客	to treat someone, to pay for someone else	10
qǐng lái	请来	please come, please bring…	10
qǐngwèn	请问	excuse me, may I ask…?	4, 10
qǐng zuò	请坐	please sit down, please have a seat	10
qǔ míngzi	取名字	to get a name, to be given a name	12
qù	去	to go	7
qúnzi	裙子	skirt	11
ránhòu	然后	(and) then, after	9
rén	人	person	1
Rìběn	日本	Japan	1
Rìběnrén	日本人	Japanese (person)	1
Rìwén	日文	Japanese (language)	1
róngyì	容易	easy	3
ròu	肉	meat	10
sān	三	3	5
sān diǎn	三点	3 o'clock	6
sānshí	三十	30	5
sānshíbā	三十八	38	5

sānshí'èr	三十二	32	5
sānshíjiǔ	三十九	39	5
sānshíliù	三十六	36	5
sānshíqī	三十七	37	5
sānshísān	三十三	33	5
sānshísì	三十四	34	5
sānshíwǔ	三十五	35	5
sānshíyī	三十一	31	5
Sānyuè	三月	March	6
shāngdiàn	商店	store, shop	11
shàng	上	up	6
shàng	上	to attend	7
shàngbān	上班	to start work, to be at work	7, 9
shàngchē	上车	get on / into (train, plane, bus, etc.)	12
Shànghǎi	上海	Shanghai	4
shàngkè	上课	to attend class	7, 9
shàngwǎng	上网	to go on the Internet	9
shǎo	少	few, little	11
shéi / shuí	谁	who	4
shénme	什么	what	4
Shénme shíhou?	什么时候？	When?	6
shēngrì	生日	birthday	6
shēngyìrén	生意人	business man / woman	12
shí	十	10	5
shíbā	十八	18	5
shí'èr	十二	12	5
Shí'èryuè	十二月	December	6
shíjiān	时间	time	9
shíjiǔ	十九	19	5
shíliù	十六	16	5

299

shíqī	十七	17	5
shísān	十三	13	5
shísì	十四	14	5
shíwǔ	十五	15	5
shíyī	十一	11	5
Shíyīyuè	十一月	November	6
Shíyuè	十月	October	6
shì	是	to be	1
shì	试	to try	11
shìde	是的	"yes, that's right"	12
shǒutào	手套	gloves	11
shòu	瘦	thin	3
shū	书	book	7
shūcài	蔬菜	vegetables	10
shūfu	舒服	comfortable	8
shuāng	双	a pair of, double, M.W. for things that come in pairs	11
shuǐ	水	water	7, 10
shuìjiào	睡觉	to go to bed, to sleep	9
shuō	说	to say, to speak	2
sījī	司机	driver (taxi, truck, etc.)	12
sì	四	4	5
Sìchuāncài	四川菜	Szechuanese food	10
sì diǎn	四点	4 o'clock	6
Sìyuè	四月	April	6
suíbiàn	随便	"it's up to you"	10
suì	岁	age, years old	5
suǒyǐ	所以	therefore, so	8
tā	他/她/它	he / she / it	1
tā de	他的/她的/它的	his / her / its	1
tāmen	他们/她们/它们	they	1

tāmen de	他们的/她们的/它们的	their	1
Táiběi	台北	Taipei	4
tài	太	too (much), extremely	11
tài duō	太多	too many	10
Tài hǎo le!	太好了！	That's great!	12
tàitai	太太	wife, Mrs., ma'am	5
tāng	汤	soup	10
Tiān'ānmén	天安门	Tiananmen Square	12
tiáo	条	M.W. for long thin things (e.g. rivers, snakes, roads, fish)	10
tīng	听	to listen	2, 7
tīng bù dǒng	听不懂	not understand	6
tuōxià	脱下	to take off (a piece of clothing)	11
wā	哇	"Wow!"	1, 11
wàzi	袜子	socks	11
wàitào	外套	overcoat	11
wánr	玩儿	to play, to have fun	7
wǎn	碗	a bowl, M.W. for things served in a bowl	10
wǎn	晚	late	9
wǎnfàn	晚饭	dinner	7
wǎnshang	晚上	evening	6
wǎng	往	to, toward	12
wǎng yòu guǎi	往右拐	turn to the right	12
wǎng zuǒ guǎi	往左拐	turn to the left	12
Wéi?	喂？	"Hello?" (on telephone)	11
Wèi!	喂！	"Hey!"	11
wèi	位	polite M.W. for counting people	10
wèizi	位子	seat	12
wén	文	language, culture, writing	1

wǒ	我	I	1
wǒ de	我的	my	1
wǒmen	我们	we	1
wǒmen de	我们的	our	1
wúliáo	无聊	bored	8
wúliáo	无聊	boring	12
wúsuǒwèi	无所谓	"it doesn't matter (to me)," "I don't care"	10
wǔ	五	5	5
wǔfàn	午饭	lunch	7
Wǔyuè	五月	May	6
wēixiǎn	危险	dangerous	12
xīyī	西医	Western doctor	12
xǐhuan	喜欢	to like	2
xǐzǎo	洗澡	to bathe (shower or bath)	9
xià	下	down	6
xià	下	to get out of / off	7
xiàbān	下班	to get off work	7, 9
xiàchē	下车	get off / out of (train, plane, bus, etc.)	12
xiàkè	下课	to get out of class	7
xiàwǔ	下午	afternoon	6
xiānsheng	先生	husband, Mr., sir	5, 10
xiànzài	现在	now	6
Xiānggǎng	香港	Hong Kong	4
xiǎng	想	to think, to want	8
xiǎo	小	small	3
xiǎojiě	小姐	Miss, lady	5, 10
xiǎopéngyou	小朋友	kids, children	7
xiézi	鞋子	shoes	11
xiě	写	to write	2
xièxie	谢谢	thank you	1

xīngfèn	兴奋	excited	8
xīngqī	星期	week	6
Xīngqī'èr	星期二	Tuesday	6
Xīngqī jǐ?	星期几？	What day (of there week)?	6
Xīngqīliù	星期六	Saturday	6
Xīngqīrì	星期日	Sunday	6
Xīngqīsān	星期三	Wednesday	6
Xīngqīsì	星期四	Thursday	6
Xīngqītiān	星期天	Sunday	6
Xīngqīwǔ	星期五	Friday	6
Xīngqīyī	星期一	Monday	6
xíng	行	possible, can work	11
xiōng-dì-jiě-mèi	兄弟姐妹	siblings	5
xiūxi	休息	to rest, to take a break	9, 12
xué	学	to study, to learn	2
xuésheng	学生	student	1
yā	鸭	duck (animal)	10
yāròu	鸭肉	duck (meat)	10
yánsè	颜色	color	11
yǎnyuán	演员	actor	12
yào	要	to want	2, 7
yě	也	also	2
yī	一	1	5
yīfu	衣服	clothes	11
yīshēng	医生	doctor	12
Yīyuè	一月	January	6
yíxià	一下	all of a sudden, in a instant	11
yìbǎi	一百	100	5
yìbiān......yìbiān......	一边……一边……	to do something while doing something else	8
yì diǎn	一点	1 o'clock	6

yìdiǎn(r)	一点(儿)	a little (bit)	2
(adj.) + yìdiǎn(r)	(adj.) + 一点(儿)	a bit more (adj.)	11
yìshùjiā	艺术家	artist	12
yìsi	意思	meaning	5
yīnwèi	因为	because, since	8
yīnwèi……suǒyǐ……	因为……所以……	(Since)…therefore…	8
yīnyuè	音乐	music	7
yīnyuèjiā	音乐家	musician	12
yǐnliào	饮料	beverage(s)	10
Yīngguó	英国	England, Britain	1
Yīngguórén	英国人	English (person)	1
Yīngwén	英文	English (language)	1
yòng kuàizi	用筷子	to use chopsticks	10
yǒu	有	to have	5
yǒushíhou	有时候	sometimes	9
yǒu yìdiǎn(r) + (adj.)	有一点(儿) + (adj.)	to be rather…, to be somewhat…, to be a bit…	11
yǒu yìsi	有意思	interesting	5
yòu	右	right	12
yòu guǎi	右拐	turn right	12
yòu……yòu……	又……又……	both one thing and another	8
yú	鱼	fish	10
yuè	月	moon, month	6
yùndòngyuán	运动员	athlete	12
zài	在	(to be) in, at, on	4
zài	再	again, once more, another	10
zài diǎn	再点	order more	10
zài hē	再喝	drink more	10
zàijiàn	再见	goodbye	1
zài lái	再来	bring more	10
zǎo	早	early	9

zǎofàn	早饭	breakfast	7
zǎoshang	早上	morning	6
zhèli / zhèr	这里/这儿	here	4
zhēn de	真的	really	6
zhīdao	知道	to know (about something)	2
Zhījiāgē	芝加哥	Chicago	4
zhí	直	straight	12
zhí zǒu	直走	go straight	12
zhǐ	只	only	2
Zhōngguó	中国	China	1
Zhōngguócài	中国菜	Chinese food	10
Zhōngguófàn	中国饭	Chinese food	7
Zhōngguórén	中国人	Chinese (person)	1
Zhōngwén	中文	Chinese (language)	1
zhōngwǔ	中午	midday, noon	6
zhōngyī	中医	traditional Chinese doctor	12
zhū	猪	pig	10
zhūròu	猪肉	pork	10
zhù	住	to live (reside)	4
zhù zài	住在	to live (reside) in / at	4
zǐsè	紫色	purple	11
zìxíngchē	自行车	bicycle	12
zǒngshì	总是	always	9
zǒu	走	to walk	12
zǒu ba	走吧	let's go	10
zǒulù	走路	to walk (on the road)	12
zuótiān	昨天	yesterday	6
zuǒ	左	left	12
zuǒ guǎi	左拐	turn left	12
zuò	做	to make / do	7
zuòfàn	做饭	to cook	9

zuòjiā	作家	author, writer	12
zuòxià	坐下	to sit down	12

III. Vocabulary Index

(English-*Pinyin*)

English	Characters	*Pinyin*	Lesson
(and) then, after	然后	ránhòu	9
(Since)…therefore…	因为……所以……	yīnwèi……suǒyǐ……	8
(to be) in, at, on	在	zài	4
"Hello?" (on telephone)	喂？	Wéi?	11
"Hey!"	喂！	Wèi!	11
"it doesn't matter (to me)," "I don't care"	无所谓	wúsuǒwèi	10
"it's up to you"	随便	suíbiàn	10
"suggestion" particle	吧	ba	8
"Take care!"; "Goodbye", "Take it easy!"	慢走	mànzǒu	12
"Wow!"	哇	wā	1, 11
"yes, that's right"	是的	shìde	12
"You are very welcome."; "You are most welcome."	不用客气	búyòng kèqi	10, 11
0	零	líng	5
1	一	yī	5
1 o'clock	一点	yì diǎn	6
10	十	shí	5
100	一百	yìbǎi	5
11	十一	shíyī	5
12	十二	shí'èr	5
13	十三	shísān	5
14	十四	shísì	5
15	十五	shíwǔ	5
16	十六	shíliù	5
17	十七	shíqī	5

18	十八	shíbā	5
19	十九	shíjiǔ	5
2	二	èr	5
2 o'clock	两点	liǎng diǎn	6
20	二十	èrshí	5
21	二十一	èrshíyī	5
22	二十二	èrshí'èr	5
23	二十三	èrshísān	5
24	二十四	èrshísì	5
25	二十五	èrshíwǔ	5
26	二十六	èrshíliù	5
27	二十七	èrshíqī	5
28	二十八	èrshíbā	5
29	二十九	èrshíjiǔ	5
3	三	sān	5
3 o'clock	三点	sān diǎn	6
30	三十	sānshí	5
31	三十一	sānshíyī	5
32	三十二	sānshí'èr	5
33	三十三	sānshísān	5
34	三十四	sānshísì	5
35	三十五	sānshíwǔ	5
36	三十六	sānshíliù	5
37	三十七	sānshíqī	5
38	三十八	sānshíbā	5
39	三十九	sānshíjiǔ	5
4	四	sì	5
4 o'clock	四点	sì diǎn	6
5	五	wǔ	5
6	六	liù	5
7	七	qī	5

8	八	bā	5
9	九	jiǔ	5
a bit more (adj.)	(adj.) + 一点(儿)	(adj.) + yìdiǎn(r)	11
a bottle, M.W. for beverages (served in bottles)	瓶	píng	10
a bowl, M.W. for things served in a bowl	碗	wǎn	10
a cent (1/100 of a kuài)	分	fēn	11
a descriptive complement used to indicate the manner, result or potential of a verb	得	de	12
a dime (1/10 of a kuài)	毛	máo	11
a dish, M.W. for dishes of food	盘	pán	10
a dollar	块	kuài	11
a glass, cup, M.W. for beverages (those served in glasses or cups)	杯	bēi	10
a little (bit)	一点(儿)	yìdiǎn(r)	2
a pair of, double, M.W. for things that come in pairs	双	shuāng	11
a place	地方	dìfang	12
able to, that's OK, that's fine	可以	kěyǐ	10, 11
accountant	会计师	kuàijìshī	12
actor	演员	yǎnyuán	12
afternoon	下午	xiàwǔ	6
again, once more, another	再	zài	10
age, years old	岁	suì	5
airplane	飞机	fēijī	12
alcohol	酒	jiǔ	7, 10

all, both, entirely	都	dōu	5, 10
all of a sudden, in a instant	一下	yíxià	11
also	也	yě	2
also have, there also is, and	还有	hái yǒu	5, 7
always	总是	zǒngshì	9
American	美国人	Měiguórén	1
American food	美国饭	Měiguófàn	7
American food	美国菜	Měiguócài	10
and	和	hé	7
anything is fine, either one is fine	都可以	dōu kěyǐ	10
April	四月	Sìyuè	6
artist	艺术家	yìshùjiā	12
athlete	运动员	yùndòngyuán	12
August	八月	Bāyuè	6
author, writer	作家	zuòjiā	12
beautiful	美	měi	3
beautiful	漂亮	piàoliang	3
because, since	因为	yīnwèi	8
beef	牛肉	niúròu	10
beer	啤酒	píjiǔ	10
Beijing	北京	Běijīng	4
Beijing food	北京菜	Běijīngcài	10
beverage(s)	饮料	yǐnliào	10
bicycle	自行车	zìxíngchē	12
big	大	dà	3
birthday	生日	shēngrì	6
black	黑色	hēisè	11
blue	蓝色	lánsè	11
boat	船	chuán	12

bon appetite, enjoy your meal	慢慢吃	mànman chī	10
book	书	shū	7
bored	无聊	wúliáo	8
boring	无聊	wúliáo	12
borrow money, lend money	借钱	jiè qián	11
both one thing and another	又……又……	yòu……yòu……	8
bottoms up, cheers	干杯	gānbēi	10
boy	男孩子	nánháizi	5
boyfriend	男朋友	nánpényou	5
breakfast	早饭	zǎofàn	7
bring more	再来	zài lái	10
brown	咖啡色	kāfēisè	11
bus	公共汽车	gōnggòng qìchē	12
business man / woman	生意人	shēngyirén	12
busy	忙	máng	8
but	可是	kěshì	4
car	汽车	qìchē	12
cheap, inexpensive	便宜	piányi	11
Chicago	芝加哥	Zhījiāgē	4
chicken (animal)	鸡	jī	10
chicken (meat)	鸡肉	jīròu	10
child	孩子	háizi	5
China	中国	Zhōngguó	1
Chinese (language)	中文	Zhōngwén	1
Chinese (person)	中国人	Zhōngguórén	1
Chinese food	中国饭	Zhōngguófàn	7
Chinese food	中国菜	Zhōngguócài	10
chopsticks	筷子	kuàizi	10
chow mein (fried noodles)	炒面	chǎomiàn	10

class	课	kè	7
close (for establishments)	关门	guānmén	10
clothes	衣服	yīfu	11
coffee	咖啡	kāfēi	7, 10
color	颜色	yánsè	11
come back	回来	huílái	10
comfortable	舒服	shūfu	8
company	公司	gōngsī	12
convenient	方便	fāngbiàn	12
correct / right	对	duì	4
cow	牛	niú	10
dangerous	危险	wēixiǎn	12
daughter	女儿	nǚ'ér	5
December	十二月	Shí'èryuè	6
delicious, tasty	好吃	hǎochī	7
delicious to drink	好喝	hǎohē	7
difficult	难	nán	3
dinner	晚饭	wǎnfàn	7
dish, food	菜	cài	10
doctor	医生	yīshēng	12
down	下	xià	6
dress	连衣裙	liányīqún	11
drink more	再喝	zài hē	10
driver (taxi, truck, etc.)	司机	sījī	12
duck (animal)	鸭	yā	10
duck (meat)	鸭肉	yāròu	10
dumpling(s)	饺子	jiǎozi	10
early	早	zǎo	9
easy	容易	róngyì	3
embarrassed	不好意思	bù hǎoyìsi	8
England, Britain	英国	Yīngguó	1

English (language)	英文	Yīngwén	1
English (person)	英国人	Yīngguórén	1
evening	晚上	wǎnshang	6
excited	兴奋	xīngfèn	8
excuse me, may I ask...?	请问	qǐngwèn	4, 10
expensive	贵	guì	11
family member	家人	jiārén	5
family, home	家	jiā	5
farmer	农民	nóngmín	12
fat	胖	pàng	3
father	爸爸	bàba	5
February	二月	Èryuè	6
female	女	nǚ	5
few, little	少	shǎo	11
fish	鱼	yú	10
fork	叉子	chāzi	10
France	法国	Fǎguó	1
French (language)	法文	Fǎwén	1
French (person)	法国人	Fǎguórén	1
French food	法国饭	Fǎguófàn	7
Friday	星期五	Xīngqīwǔ	6
fried rice	炒饭	chǎofàn	10
friend(s)	朋友	péngyou	5, 7
from (place) to (place)	从 (place) 到 (place)	cóng (place) dào (place)	12
fruit juice	果汁	guǒzhī	10
full	饱	bǎo	8
fun	好玩儿	hǎowánr	7
German (language)	德文	Déwén	1
German (person)	德国人	Déguórén	1
Germany	德国	Déguó	1

get off / out of (train, plane, bus, etc.)	下车	xiàchē	12
get on / into (train, plane, bus, etc.)	上车	shàngchē	12
girl	女孩子	nǔháizi	5
girlfriend	女朋友	nǔpéngyou	5
gloves	手套	shǒutào	11
go straight	直走	zhí zǒu	12
good	好	hǎo	1
good friends	好朋友	hǎo péngyou	7
goodbye	再见	zàijiàn	1
good-looking, nice to look at, a good read, good to watch	好看	hǎokàn	3, 7
gray	灰色	huīsè	11
green	绿色	lǜsè	11
guest, customer	客人	kèrén	10
half	半	bàn	6
happens to be (emphasizes that something is precisely or exactly what is stated)	就是	jiù shì	6
happy	快乐	kuàilè	3
happy	高兴	gāoxìng	8
hat	帽子	màozi	11
he / she / it	他/她/它	tā	1
hello	你好	nǐ hǎo	1
here	这里/这儿	zhèli / zhèr	4
his / her / its	他的/她的/它的	tā de	1
Hong Kong	香港	Xiānggǎng	4
How many?	几	jǐ	5
How many (of something)?	几个？	Jǐ ge?	5
How many months?	几个月？	Jǐ ge yuè?	6

How many weeks?	几个星期？	Jǐ ge xīngqī?	6
How many years old?	几岁？	Jǐ suì?	5
how much money, how much (is it)	多少钱	duōshao qián	11
how much, how many	多少	duōshao	11
hungry	饿	è	8
husband, Mr., sir	先生	xiānsheng	5, 10
I	我	wǒ	1
immediately	马上	mǎshàng	10
in that case, then	那么	nàme	10
intelligent	聪明	cōngmíng	3
interesting	有意思	yǒu yìsi	5
it doesn't matter, it's OK	没有关系	méiyǒu guānxi	5, 10
it's OK, it's alright, it's fine	还可以	hái kěyǐ	11
jacket	夹克	jiākè	11
January	一月	Yīyuè	6
Japan	日本	Rìběn	1
Japanese (language)	日文	Rìwén	1
Japanese (person)	日本人	Rìběnrén	1
July	七月	Qīyuè	6
June	六月	Liùyuè	6
kids, children	小朋友	xiǎopéngyou	7
language, culture, writing	文	wén	1
late	晚	wǎn	9
lawyer	律师	lǜshī	12
left	左	zuǒ	12
let's go	走吧	zǒu ba	10
London	伦敦	Lúndūn	4
Los Angeles	洛杉矶	Luòshānjī	4
lunch	午饭	wǔfàn	7

M.W. for events, items and clothes	件	jiàn	11
M.W. for long thin things (e.g. rivers, snakes, roads, fish)	条	tiáo	10
M.W. for saying the number of things	个	ge	5
M.W. for stores, restaurants & businesses	家	jiā	11, 12
male	男	nán	5
many, much	多	duō	11
March	三月	Sānyuè	6
May	五月	Wǔyuè	6
meaning	意思	yìsi	5
meat	肉	ròu	10
menu	菜单	càidān	10
midday, noon	中午	zhōngwǔ	6
minute(s)	分	fēn	6
Miss, lady	小姐	xiǎojiě	5, 10
Monday	星期一	Xīngqīyī	6
moon, month	月	yuè	6
morning	早上	zǎoshang	6
mother	妈妈	māma	5
motorcycle	摩托车	mótuōchē	12
movie	电影	diànyǐng	7
music	音乐	yīnyuè	7
musician	音乐家	yīnyuèjiā	12
my	我的	wǒ de	1
nearby (someplace), in the vicinity of (a place)	_____的附近	_____ de fùjìn	12
nearby, in the vicinity	附近	fùjìn	12
nervous	紧张	jǐnzhāng	8
never	从不	cóng bù	9

New York	纽约	Niǔyuē	4
no problem	没有问题	méiyǒu wèntí	11
noodles	面	miàn	10
not	不	bù	1
not bad, pretty good	不错	búcuò	11
not good	不好	bù hǎo	1
not good sounding	难听	nántīng	7
not interesting, boring	没有意思	méiyǒu yìsi	5
not possible, can't work	不行	bù xíng	11
not so, not so	哪里哪里	nǎli nǎli	1
not tasty	难吃	nánchī	7
not tasty to drink	难喝	nánhē	7
not understand	听不懂	tīng bù dǒng	6
November	十一月	Shíyīyuè	6
now	现在	xiànzài	6
number, date	号	hào	6
nurse	护士	hùshi	12
o'clock	点	diǎn	6
occasionally	偶尔	ǒu'ěr	9
October	十月	Shíyuè	6
office	办公室	bàngōngshì	12
often	常常	chángcháng	9
old friends	老朋友	lǎo pényou	7
older brother	哥哥	gēge	5
older sister	姐姐	jiějie	5
only	只	zhǐ	2
open (for establishments)	开门	kāimén	10
or	还是	háishi	8
or	或是	huòshi	8
orange	橙色	chéngsè	11
order more	再点	zài diǎn	10

other	别的	biéde	11
our	我们的	wǒmen de	1
overcoat	外套	wàitào	11
pants	裤子	kùzi	11
parents	爸爸妈妈	bàba māma	5
Paris	巴黎	Bālí	4
peaceful, quiet	安静	ānjìng	12
person	人	rén	1
pig	猪	zhū	10
pink	粉红色	fěnhóngsè	11
please come, please bring…	请来	qǐng lái	10
please sit down, please have a seat	请坐	qǐng zuò	10
polite M.W. for counting people	位	wèi	10
popular, fashionable	流行	liúxíng	11
pork	猪肉	zhūròu	10
possible, can work	行	xíng	11
professor	教授	jiàoshòu	12
purple	紫色	zǐsè	11
really	真的	zhēn de	6
red	红色	hóngsè	11
relations, connections, to matter	关系	guānxi	5
restaurant	饭馆	fànguǎn	10
rice wine	米酒	mǐjiǔ	10
rice, meal	饭	fàn	7, 10
right	右	yòu	12
sad	难过	nánguò	3, 8
San Francisco	旧金山	Jiùjīnshān	4
Saturday	星期六	Xīngqīliù	6

seat	位子	wèizi	12
September	九月	Jiǔyuè	6
Shanghai	上海	Shànghǎi	4
shirt	衬衫	chènshān	11
shoes	鞋子	xiézi	11
short	矮	ǎi	3
shorts	短裤子	duǎn kùzi	11
siblings	兄弟姐妹	xiōng-dì-jiě-mèi	5
skirt	裙子	qúnzi	11
small	小	xiǎo	3
so so	马马虎虎	mǎmahūhū	1
socks	袜子	wàzi	11
soda	汽水	qìshuǐ	10
sometimes	有时候	yǒushíhou	9
son	儿子	érzi	5
sorry	对不起	duìbuqǐ	4
sounds good, pretty sound, nice to listen to	好听	hǎotīng	7
soup	汤	tāng	10
spicy	辣	là	10
store, shop	商店	shāngdiàn	11
straight	直	zhí	12
student	学生	xuésheng	1
stupid	笨	bèn	3
suburbs, outskirts (of a city)	郊外	jiāowài	12
subway, metro	地铁	dìtiě	12
Sunday	星期日	Xīngqīrì	6
Sunday	星期天	Xīngqītiān	6
Szechuanese food	四川菜	Sìchuāncài	10
Taipei	台北	Táiběi	4
tall / high	高	gāo	3

taxi	出租车	chūzūchē	12
tea	茶	chá	7, 10
teacher	老师	lǎoshī	1
television	电视	diànshì	7
thank you	谢谢	xièxie	1
That's great!	太好了！	Tài hǎo le!	12
that's not necessary, there is no need	不用	búyòng	10
that's OK, it doesn't matter	没关系	méi guānxi	4
that's right; you've got it right	对啊	duì a	11
the bill (in a restautant)	买单	mǎidān	10
The Forbidden City, The palace Museum, former Chinese imperial palace	故宫	Gùgōng	12
the U.S.A.	美国	Měiguó	1
their	他们的/她们的/它们的	tāmen de	1
there	那里/那儿	nàli / nàr	4
therefore, so	所以	suǒyǐ	8
they	他们/她们/它们	tāmen	1
thin	瘦	shòu	3
thirsty	渴	kě	8
Thursday	星期四	Xīngqīsì	6
Tiananmen Square	天安门	Tiān'ānmén	12
time	时间	shíjiān	9
tired	累	lèi	8
to, toward	往	wǎng	12
to attend	上	shàng	7
to attend class	上课	shàngkè	7, 9
to bathe (shower or bath)	洗澡	xǐzǎo	9
to be	是	shì	1

to be rather…, to be somewhat…, to be a bit…	有一点(儿) + (adj.)	yǒu yìdiǎn(r) + (adj.)	11
to buy	买	mǎi	11
to close	关	guān	10
to come	来	lái	11
to come from (a place / country)	从 (place) 来的	cóng (place) lái de	12
to cook	做饭	zuòfàn	9
to do something while doing something else	一边……一边……	yìbiān…… yìbiān……	8
to drink	喝	hē	7
to drive a car	开车	kāichē	9, 12
to eat	吃	chī	7
to eat	吃饭	chīfàn	8, 9
to eat breakfast	吃早饭	chī zǎofàn	9
to get a name, to be given a name	取名字	qǔ míngzi	12
to get off work	下班	xiàbān	7, 9
to get out of / off	下	xià	7
to get out of class	下课	xiàkè	7
to get somewhere, to pass by	过去	guòqù	12
to get up, to get out of bed	起床	qǐchuáng	9
to go	去	qù	7
to go (somewhere)	到 (place) 去	dào (place) qù	12
to go home	回家	huíjiā	9
to go in	进去	jìnqù	11
to go on the Internet	上网	shàngwǎng	9
to go to bed, to sleep	睡觉	shuìjiào	9
to have	有	yǒu	5
to have a look	看看	kànkan	11
to have a meeting	开会	kāihuì	9

to know (a skill)	会	huì	2, 12
to know (about something)	知道	zhīdao	2
to like	喜欢	xǐhuan	2
to listen	听	tīng	2, 7
to live (reside)	住	zhù	4
to live (reside) in / at	住在	zhù zài	4
to make / do	做	zuò	7
to make a telephone call (to)	打电话(给)	dǎ diànhuà (gěi)	9, 11
to meet (up)	见面	jiànmiàn	11
to not have	没有	méiyǒu	5
to open	开	kāi	10
to order food	点菜	diǎncài	10
to pick someone up (at a place)	接	jiē	11
to play, to have fun	玩儿	wánr	7
to put (a piece of clothing) on	穿上	chuānshàng	11
to read a book	看书	kàn shū	7
to rest, to take a break	休息	xiūxi	9, 12
to say, to speak	说	shuō	2
to see, to read, to look at, to watch	看	kàn	2, 7
to sell	卖	mài	11
to sit down	坐下	zuòxià	12
to start work, to be at work	上班	shàngbān	7, 9
to stroll	逛	guàng	11
to study, to learn	学	xué	2
to take off (a piece of clothing)	脱下	tuōxià	11
to teach	教	jiāo	2
to tell, to inform	告诉	gàosu	12

to think, to want	想	xiǎng	8
to treat someone, to pay for someone else	请	qǐng	10
to treat someone, to pay for someone else	请客	qǐngkè	10
to try	试	shì	11
to use chopsticks	用筷子	yòng kuàizi	10
to wait	等	děng	11
to walk	走	zǒu	12
to walk (on the road)	走路	zǒulù	12
to want	要	yào	2, 7
to wear	穿	chuān	11
to wear (caps, gloves, glasses, etc.)	戴	dài	11
to wear clothes	穿衣服	chuān yīfu	11
to window-shop	逛街	guàngjiē	11
to work on the computer	打电脑	dǎ diànnǎo	9
to write	写	xiě	2
today	今天	jīntiān	6
tofu	豆腐	dòufu	10
together	跟……一起	gēn……yìqǐ	8
Tokyo	东京	Dōngjīng	4
tomorrow	明天	míngtiān	6
too (much), extremely	太	tài	11
too many	太多	tài duō	10
top, apex, crown of the head, M.W. for hats	顶	dǐng	11
traditional Chinese doctor	中医	zhōngyī	12
train	火车	huǒchē	12
troublesome, "a pain"	麻烦	máfan	12
Tuesday	星期二	Xīngqī'èr	6
turn left	左拐	zuǒ guǎi	12

turn right	右拐	yòu guǎi	12
turn to the left	往左拐	wǎng zuǒ guǎi	12
turn to the right	往右拐	wǎng yòu guǎi	12
ugly	丑	chǒu	3
unattractive	难看	nánkàn	3, 7
understand	懂	dǒng	1
underwear	内裤	nèikù	11
up	上	shàng	6
usually	平常	píngcháng	9
vegetables	蔬菜	shūcài	10
vegetarian	吃素	chīsù	10
very few, very little	很少	hěn shǎo	11
very good	很好	hěn hǎo	1
very many, very much	很多	hěn duō	10, 11
wait a moment	等一下	děng yíxià	11
waiter / waitress	服务员	fúwùyuán	12
water	水	shuǐ	7, 10
we	我们	wǒmen	1
Wednesday	星期三	Xīngqīsān	6
week	星期	xīngqī	6
welcome, you honor us with your presence	欢迎光临	huānyíng guānglín	11
Western doctor	西医	xīyī	12
what	什么	shénme	4
What day (of the month)?	几号？	Jǐ hào?	6
What day (of there week)?	星期几？	Xīngqī jǐ?	6
What month?	几月？	Jǐ yuè?	6
What time?	几点？	Jǐ diǎn?	6
What year?	哪一年？	Nǎ yì nián?	6
when (for indicative sentence)	的时候	de shíhou	9
When?	什么时候？	Shénme shíhou?	6

where	哪里/哪儿	nǎli / nǎr	4
which	哪	nǎ	4
white	白色	báisè	11
who	谁/谁	shéi / shuí	4
wife, Mrs., ma'am	太太	tàitai	5
wine	葡萄酒	pútáojiǔ	10
with, and	跟	gēn	8
work shift	班	bān	7
would rather	宁可	nìngkě	10
Year	年	nián	6
yellow	黄色	huángsè	11
yesterday	昨天	zuótiān	6
you	你	nǐ	1
you (formal)	您	nín	11
you all	你们	nǐmen	1
you're welcome	不客气	bú kèqi	1
younger brother	弟弟	dìdi	5
younger sister	妹妹	mèimei	5
your	你的	nǐ de	1
your (plural)	你们的	nǐmen de	1

IV. Answer Key

Lesson One

Auditory Exercise - (Page 4)
Part One:

1. ╱   2. –   3. ╲   4. ˅

5. ╲   6. ╱   7. –   8. ˅

9. ╱   10. –

Part Two:

11. māng   12. tā   13. nān   14. dāo

15. lāi   16. dān   17. bāo   18. bāng

19. lān   20. māi

Chit-Chat Practice 1.1

1.   Bú shì. Bob shì Měiguórén.

2.   Bú shì. Lili shì Zhōngguórén.

3.   Shì. Bob shì xuésheng.

4.   Bú shì. Lili shì Yīngwén lǎoshī.

5.   Shì. Lili shì Yīngwén lǎoshī.

6.   Lili dǒng Yīngwén.

7.   Bob dǒng Zhōngwén.

Chit-Chat Practice 1.2

1.   Jen shì Zhōngwén xuésheng ma?

2.   Xiǎoměi shì lǎoshī ma?

3.   Jen de Zhōngwén hǎo ma?

Chit-Chat Practice 1.3

Sample Answers (answers will vary)

1.   Wǒ hěn hǎo, xièxie. Nǐ ne?

2.   Wǒ jiào (your name).

3.   Shì. Wǒ shì Měiguórén.

4.   Bú shì. Wǒ bú shì Zhōngguórén.

5.   Shì. Wǒ shì Zhōngwén xuésheng.

6.   Wǒ de Yīngwén hěn hǎo.

7.   Wǒ de Zhōngwén bù hǎo.

Lesson Two

Sound Differentiation Exercise - (Page 23)

1. sòng	2. zǒu	3. sài	4. cái
5. zì	6. sì	7. zāng	8. zǎo
9. cā	10. sǎng	11. sān	12. zé
13. zēng	14. cén	15. cǎn	16. zài
17. sào	18. cóng	19. cì	20. zěn

Chit-Chat Practice 2.1

Sample Answers (answers will vary)

1.   Wǒ hěn xǐhuan Zhōngguó.

2.   Wǒ xué Zhōngwén.

3.   Wǒ huì Yīngwén. Wǒ shì Měiguórén.

4.   Wǒ huì yìdiǎnr.

5.   Wǒ bú yào. Wǒ yào xué Zhōngwén.

6.   Wǒ bú huì xiě.

Chit-Chat Practice 2.1 - Brain Stretcher

1.   We are looking at them.

2.   He said "hello."

3.   I am writing my name.

4.   I want to speak German.

5.   I am listening to the teacher speaking in Chinese.

6.   He doesn't know how to write.

7.   He only knows how to speak.

Chit-Chat Practice 2.2

1.   Tim shì Měiguórén ma?

      Tim shì bú shì Měiguórén?

2.   Tim xué Zhōngwén ma?

Tim xué bù xué Zhōngwén?

3.   Tim huì xiě Zhōngwén ma?

      Tim huì bú huì xiě Zhōngwén?

4.   Tim xǐhuan xué Zhōngwén ma?

      Tim xǐ bù xǐhuan xué Zhōngwén?

5.   Junli huì shuō Yīngwén ma?

      Junli huì bú huì shuō Yīngwén?

Lesson Three

Sound Differentiation Exercise - (Page 40)

1. guāi	2. kàn	3. hēi	4. gǎi
5. kàng	6. guó	7. huán	8. kǎ
9. hǎo	10. hóng	11. gòu	12. gē
13. gēng	14. huā	15. huǒ	16. huáng
17. guāng	18. kuài	19. hěn	20. guì

Chit-Chat Practice 3.1 & 3.2

Sample Answers (answers may vary)

1.   Tā hěn piàoliang.

2.   Yáo Míng hěn gāo.

3.   Tā hěn hǎokàn.

4.   Kǒngzǐ hěn cōngmíng.

5.   Tā bú pàng.

6.   Gōngfu bù róngyì.

7.   Tā bù nánguò yě bú kuàilè.

8.   Tā hěn ǎi.

9.   Měiguó hěn měi.

10.   Tā hěn kuàilè.

Grammar Grove - (Page 47)

Translation of pattern drill

2.   England is smaller than the U.S.

3.   The teacher is smarter than the student.

4. Your English is better than my Chinese.

5. They are fatter than us.

6. You (all) are shorter than them.

7. Beijing is prettier than Shanghai.

8. Learning Chinese is more difficult than learning English.

9. Speaking Chinese is easier than speaking English.

10. Germans are taller than Americans.

11. French is harder to learn than English.

12. Reading English is easier than reading Chinese.

Lesson Four

Sound Differentiation Exercise - (Page 60)

1. xiǎng	2. jiāo	3. ròu	4. zhōng
5. shéi	6. qǐng	7. xìng	8. chá
9. xīn	10. shàng	11. rén	12. jiàn
13. chē	14. jiǔ	15. zhǎo	16. xiè
17. shān	18. xià	19. shēng	20. qióng

Chit-Chat Practice 4.1

1. Tā shì Táiwānrén.

2. Bú duì. Tā bù jiāo Yīngwén.

3. Duì. Tā jiāo Zhōngwén.

4. Tā lǎoshī de Yīngwén míngzi jiào "Nancy."

5. Ann bù zhīdao tā lǎoshī de Zhōngwén míngzi.

6. Ann de lǎoshī hěn piàoliang.

7. Tā zhù zài Zhījiāgē.

8. Bú duì. Ann hěn xǐhuan Zhījiāgē.

Chit-Chat Practice 4.2

1. Nǐ huì shuō Zhōngwén ma?

2. Nǐ zài nǎr xué Zhōngwén?

3. Nǐ zhù zài Měiguó nǎr?

4. Zhōngwén nán bù nán xué?

5. Nǐ yào qù Zhōngguó ma?

6. Nǐ zhù zài Zhōngguó nǎr?

7. Nǐ xǐhuan xué Yīngwén ma?

8. Běijīng hěn dà ma?

9. Zhōngwén bǐ Yīngwén nán ma?

Lesson Five

Sound Differentiation Exercise - (Page 78)

1. biào	2. yě	3. dù	4. duō
5. niáng	6. diū	7. liù	8. luàn
9. tiān	10. yī	11. píng	12. wèn
13. liáng	14. yǒu	15. yīng	16. bié
17. tīng	18. nián	19. lún	20. lín

Chit-Chat Practice 5.1

1. Andy yǒu gēge.

2. Tā de gēge yǒu tàitai.

3. Tā de tàitai hěn piàoliang.

4. Bú shì. Tā de tàitai shì Zhōngguórén.

5. Tā de gēge bú huì shuō Zhōngwén.

6. Tā gēge de tàitai Yīngwén hěn hǎo.

7. Andy de bàba māma zhù zài Niǔyuē.

8. Andy yǒu jiějie mèimei.

9. Tāmen zhù zài Niǔyuē.

Chit-Chat Practice 5.2

1. Wáng Jiān de jiā yǒu liù ge rén.

2. Wáng Jiān zuì dà.

3. Tā de dìdi zuì xiǎo.

4. Tā èrshíwǔ suì.

5. Tā de dìdi shí'èr suì.

6. Wáng Jiān de mèimeimen huì yìdiǎnr.

7. Tā de bàba māma dōu bú huì shuō Yīngwén.

8. Bú shì. Tā de bàba māma shì Fǎguórén.

9. Bú duì. Zài Nandy de jiā tāmen shuō Fǎwén.

Lesson Six

Sound Differentiation Exercise - (Page 104)

1. bō	2. dǒng	3. tè	4. dōu
5. mèi	6. fēn	7. lěng	8. mén
9. lóu	10. tòng	11. děng	12. bèi
13. néng	14. lèi	15. lóng	16. fēng
17. mǒu	18. dé	19. fó	20. téng

Module 6.1

3. èr líng líng jiǔ nián, Jiǔyuè qī hào, Xīngqīyī, zǎoshang jiǔ diǎn shí fēn

4. èr líng líng jiǔ nián, Jiǔyuè shí hào, Xīngqīsì, xiàwǔ yì diǎn sìshí fēn

5. èr líng líng jiǔ nián, Jiǔyuè shí'èr hào, Xīngqīliù, xiàwǔ liǎng diǎn èrshí fēn.

6. èr líng líng jiǔ nián, Jiǔyuè shíliù hào, Xīngqīsān, zǎoshang shíyī diǎn sìshíwǔ fēn

7. èr líng líng jiǔ nián, Jiǔyuè shíbā hào, Xīngqīwǔ, zhōngwǔ shí'èr diǎn èrshí fēn

8. èr líng líng jiǔ nián, Jiǔyuè èrshí hào, Xīngqītiān, zhōngwǔ shí'èr diǎn

9. èr líng líng jiǔ nián, Jiǔyuè èrshísì hào, Xīngqīsì, wǎnshang jiǔ diǎn bàn

10. èr líng líng jiǔ nián, Jiǔyuè èrshíjiǔ hào, Xīngqī'èr, zǎoshang shí diǎn èrshíwǔ fēn

11. èr líng yī líng nián, Liùyuè yī hào, Xīngqī'èr, wǎnshang bā diǎn shí fēn

12. èr líng yī líng nián, Liùyuè wǔ hào, Xīngqīliù, xiàwǔ liǎng diǎn èrshí fēn

13. èr líng yī líng nián, Liùyuè liù hào, Xīngqīrì, zǎoshang qī diǎn sānshíwǔ fēn

14. èr líng yī líng nián, Liùyuè jiǔ hào, Xīngqīsān, wǎnshang bā diǎn wǔshí fēn

15. èr líng yī líng nián, Liùyuè shísì hào, Xīngqīyī, zǎoshang bā diǎn bàn

16. èr líng yī líng nián, Liùyuè shí bā hào, Xīngqīwǔ, wǎnshang shíyī diǎn èrshíbā fēn

17. èr líng yī líng nián, Liùyuè èrshí'èr hào, Xīngqī'èr, zhōngwǔ shí'èr diǎn

18. èr líng yī líng nián, Liùyuè èrshísì hào, Xīngqīsì, wǎnshang liù diǎn sìshí fēn

19. èr líng yī líng nián, Liùyuè èrshíqī hào, Xīngqītiān, zǎoshang liǎng diǎn sānshíwǔ fēn

20. èr líng yī líng nián, Liùyuè sānshí hào, Xīngqīsān, wǎnshang shí diǎn sānshíwǔ fēn

Chit-Chat Practice 6.2

1. Lisa de shēngrì shì Sānyuè yī hào.
   Wǒ de shēngrì shì (month) (day).

2. Lisa èrshíwǔ suì.
   Wǒ (your age number) suì.

3. Lisa māma de shēngrì shì Bāyuè èrshíbā hào.
   Wǒ māma de shēngrì shì (month) (day).

4. Lisa bàba de shēngrì shì Liùyuè shíjiǔ hào.
   Wǒ bàba de shēngrì shì (month) (day).

Chit-Chat Practice 6.3

1. Míngtiān.
2. Yī jiǔ jiǔ bā nián.
3. Jiǔyuè èrshísān hào.
4. Xiàwǔ sān diǎn bàn.
5. Xīngqītiān / Xīngqīrì.
6. Xiànzài.
7. Shíyuè.
8. Sān ge xīngqī.
9. Zǎoshang qī diǎn èrshí fēn.
10. Liù ge yuè.
11. Èr líng líng yī nián.
12. Xià ge xīngqī.

Chit-Chat Practice 6.4

去年三月 qùnián Sānyuè	March of last year
上上个星期三 shàngshàng ge Xīngqīsān	Wednesday of the week before last
下个月五号 xià ge yuè wǔ hào	the 5th of next month
晚上八点三十五分 wǎnshang bā diǎn sānshíwǔ fēn	8:35 at night
六个月 liù ge yuè	six months
下个星期日 xià ge Xīngqīrì	next Sunday
今年五月 jīnnián Wǔyuè	May of this year
下下个星期一 xiàxià ge Xīngqīyī	Monday of the week after next
明年六月 míngnián Liùyuè	June of next year
这个月七号 zhèi ge yuè qī hào	the 7th of this month
两个月 liǎng ge yuè	two months
后年二月 hòunián Èryuè	February of the year after next

Lesson Seven

Sound Differentiation Exercise - (Page 124)

1. yù 2. qún 3. jué 4. qù

5. xué 6. yún 7. yuǎn 8. xuǎn

9. nǔ 10. jù 11. yuè 12. jūn

13. lù 14. què 15. juān 16. xù

17. lüè 18. quán 19. xún 20. nüè

Module 7.1

2.　Tā zuòfàn.

3.　Tā hē kāfēi.

4.　Tāmen shàngkè.

5.　Wǒ kàn diànyǐng.

6.　Tā chīfàn.

7.　Tā tīng yīnyuè.

8.　Tāmen xiàkè.

9.　Tā hē shuǐ.

10.　Tāmen kàn diànshì.

11.　Tā shàngbān.

12.　Wǒ hē chá.

13.　Wǒmen shàngkè.

14.　Tāmen kàn diànyǐng.

15.　Tāmen wánr.

16.　Tā tīng yīnyuè.

17.　Tā kàn diànshì.

18.　Tā kàn shū.

19.　Tāmen kàn péngyou.

20.　Wǒ zuòfàn.

Module 7.2

Sample Answers (answers will vary)

1.　Wǒ bàba hěn hǎokàn.

2.　Měiguó yīnyuè hěn hǎotīng.

3.　Xué Zhōngwén hěn hǎowánr.

4.　Fǎguófàn hěn hǎochī.

5.　Kāfēi bù nánhē. Kāfēi hěn hǎohē.

6.　Xiǎopéngyou bú huì zuòfàn.

7.　Wǒ de lǎo péngyou zài Niǔyuē.

8.　Wǒ yì diǎn chī wǔfàn.

Appendix IV

Lesson Eight

Sound Differentiation Exercise - (Page 148)

1. chuī	2. rú	3. suān	4. zú
5. cuò	6. zuǐ	7. zhǔn	8. shuāng
9. chū	10. zhuǎ	11. shuāi	12. ruǎn
13. zhuàng	14. cuī	15. suǒ	16. zhù
17. shuō	18. ruò	19. shuǐ	20. zhuǎn

Module 8.1

1. Tā huì shuō Fǎwén yě huì shuō Yīngwén.
2. Nǐ de tàitai yòu piàoliang yòu cōngmíng.
3. Wǒ qù tā jiā chīfàn X kàn diànshì.
4. Tā zài Fǎguó yìbiān gōngzuò yìbiān xué Fǎwén.
5. Tā míngnián yào xué Rìwén, Zhōngwén hái yǒu / gēn Déwén.
6. Tā hé / gēn tā de nǚpéngyou zhù zài Lúndūn.
7. Wǒ jiějie hé / gēn tā de xiānsheng yìqǐ gōngzuò.
8. Wǒ huì kàn X / yě huì xiě Zhōngwén.
9. Xiǎopéngyou shàngkè yìbiān kàn shū yìbiān xiě zì.
10. Nǐ xǐhuan kàn shū, tīng yīnyuè, hái yǒu shénme?

Module 8.2

2. Tā hěn gāoxìng.
3. Tāmen hěn wúliáo.
4. Tā hěn nánguò.
5. Wǒ hěn kě.
6. Tā hěn xīngfèn.
7. Tā hěn máng.
8. Tā hěn bù hǎoyìsi.
9. Wǒmen hěn wúliáo.
10. Tā hěn shūfu.
11. Tāmen hěn jǐnzhāng.
12. Tā hěn lèi.
13. Tā hěn nánguò.

14.   Tā hěn gāoxìng.

15.   Tā hěn máng.

16.   Tā hěn kě.

17.   Tā hěn bù hǎoyìsi.

18.   Tā hěn wúliáo.

19.   Wǒ hěn jǐnzhāng.

20.   Tā hěn gāoxìng.

Chit-Chat Practice 8.3

1.   Yīnwèi tā dùzi è le.

2.   Tā xiǎng gēn péngyou qù chīfàn.

3.   Yīnwèi tā hěn lèi.

4.   Yīnwèi tā gōngzuò de hěn wǎn.

5.   Tā xiǎng zài jiā kàn diànshì.

6.   Tā juéde zài jiā kàn diànshì hěn wúliáo.

7.   Yīnwèi míngtiān hòutiān tā de gōngzuò hěn máng.

8.   Tā juéde zài jiā kàn diànshì hěn shūfu.

9.   Tā xiǎng qù kàn diànyǐng.

Lesson Nine

Sound Differentiation Exercise - (Page 167)

1. bāngmáng	2. nǚrén	3. chángcháng	4. wúliáo
5. míngtiān	6. pīnyīn	7. tiānqì	8. ǒu'ěr
9. māma	10. méiyǒu	11. ránhòu	12. hǎochī
13. jiějie	14. fācái	15. gōngxǐ	16. xuéxiào
17. péngyou	18. xǐhuan	19. kěshì	20. tiānqì

Module 9.1

2.   Tā zǎoshang qī diǎn shí fēn xǐzǎo.

3.   Tā zǎoshang qī diǎn bàn chī zǎofàn hē kāfēi.

4.   Tā zǎoshang bā diǎn wǔ fēn yìbiān zuò huǒchē yìbiān kàn shū.

5.   Tā zǎoshang bā diǎn sìshíwǔ fēn zǒulù qù gōngzuò.

6.   Tā zǎoshang jiǔ diǎn dǎ diànhuà.

7.   Tā zǎoshang shí diǎn bàn kāihuì.

8.   Tā zhōngwǔ shí'èr diǎn yìbiān xiūxi yìbiān chī wǔfàn.

9.   Tā xiàwǔ yì diǎn dǎ diànnǎo.

10. Tā xiàwǔ wǔ diǎn bàn xiàbān.

11. Tā xiàwǔ wǔ diǎn wǔshí fēn zuò huǒchē.

12. Tā wǎnshang liù diǎn bàn huíjiā.

13. Tā wǎnshang qī diǎn zuò wǎnfàn.

14. Tā wǎnshang qī diǎn bàn yìbiān chī wǎnfàn yìbiān kàn diànshì.

15. Tā wǎnshang shíyī diǎn shuìjiào.

Word Workshop - (Page 171)

3.   When I see my friends, I am happy.

4.   When I eat dinner, I don't watch TV.

Module 9.2

1.   Tā chángcháng qù kàn tā de māma.

2.   Wǒ ǒu'ěr huí Zhōngguó qù kàn lǎo péngyou.

3.   Tā yǒushíhou gēn péngyou qù hē jiǔ.

4.   Tā cóng bú shàngwǎng.

5.   Tā píngcháng zuò gōnggòng qìchē qù gōngzuò, kěshì yǒushíhou tā kāichē qù.

6.   Tā měi tiān xiàbān yǐhòu zǒngshì qù kàn tā de nánpéngyou.

7.   Tā píngcháng qī diǎn qǐchuáng, kěshì yǒushíhou tā jiǔ diǎn cái qǐchuáng.

Lesson Ten

Sound Differentiation Exercise - (Page 189)

1. xīngqī	2. tāmen	3. píjiǔ	4. piányi
5. máfan	6. xǐhuan	7. měilì	8. xiàtiān
9. Měiguó	10. hē jiǔ	11. jìde	12. kuàilè
13. zhīdao	14. xiàwǔ	15. shuǐguǒ	16. bàba
17. fàndiàn	18. qiánmiàn	19. pángbiān	20. jiārén

Module 10.1

1. Wúsuǒwèi.

2. Qǐng zuò.

3. Dōu kěyǐ.

4. Qǐngwèn.

5. Suíbiàn.

6. Wǒ dōu xǐhuan.

7. Búyòng kèqi.

8. Méiyǒu wèntí.

9. Wǒmen zǒu ba!

10. Méiyǒu guānxi.

Chit-Chat Practice 10.2

2. Nǐ xiǎng zài jiā háishi zài fàndiàn chīfàn.

3. Wúsuǒwèi.

4. Jīntiān wǎnshang wǒ nìngkě qù fàndiàn chīfàn.

5. Hǎo a. Nǐ xiǎng chī Sìchuān cài ma?

6. Suíbiàn.

7. Hǎo. Wǒmen qù Sìchuān fànguǎn ba.

8. Zǒu ba.

9. Qǐngwèn, nǐmen jǐ wèi?

10. Wǒmen liǎng wèi.

11. Qǐng zuò.

12. Xièxie.

13. Bú yòng kèqi.

14. Qǐng lái càidān.

15. Nǐmen xiǎng chī shénme?

Chit-Chat Practice 10.3

1. Tāmen xiǎng hē chá hái yǒu píjiǔ.

2. Tāmen diǎnle Zhōngguó píjiǔ.

3. Lisa xiǎng chī jīròu.

4. Lisa hěn xǐhuan chī là.

5. Yīnwèi Lisa bù chī zhūròu.

6.   Chǎomiàn.

7.   Tāmen diǎnle gōngbǎo jīdīng hái yǒu chǎomiàn.

8.   Tāmen diǎnle suānlàtāng.

Chit-Chat Practice 10.4

Entering restaurant -

1. Waitress: Nǐmen jǐ wèi?

2. You: Wǒmen liǎng wèi.

3. Waitress: Qǐng zuò.

4. You & Friend: Xièxie.

At table getting drink order -

1. Waitress: Nǐmen xiǎng hē shénme?

2. You: Wǒ xiǎng hē guǒzhī.

3. Friend: Wǒ xiǎng hē pútáojiǔ.

At table getting food order -

1. Waitress: Nǐmen xiǎng chī shénme?

2. You: Wǒ xiǎng chī chǎomiàn hái yǒu suānlàtāng.

3. Friend: Wǒ xiǎng chī gōngbǎo jīdīng hái yǒu chǎofàn.

Talking with friend about food -

 1. You: Mànman chī.

 2. Friend: Mànman chī.

 3. You: Gōngbǎo jīdīng là ma?

 4. Friend: Yǒu yìdiǎnr là. Chǎomiàn ne?

 5. You: Hěn hǎochī. Nǐ yào zài diǎn cài ma?

 6. Friend: Búyòng. Cài tài duō le.

 7. You: Wǒ yě yào yì bēi pútáojiǔ.

 8. Friend: Xiǎojiě, qǐng lái yì bēi pútáojiǔ.

 9. You: Xièxie, nǐ yě yào yì bēi ma?

10. Friend: Búyòng.

11. You: Xiǎojiě qǐng yě lái liǎng wǎn fàn.

Finishing up meal -

1. Friend: Nǐ chībǎo le ma?

2. You: Wǒ chībǎo le. Xiǎojiě qǐng lái mǎidān.

3. Friend: Wǒ qǐngkè.

4. You: Xièxie. Zǒu ba.

Lesson Eleven

Module 11.1

2.   Zhè shì yì shuāng lánsè de xiézi.

3.   Zhè shì yì tiáo hēisè de kùzi.

4.   Zhè shì yí jiàn huángsè de qúnzi.

5.   Zhè shì yí jiàn fěnhóngsè de chènshān.

6.   Zhè shì yì tiáo báisè de duǎn kùzi.

7.   Zhè shì yì shuāng chéngsè de shǒutào.

8.   Zhè shì yí jiàn huīsè de jiākè.

9.   Zhè shì yì dǐng lǜsè de màozi.

10.   Zhè shì yí jiàn zǐsè de wàitào.

11.   Zhè shì yì tiáo hóngsè de nèikù.

12.   Zhè shì yì tiáo kāfēisè de kùzi.

13.   Zhè shì yí jiàn lánsè de qúnzi.

14.   Zhè shì yì shuāng hēisè de xiézi.

15.   Zhè shì yí jiàn huángsè de chènshān.

16.   Zhè shì yí jiàn báisè de liányīqún.

17.   Zhè shì yì shuāng chéngsè de wàzi.

18.   Zhè shì yí jiàn lǜsè de jiākè.

19.   Zhè shì yí jiàn huīsè de wàitào.

20.   Zhè shì yì tiáo zǐsè de duǎn kùzi.

Module 11.2

2.   Xiǎoměi hěn xǐhuan chuān lánsè de duǎn kùzi, kěshì tā bù xǐhuan chuān báisè de.

3.   Xiǎoměi hěn xǐhuan chuān fěnhóngsè de qúnzi, kěshì tā bù xǐhuan chuān hēisè de.

4. Xiǎoměi hěn xǐhuan chuān hóngsè de liányīqún, kěshì tā bù xǐhuan chuān huángsè de.

5. Xiǎoměi hěn xǐhuan dài chéngsè de shǒutào, kěshì tā bù xǐhuan dài huīsè de.

6. Xiǎoměi hěn xǐhuan dài kāfēisè de màozi, kěshì tā bù xǐhuan dài hēisè de.

Module 11.3

2. Zhèi jiàn jiākè duōshao qián?
Zhèi jiàn jiākè qīshíwǔ kuài liù máo.

3. Zhèi tiáo kùzi duōshao qián?
Zhèi tiáo kùzi sìshíwǔ kuài èr máo wǔ.

4. Zhèi dǐng màozi duōshao qián?
Zhèi dǐng màozi shí'èr kuài sān máo wǔ.

5. Zhèi tiáo duǎn kùzi duōshao qián?
Zhèi tiáo duǎn kùzi shíyī kuài yì máo jiǔ.

6. Zhèi shuāng wàzi duōshao qián?
Zhèi shuāng wàzi liǎng kuài yì máo èr.

7. Zhèi shuāng shǒutào duōshao qián?
Zhèi shuāng shǒutào wǔ kuài.

8. Zhèi jiàn wàitào duōshao qián?
Zhèi jiàn wàitào yìbǎi èrshíyī kuài qī máo wǔ.

9. Zhèi tiáo nèikù duōshao qián?
Zhèi tiáo nèikù sān kuài liù máo qī.

10. Zhèi jiàn liányīqún duōshao qián?
Zhèi jiàn liányīqún sānshí'èr kuài sān máo wǔ.

11. Zhèi dǐng màozi duōshao qián?
Zhèi dǐng màozi bā kuài èr máo wǔ.

12. Zhèi shuāng wàzi duōshao qián?
Zhèi shuāng wàzi yí kuài sān máo qī.

13. Zhèi jiàn chènshān duōshao qián?
Zhèi jiàn chènshān shí kuài jiǔ máo bā.

14. Zhèi jiàn jiākè duōshao qián?
Zhèi jiàn jiākè èrshíliù kuài sì máo wǔ.

15. Zhèi tiáo qúnzi duōshao qián?

Zhèi tiáo qúnzi sānshíbā kuài èr máo èr.

16. Zhèi tiáo kùzi duōshao qián?

Zhèi tiáo kùzi shíwǔ kuài èr máo sān.

17. Zhèi jiàn liányīqún duōshao qián?

Zhèi jiàn liányīqún shíjiǔ kuài sì máo sì.

18. Zhèi tiáo duǎn kùzi duōshao qián?

Zhèi tiáo duǎn kùzi jiǔ kuài jiǔ máo wǔ.

19. Zhèi jiàn wàitào duōshao qián?

Zhèi jiàn wàitào liùshíqī kuài bā máo bā.

20. Zhèi shuāng wàzi duōshao qián?

Zhèi shuāng wàzi liǎng kuài liǎng máo.

Module 11.4

1. Nèi jiā shāngdiàn yǒu Yìdàlì de chènshān.
2. Nèi jiàn Yìdàlì de chènshān hěn guì.
3. Nèi jiàn Yìdàlì de chènshān liǎnbǎi liùshí kuài.
4. Jenny hěn xǐhuan, kěshì tā juéde nèi jiàn tài guì.
5. Duì. Shāngdiàn mài nǚháizi de kùzi.
6. Jenny xiǎng mǎi hēisè de kùzi.
7. Nèi tiáo hēisè de kùzi liǎngbǎi wǔshí'èr kuài.
8. Jenny hěn xǐhuan, kěshì tā juéde tài dà.

Chit-Chat Practice 11.5

3. You: Hěn hǎo. Nǐ ne?
4. You: Wǒ zài kàn shū. Wǒ hěn wúliáo.
5. You: Hěn hǎo. Wǒmen jǐ diǎn jiànmiàn?
6. You: Hǎo. Wǒmen zài nǎr jiànmiàn?
7. You: Hěn hǎo. Wǒmen sān diǎn jiàn.
8. You: Nèi jiàn hěn hǎokàn. Nǐ xiǎng mǎi ma?
9. You: Méiyǒu guānxi. Wǒ kěyǐ jiè nǐ qián.
10. You: Wǒ xiǎng mǎi yì tiáo kùzi.
11. You: Wǒ bù xǐhuan nèige yánsè. Wǒ xiǎng mǎi hēisè de kùzi.
12. You: Hǎo, zǒu ba!

Lesson Twelve

Chit-Chat Practice 12.1

1. Tā zuò gōnggòng qìchē qù gōngzuò. Yǒushíhou tā huì zǒulù huòshi qí zìxíngchē qù.
2. Tā juéde zuò Jiùjīnshān de gōnggòng qìchē hěn fāngbiàn.
3. Yīnwèi tā kāichē de shíhou kěyǐ tīng yīnyuè huòshi dǎ diànhuà gěi péngyoumen, suǒyǐ tā bù juéde hěn wúliáo.
4. Tā zài Niǔyuē zuò dìtiě hěn bù fāngbiàn, yīnwèi píngcháng rén hěn duō suǒyǐ méiyǒu wèizi.
5. Dìtiě yǒu wèizi de shíhou tā huì zuòxià, yìbiān xiūxi yìbiān kàn shū.
6. Tā gēn péngyoumen zài Niǔyuē de fànguǎn chīfàn yǐhòu tāmen huì zuò chūzūchē huíjiā.
7. Yīnwèi Jiùjīnshān de chūzūchē hěn guì, suǒyǐ tā bù cháng zuò.
8. Tā juéde qí mótuōchē hěn fāngbiàn yě hěn hǎowánr, kěshì yǒu yìdiǎnr wēixiǎn.
9. Tā xǐhuan zuò chuán yīnwèi tā juéde zuò chuán yòu ānjìng yòu shūfu.
10. Tā juéde zuò fēijī hěn bù shūfu, kěshì hěn fāngbiàn.

Chit-Chat Practice 12.2

1. Judy zài Běijīng Dàxué xué Zhōngwén.
2. Tā xué yì nián le.
3. Yīnwèi tā méiyǒu shíjiān hǎohǎor xué.
4. Tā xiànzài zài Běijīng xué de kuài yìdiǎnr.
5. Tā xué de bù hǎo yīnwèi shàngkè de shíhou lǎoshī chángcháng shuō Zhōngwén.
6. Bù. Judy de Zhōngwén bǐ Jiàn'ān de Yīngwén hǎo.
7. Judy xiǎng qù Gùgōng.
8. Jiàn'ān gōngzuò de dìfang zài Gùgōng de fùjìn.
9. Jiàn'ān xiàwǔ hé wǎnshang gōngzuò.
10. Yīnwèi Jiàn'ān huì gàosu Judy zěnme qù Gùgōng.
11. Judy yào wǎng qián zǒu, zài Tiān'ānmén wǎng yòu guǎi.

Module 12.3

2. Tā shì yīshēng.
3. Tā shì yīnyuèjiā.
4. Tā shì shēngyìrén.
5. Tā shì hùshi.
6. Tā shì jiàoshòu.
7. Tā shì yìshùjiā.
8. Tā shì sījī.
9. Tā shì lǜshī.
10. Tā shì zuòjiā.
11. Tā shì nóngmín.
12. Tā shì yǎnyuán.
13. Tā shì fúwùyuán.
14. Tā shì yùndòngyuán.
15. Tā shì zhōngyī.
16. Tā shì kuàijìshī.

Chit-Chat Practice 12.4

1. Wǒ xìng (your last name), jiào (your first name).
2. If you have a Chinese name, say it. If not, you should have written: Wǒ méiyǒu Zhōngwén míngzi.
3. Bú shì. Wǒ lái Zhōngguó xué Zhōngwén.
4. Wǒ zài Běijīng Dàxué xué.
5. Wǒ lái liǎng ge yuè le.
6. Wǒ xué Zhōngwén sān nián le.
7. Wǒ zhù zài Luòshānjī.
8. Wǒ shì yǎnyuán.
9. Wǒ èrshíjiǔ suì.
10. Wǒ méiyǒu háizi.
11. Zhōngwén bù nánxué.

V. Countries List

Countries · Cities

国家　　都市
guójiā　dūshì

Afghanistan	阿富汗 Āfùhàn
Albania	阿尔巴尼亚 Ā'ěrbāníyà
Algeria	阿尔及利亚 Ā'ěrjílìyà
Amsterdam	阿姆斯特丹 Āmǔsītèdān
Angola	安哥拉 Āngēlā
Argentina	阿根廷 Āgēntíng
Armenia	亚美尼亚 Yàměiníyà
Athens	雅典 Yǎdiǎn
Auckland	奥克兰 Àokèlán
Australia	澳大利亚 Àodàlìyà
Austria	奥地利 Àodìlì
Azerbaijan	阿塞拜疆 Āsàibàijiāng
Baghdad	巴格达 Bāgédá
Bahamas	巴哈马 Bāhāmǎ
Bahrain	巴林 Bālín
Bangkok	曼谷 Màngǔ
Bangladesh	孟加拉国 Mèngjiālāguó
Barcelona	巴赛罗那 Bāsàiluónà
Beijing	北京 Běijīng
Beirut	贝鲁特 Bèilǔtè
Belarus	白俄罗斯 Bái'éluósī
Belgium	比利时 Bǐlìshí
Belize	伯利兹 Bólìzī
Berlin	柏林 Bólín
Bermuda	百慕大 Bǎimùdà
Bern	伯尔尼 Bó'ěrní
Bhutan	不丹 Bùdān
Bolivia	玻利维亚 Bōlìwéiyà
Bonn	波恩 Bō'ēn
Bosnia and Herzegovina	波斯尼亚和黑塞哥维那 Bōsīníyà hé Hēisàigēwéinà
Brazil	巴西 Bāxī
Brunei	文莱 Wénlái

Budapest	布达佩斯 Bùdápèisī
Buenos Aires	布宜诺斯艾利斯 Bùyínuòsī'àilìsī
Bulgaria	保加利亚 Bǎojiālìyà
Burundi	布隆迪 Bùlóngdí
Cairo	开罗 Kāiluó
Cambodia	柬埔寨 Jiǎnpǔzhài
Cameroon	喀麦隆 Kāmàilóng
Canada	加拿大 Jiānádà
Chad	乍得 Zhàdé
Chicago	芝加哥 Zhījiāgē
Chile	智利 Zhìlì
China	中国 Zhōngguó
Colombia	哥伦比亚 Gēlúnbǐyà
Congo, Democratic Republic of the	刚果民主共和国 Gāngguǒ Mínzhǔ Gònghéguó
Congo, Republic of the	刚果共和国 Gāngguǒ Gònghéguó
Copenhagen	哥本哈根 Gēběnhāgēn
Costa Rica	哥斯达黎加 Gēsīdálíjiā
Cote d'Ivoire	科特迪瓦 Kētèdíwǎ
Croatia	克罗地亚 Kèluódìyà
Cuba	古巴 Gǔbā
Cyprus	塞浦路斯 Sàipǔlùsī
Czech Republic	捷克 Jiékè
Denmark	丹麦 Dānmài
Dominican Republic	多米尼加 Duōmǐníjiā
Dubai	迪拜 Díbài
Dublin	都柏林 Dūbólín
East Timor	东帝汶 Dōng Dìwèn
Ecuador	厄瓜多尔 Èguāduō'ěr
Egypt	埃及 Āijí
El Salvador	萨尔瓦多 Sà'ěrwǎduō
Estonia	爱沙尼亚 Àishāníyà
Ethiopia	埃塞俄比亚 Āisài'ébǐyà
Fiji	斐济 Fěijì
Finland	芬兰 Fēnlán
France	法国 Fǎguó
Gabon	加蓬 Jiāpéng
Gambia	冈比亚 Gāngbǐyà
Georgia	格鲁吉亚 Gélǔjíyà
Germany	德国 Déguó

Ghana	加纳 Jiānà
Greece	希腊 Xīlà
Greenland	格陵兰 Gélínglán
Grenada	格林纳达 Gélínnàdá
Guam	关岛 Guāndǎo
Guangzhou	广州 Guǎngzhōu
Guatemala	危地马拉 Wēidìmǎlā
Guinea	几内亚 Jǐnèiyà
Guyana	圭亚那 Guīyànà
Hague	海牙 Hǎiyá
Haiti	海地 Hǎidì
Hanoi	河内 Hénèi
Helsinki	赫尔辛基 Hè'ěrxīnjī
Ho Chi Minh City	胡志明市 Húzhìmíngshì
Holy See (Vatican City)	梵蒂冈 Fàndìgāng
Honduras	洪都拉斯 Hóngdūlāsī
Hong Kong	香港 Xiānggǎng
Hungary	匈牙利 Xiōngyálì
Iceland	冰岛 Bīngdǎo
India	印度 Yìndù
Indonesia	印度尼西亚 Yìndùníxīyà
Iran	伊朗 Yīlǎng
Iraq	伊拉克 Yīlākè
Ireland	爱尔兰 Ài'ěrlán
Israel	以色列 Yǐsèliè
Italy	意大利 Yìdàlì
Jakarta	雅加达 Yǎjiādá
Jamaica	牙买加 Yámǎijiā
Japan	日本 Rìběn
Java	爪哇 Zhǎowā
Jordan	约旦 Yuēdàn
Kaohsiung	高雄 Gāoxióng
Kashmir	克什米尔 Kèshímǐěr
Kazakhstan	哈萨克斯坦 Hāsàkèsītǎn
Kenya	肯尼亚 Kěnníyà
Korea, North	朝鲜 Cháoxiǎn
Korea, South	大韩民国(韩国) Dàhánmínguó (Hánguó)
Kuala Lumpur	吉隆坡 Jílóngpō
Kuwait	科威特 Kēwēitè

Kyoto	京都 Jīngdū
Kyrgyzstan	吉尔吉斯斯坦 Jí'ěrjísīsītǎn
Laos	老挝 Lǎowō
Latvia	拉脱维亚 Lātuōwéiyà
Lebanon	黎巴嫩 Líbānèn
Lesotho	莱索托 Láisuǒtuō
Liberia	利比里亚 Lìbǐlǐyà
Libya	利比亚 Lìbǐyà
Liechtenstein	列支敦士登 Lièzhīdūnshìdēng
Lithuania	立陶宛 Lìtáowǎn
London	伦敦 Lúndūn
Los Angeles	洛杉矶 Luòshānjī
Luxembourg	卢森堡 Lúsēnbǎo
Macao	澳门 Àomén
Macedonia	马其顿 Mǎqídùn
Madagascar	马达加斯加 Mǎdájiāsījiā
Madrid	马德里 Mǎdélǐ
Malawi	马拉维 Mǎlāwéi
Malaysia	马来西亚 Mǎláixīyà
Maldives	马尔代夫 Mǎ'ěrdàifū
Malta	马耳他 Mǎ'ěrtā
Manila	大马尼拉市 Dàmǎnílāshì
Marshall Islands	马绍尔群岛 Mǎshào'ěr Qúndǎo
Mauritania	毛里塔尼亚 Máolǐtǎníyà
Mauritius	毛里求斯 Máolǐqiúsī
Melbourne	墨尔本 Mò'ěrběn
Mexico	墨西哥 Mòxīgē
Moldova	摩尔多瓦 Mó'ěrduōwǎ
Monaco	摩纳哥 Mónàgē
Mongolia	蒙古 Měnggǔ
Morocco	摩洛哥 Móluògē
Moscow	莫斯科 Mòsīkē
Mozambique	莫桑比克 Mòsāngbǐkè
Namibia	纳米比亚 Nàmǐbǐyà
Nanjing	南京 Nánjīng
Nauru	瑙鲁 Nǎolǔ
Nepal	尼泊尔 Níbó'ěr
Netherlands	荷兰 Hélán
New Delhi	新德里 Xīndélǐ

New York	纽约	Niǔyuē
New Zealand	新西兰	Xīnxīlán
Nicaragua	尼加拉瓜	Níjiālāguā
Niger	尼日尔	Nírì'ěr
Nigeria	尼日利亚	Nírìlìyà
Norway	挪威	Nuówēi
Oman	阿曼	Āmàn
Osaka	大阪	Dàbǎn
Oslo	奥斯陆	Àosīlù
Pakistan	巴基斯坦	Bājīsītǎn
Palau	帕劳	Pàláo
Palestine	巴勒斯坦	Bālèsītǎn
Panama	巴拿马	Bānámǎ
Papua New Guinea	巴布亚新几内亚	Bābùyà Xīnjǐnèiyà
Paraguay	巴拉圭	Bālāguī
Paris	巴黎	Bālí
Peru	秘鲁	Bìlǔ
Philippines	菲律宾	Fēilùbīn
Poland	波兰	Bōlán
Polynesia	波利尼西亚	Bōlìníxīyà
Portugal	葡萄牙	Pútáoyá
Prague	布拉格	Bùlāgé
Puerto Rico	波多黎各	Bōduōlígè
Pyongyang	平壤	Píngrǎng
Qatar	卡塔尔	Kǎtǎ'ěr
Rio de Janeiro	里约热内卢	Lǐyuē Rènèilú
Romania	罗马尼亚	Luómǎníyà
Rome	罗马	Luómǎ
Russia	俄罗斯	Éluósī
Rwanda	卢旺达	Lúwàngdá
San Francisco	旧金山	Jiùjīnshān
San Marino	圣马力诺	Shèngmǎlìnuò
Saudi Arabia	沙特阿拉伯	Shātè Ālābó
Senegal	塞内加尔	Sàinèijiā'ěr
Seoul	首尔	Shǒu'ěr
Shanghai	上海	Shànghǎi
Sierra Leone	塞拉利昂	Sàilālì'áng
Sikkim	锡金	Xījīn
Singapore	新加坡	Xīnjiāpō

Slovakia	斯洛伐克	Sīluòfákè
Slovenia	斯洛文尼亚	Sīluòwénníyà
Solomon Islands	所罗门群岛	Suǒluómén Qúndǎo
Somalia	索马里	Suǒmǎlǐ
South Africa	南非	Nánfēi
Spain	西班牙	Xībānyá
Sri Lanka	斯里兰卡	Sīlǐlánkǎ
Stockholm	斯德哥尔摩	Sīdégē'ěrmó
St. Petersburg	圣彼得堡	Shèngbǐdébǎo
Sudan	苏丹	Sūdān
Suriname	苏里南	Sūlǐnán
Swaziland	斯威士兰	Sīwēishìlán
Sweden	瑞典	Ruìdiǎn
Switzerland	瑞士	Ruìshì
Sydney	悉尼	Xīní
Syria	叙利亚	Xùlìyà
Taichung	台中	Táizhōng
Taipei	台北	Táiběi
Taiwan	台湾	Táiwān
Tajikistan	塔吉克斯坦	Tǎjíkèsītǎn
Tanzania	坦桑尼亚	Tǎnsāngníyà
Thailand	泰国	Tàiguó
Tibet	西藏	Xīzàng
Tokyo	东京	Dōngjīng
Tonga	汤加	Tāngjiā
Tunisia	突尼斯	Tūnísī
Turkey	土耳其	Tǔ'ěrqí
Turkmenistan	土库曼斯坦	Tǔkùmànsītǎn
Uganda	乌干达	Wūgāndá
Ukraine	乌克兰	Wūkèlán
Union of Myanmar (Burma)	缅甸	Miǎndiàn
United Arab Emirates	阿拉伯联合酋长国	Ālābó Liánhé Qiúzhǎngguó
United Kingdom	英国	Yīngguó
United States	美国	Měiguó
Uruguay	乌拉圭	Wūlāguī
Uzbekistan	乌兹别克斯坦	Wūzībiékèsītǎn
Vancouver	温哥华	Wēngēhuá
Vanuatu	瓦努阿图	Wǎnǔ'ātú
Venezuela	委内瑞拉	Wěinèiruìlā

Vienna	维也纳	Wéiyěnà
Vietnam	越南	Yuènán
Warsaw	华沙	Huáshā
Washington, DC	华盛顿哥伦比亚特区	Huáshèngdùn Gēlúnbǐyà Tèqū
Western Samoa	西萨摩亚	Xīsàmóyà
Yemen	也门	Yěmén
Zambia	赞比亚	Zànbǐyà
Zimbabwe	津巴布韦	Jīnbābùwéi